TOWN PLANNING IN ANCIENT INDIA

TOWN PLANNING IN ANCIENT INDIA

BINODE BEHARI DUTT

Town Planning in Ancient India

ISBN : 978-81-8205-487-5

Reprinted in 2009 in India by
Isha Books
B-63, 1st Floor
New Gupta Colony,
Near DDA Market,
Delhi - 110009
First Published in 1925

Printed at : Vishal Kaushik Printers, Delhi

पितृदेवस्य

मातृदेव्याश्च

श्रीचरणारविन्देषु ।

INTRODUCTORY NOTE

Since the fundamental discovery of the world-importance of Sanskrit, not only for the philology of the Indo-European languages, but for the past of Aryan culture, there have been not a few further disclosures of the great past of India, and of the high levels attained, once and again, by its many and varied civilisations. Yet with all this increasing appreciation of ancient India—and not only among her own children, but throughout the world—most still tend to think her achievements as all in the range of the subjective life, as of religion, philosophy and poetry, and as without parallels on the material and constructive side, of man's life and work: or at any rate that while princes and men of fortune may have attained to artistic magnificence of life, the ordinary life of the people was poor and deficient; as, alas, so much to-day.

Hence the value and significance of this book, as bringing out—not for the first time, but more clearly and extensively than heretofore—the evidence of a planned, organised and orderly life for all the people, in village, town and city alike. What better test, and proof, of true and general civilisation? Given such ordered communitary life—and with adequate homes, as we also know,—we cannot but see that the conditions of health and well-being have of old been realised; and these not only long before our present mingled dilapidation of the past and confusion of the present, but on a level ahead of our present practical endeavours. We understand better too how such communities have been truly educated, in religion and philosophy, in literature and art, and these with many and varied flowers, of which the few that remain are evidence of the many that have been lost. The historical value of this scholarly book is thus manifest and real.

Yet beyond this, it is a sign of the times, and in the movement of our age. In well-nigh every country there is being recovered the best traditions of its past; and these not merely for memory's sake, but towards the future also. And so in India. Why should not every village—in time even every villager—be helped to know that things were once better than now; and that there was ordered beauty here of old, whatever be the tumble-down confusion and insanitation of to-day?

India is indeed at the outset of a reconstruction movement, say rather, of a Reconstructive Period. It is no doubt a good beginning to revive domestic industries, but it is a yet better advance to be renewing the villages themselves; and these from agriculture homewards and towards the associated life; a life co-operative alike towards material efficiency and well-being and towards renewed and advancing culture. So while the Indian people are rightly cheered to have their foremost political leader insisting on the revival of home industries, they will soon be yet more rejoiced to know how their foremost poet—a world-poet as well, a creative educationalist too, making the first Applied Faculty of his new University—and a new one for all Universities—that of Village Reconstruction. In this great initiative of Indian renewal, Mr. Dutt's book here before us has its definite place and use, since so full of historical information and that of practical suggestiveness. Thus, despite its studious calm, it brings inspiration for the opening generation; since in this a happily increasing number are preparing themselves for action. And this in no mere political sense; but above all as constructive citizens of their communities, in social service, local, regional and civic; and thus widening, to Indian; indeed thence even to stimulus and encouragement in lands beyond.

Limits of space prevent me from entering here upon the definite theses of this book, chapter by chapter. But this is not needed; for they are at once presented with due scholarship for the learned, and stated with due simplicity and clearness for the general reader. And all in such a way as to invite their co-operation; and this in the right spirit, of constructive renewal, in which scholar and peasant have each their part.

PATRICK GEDDES

FOREWORD

"No study has so potent an influence in forming a nation's mind and a nation's character as a critical and careful study of its past history."

R. C. Dutt, (*Early Hindu Civilisation*)

To-day is Saturday and one of these Saturdays, in the month of Āshāḍha, the planets, satellites, and constellations of the Universe conjoined and evolved into an aspect and configuration favourable for the physical manifestation of this Self until then immanent in it and I was ushered into mundane existence. It is a well-known immemorial doctrine of Hinduism that every Hindu is born to a debt to the sage savants, Ṛshis, of old and hallowed memory. These selfless souls laid humanity under a sacred obligation by communicating the fruits of their profound meditation and beatific realisation to their disciples as well as by preserving them in treatises. And it is the pious duty of every Hindu to pay off this holy debt by acquiring and assimilating them through study and devotion as also by disseminating them broadcast among mankind. This is the only recompense which our intellectual forebears may expect of us for their labours and gratuitous services.

Rather, this is the utmost that we may do to them in return for the inestimable services which they have thereby rendered to us simply out of love. I do not know whether I shall be instrumental to adulterating and profaning its religious sanctity and obligatoriness when I make bold to interpret this scriptural injunction as an essentially Hindu method of preserving the lore and culture of the ancient savant seers and providing for their transmission to posterity, perpetuation and promulgation. It is the bounden duty, therefore, of every Indian, specially of a Hindu, to rescue from oblivion, from the ravages of time and tyrants, the sciences which our ancesters, thousand years ago, knew, the culture which they evolved, the practices which they observed, and the achievements which they made in the social and political fields. We must know and spread what they knew and thought, said and wrote, attained and accomplished. It is by such action that we shall be able to discharge ourselves in some measure from obligations to them and prove ourselves as their worthy descendants. We shall be justified in declaring ourselves as their true heirs not as much by pointing to the movables and immovables inherited as pre-eminently by our acquisition and realisation in life of their culture and wisdom which constitutes our true heritage and patrimony. It is by *kshema* (preservation and consolidation of what one possesses) that India can be qualified for *yoga* (fresh acquisition). Her glorious Past must be resuscitated and rehabilitated in her Present that a far more glorious Future may blossom out of it. Thus will her life be flowing, undammed and unchoked, rupturously from times immemorial to æons immortal. It is this spirit which has always inspired this humble worker in his exploration into a hitherto neglected field of Indian Śilpa, some results of which he has essayed to shapen, systematise, and embody in the following pages.

Though India's Past had then, as it has now, a great fascination for me, yet it was not this spirit which impelled me to commence work in this line. It is an accident that drew me to it. Some years ago Prof. Patrick Geddes organised town-planning exhibitions in some important metropolises of India. The Calcutta exhibition aroused the imagination of a revered brother of mine who urged me to investigate what progress ancient India might have made in the field of civic science. The present writer who had till then come across only florid and fantastic descriptions of forts and capitals in the Epics and the Purāṇas, and scrappy treatment of the science in the latter works, did not feel himself encouraged to launch upon such a venture as these materials, until then the only within his knowledge, could, in his opinion, be hardly developed into even a decent monograph on the subject to be placed beside the bulky volumes that the West has of late contributed to its parallel there. The result, he thought, would hardly repay the ardous labour involved. The optimistic enthusiasm of my brother was not however to be damped by such diffident and discouraging considerations which, as he truly thought, ignorance usually engenders. He continued to goad and exhort me until I had perforce to direct my attention to it. I was really unprepared for the happy disillusionment which awaited me and followed soon after the commencement of the investigation. A vast splendid landscape of ancient India, quite unknown to me, opened up before my admiring eyes. The materials began to accumulate with unexpected rapidity and to-day they baffle my anxiety and capacity to bring them all together. I have met, in references, with many works, published and unpublished, which with all my efforts I have failed to get at. The materials to my hand are however enough for writing a good volume on the subject and, reserving the unsecured materials for its further improvement and future edition, I have thought it wise to put the results of my labour up to this day in black and white and to place them before the critical world. No one is more conscious of the defects and shortcomings of this book than its humble author. He hopes however, with the generous assistance of his sympathetic readers, to improve and develop the volume into its full dimensions in its future editions.

I have not hesitated whenever necessary to draw upon the descriptions of towns and cities founded during the Indo-Moslem regime, in order to illustrate the principles of town-planning known to ancient India. That sums up as well my attitude towards the towns that sprang up during what is commonly called as the Buddhist period of Indian history. I do not for myself think that the Buddhist culture, both in its phases of art and religion, has any serious contra-Hinduistic air about it as a distinct growth, devoid of any organic affinity of origin and development with the pre-Buddhistic Hindu culture of the land. Positively speaking, I believe, on the contrary, that, whatever may some scholars make of a distinctive Buddhist school, the Buddhist culture is an offshoot of, a growth out of the mighty tree of Hinduism. It possibly perished when it sought to disown its parent tree altogether. There may be some special features of Indian town-planning which may be credited to the Buddhists. I have not as yet succeeded in sifting out and ascertaining these special contributions. Whatever they might be, they were not certainly innovations subversive of the fundamentals of the science that were recognised and passed current prior to the spread of Buddhism in this land. They were, at most, improvements and embellishments upon the original fabric. All the existing treatises that are directly concerned with the treatment of the science as well as those that have contented themselves with its passing notice, bear strong testimony of their origin and composition under Hindu influence. This is evident from the shabby treatment which they have vouchsafed to the Buddhist fanes and institutions in allocation of the sites of a city. And the materials that have hitherto come to my knowledge will not justify me in building up a Buddhist school of Indian town-planning.

There is however no such cogent reason for classifying the Indo-Moslem towns and capitals in the category of ancient Indian cities. But I am not aware of a Saracenic school of town-planning that may present remarkable marks of differentiation. The Moslem rulers of India had had to establish few new towns. Of these, many bear impressions of the town-planning traditions of

India. Again many towns which go under Islamic denominations, or might have been extended and improved into seats of Moslem administration, evince characteristics which can be traced or likened to the Hindu system of town-planning. It is to these alone that I have referred to by way of illustrative examples, without losing myself in disquisitions about the propriety thereof.

I have very keenly felt the want of illustrative plans of ancient Indian towns. The plans that have been prepared by the department of the Archæological Survey of India, may hardly be said to have been drawn up to indicate the methods of town-planning in ancient India. Only the map of Jaipur, to my knowledge, is fitted for this purpose. The Department of the Archæological Survey of India, as the only competent body, should undertake this task, following the example of similar bodies of the West, *e.g.*, of Germany. It is German excavations of the towns of the Græco-Roman world that have facilitated the study of their plans. Unless and until such plans of ancient Indian towns are forthcoming, any investigation into Indian town-planning will obviously remain more or less of a theoretical, even conjectural and hypothetical, character, bereft of that strength which illustrations of actual executions and achievements alone can impart and assure. I shall be highly obliged if any of the kind readers of these pages to whom the subject may appeal as one of interest and importance, supply me with such illustrative plans so that they may be utilised and incorporated in future editions of this volume. Needless to add, the writer shall only be too glad to acknowledge with gratitude his debt to him.

A few scholars have preceded me in tackling this subject. Mr. Rāmrāz dwelt upon it in passing in his classical monograph on Hindu architecture. He drew mainly upon the Mānasāra in this matter and I venture to say that he only touched the fringe of this vast subject. Mr. Havell in his "Aryan Rule in Ancient India" and "Ancient and Mediaval Architecture", have merely transcribed what Rāmrāz wrote two score years before him, with a few new points here and there derived from Kauṭilya's Arthaśāstra and the Jātakas. Dr. P. K. Acharyya who have followed them up has barely touched upon the subject in his "Summary of the Mānasāra." The first scholar who has therefore seriously essayed to deal with this subject is Mr. Venkatarama Iyer of the Madras University whose "Town-planning in Ancient Deccan", in its own sphere, is an eminently good work. Unfortunately he has contented himself in localising his investigations exclusively in the field of the vernacular Tamil literature and has reviewed and presented the descriptions of towns and villages made therein from the stand-point of town-planning. He has not widened his exploration into the vast field which the Śilpa Śāstras cover about this subject, although, as an inhabitant of the Deccan which is rich with these works, he was eminently posted for this task and specially so, when we bear in mind that the descendants of the old school of masons and artisans who are alone conversant to-day with the technical terms abounding in the orthodox treatises on Śilpa, were within easy reach of him. As regards his own sphere of exploration too, he had been anticipated, in some measure, by Mr. V. Kanaksavai Pillai who had compiled, in his book, "Tamils Eighteen Hundred Years Ago", the descriptions of ancient towns and villages that could possibly be met with in Tamil literature. The credit of Mr. Iyer lies principally therefore in surveying the same field, of course, on a fuller and grander scale, from a different view-point and consequently in its method of presentation. Notwithstanding all these, his work deserves credit for the materials which it contains, much of which is not available elsewhere. Prof. Radhakamal Mukerjee contributed two or three articles relating to this subject to the *Modern Review* and, in these, he surveyed the subject from the stand-point of an exponent of Hindu communalism that he is. Prof. Patrick Geddes also contributed to the same journal an informed and instructive article on temple-cities of India. I think I need not offer words of apology for freely and copiously drawing upon the works of my predecessors which I must, if I am to make my treatise as complete, exhaustive, and up-to-date as is possible under the present circumstances. I feel sincere pleasure in remembering my indebtedness to them.

The method of transliteration followed in this book tallies substantially with the current system, with a very few deviations. The following may however require special notice :

ṅ for ङ
ṁ for ञ
ṇ for ण
ś for श

When I think of offering my sincere thanks to those who have assisted me in my work, the outstanding figure that shines forth first in my mind is that of one who suggested this subject to me for research. Not content with electrifying away the lethargy and procrastination of the writer with his own enthusiasm, he has collected many materials for him, studied much of them himself, gone through the chapters one by one, carefully criticised them, suggested many hints for improvement, and has patiently borne the tedious drudgery of seeing the book through the press and correcting the proofs. In a word, he has worked for me; he has worked through me. But my relation with him is such that my Hindu instinct precludes me from marring its sanctity and naturalness with any expression that may, even remotely, smack of ceremoniousness. Ours is a natural bond in which reciprocal assistance and co-operation is a divine duty. Therefore bowing to him in reverence I turn to the first man who claims my heart-felt thanks. I gratefully acknowledge the invaluable assistance which Mr. O C. Gangooly, the gifted editor of the *Rupam*, has rendered me by allowing me to use and utilise his manuscript copy of the Mānasāra. Prof. Radhakamal Mukerjee and Prof. Beni Madhav Barua have also laid me under obligation by supplying me with references of books that may have dealt with the subject of my investigation. Last but not the least to whom my heart goes out to offer its sincere tribute of gratefulness is Prof. Patrick Geddes who has obliged this juvenile author, unknown to fame as he is, by consenting to write the introduction which adorns these pages at a time when he was seriously ill and was hurrying through his pre-occupations to go home in order to recoup his shattered health. He is pre-eminently the fittest person, as one who first kindled the imagination of the inspiring genius of this thesis, to act as the priest of introducing it to the public with his benedictions.

In fine, I invite suggestions for improvement, helpful criticism, and supply of new materials all of which will be received with gratitude.

Saturday,
The 20th September, 1924

BINODE BEHARI DUTT,
Vil. Kanungoepara,
P.O. Saroatali,
Chittagong.
(India)

CONTENTS

Chapter I

Introductory

Chapter II

The Origin and Growth of Indian Cities

CHAPTER III

Preliminary to City-Foundation: Survey of the City

CHAPTER IV

On Boundaries and Approaches

CHAPTER V

Streets and their Planning

CHAPTER VI

Site-planning and Folk-planning

CHAPTER VII

Improvement and Expansion of Towns

Chapter VIII

The Village

CHAPTER IX

Of Buildings and Building Bye-Laws

CHAPTER X

Of Centres and Enclosed Places

CHAPTER XI

Individuality of Indo-Aryan Towns

CHAPTER XII

City as the Expression of Civic Life—Interpretation of Civic Architecture: Cultural and Socio-political

Appendix A

Some Noted Ancient Indian Towns

Appendix B

Camps

Appendix C

Distribution of City-Gates

List of Illustrations and Diagrams

CHAPTER I

INTRODUCTORY

THE subject of Indo-Aryan town-planning is treated particularly in the Śilpa Śāstras and incidentally in the Purāṇas, the two great Epics of India, treatises on Astronomy and Astrology, the Nīti Śāstras and Smṛti Śāstras, i.e., works of Sociology in its widest sense. The Śilpa Śāstras that have survived the ravages of time and vandalism of tyrants, leaving out the not inconsiderable number of the extinct ones that live only in references in the extant treatises, may be computed at hundreds. Vāstu Vidyā or Vāstu Śāstra—the science of residence or abode, strictly speaking,—forms a subdivision of the Śilpa Śāstra. The radical connotation of the word 'vāstu' is very wide and the range of discourses in the Vāstu Śāstra is so comprehensive that Vāstu Vidyā is almost coextensive with the Śilpa Śāstra. Mānasāra defines: "The place where men and gods reside is called Vāstu" (from the Sanskrit root, 'vas', to reside, to sit). This includes ground (dharā), building (harmya), conveyance (yāna), and couch (paryaṅka). Of these, the ground is the principal subject; for, nothing can be built without ground as a support. The building (harmya) includes 'prāsāda', 'maṇḍapa', 'sabhā', 'śālā', 'prapā', and 'araṅga'.[1] That is to say, Vāstu Vidyā contains within its category the science of civil and military engineering, architecture, building, construction of carriages, cots, chairs, and couches, and sometimes sculpture and iconography too. Notwithstanding the absence of direct reference to town-planning in the above list, since town-planning concerns only 'dharā', and 'harmya', it certainly falls under Vāstu Vidyā. But the universal importance of building architecture is so great that domestic engineering formed a distinct subject by itself

[1] Mānasāra, Ch. III. *Vide* Dr. P. K. Acharyya's 'A Summary of the Mānasāra'. The existing manuscripts of the Mānasāra retain the word 'araṅga' which, in my opinion, should be 'raṅga'. *Cf.* the Mayamata Ch. II. :—

अमर्त्याश्चैव मर्त्याश्च यत्र यत्र वसन्ति हि ।
तद्वस्त्विति मतं तज्ज्ञैस्तद्भेदं च वदाम्यहम् ॥ १ ॥
भूमिप्रासादयानानि शयनं च चतुर्विधम् ।
भूरेव मुख्यवस्तु स्यात् तत्र जातानि यानि हि ॥ २ ॥
प्रासादादीनि वास्तूनि वस्तुत्वात् वस्तुसंश्रयात् ।
वस्तून्येव हि तान्येव प्रोक्तान्यस्मिन् पुरातनैः ॥ ३ ॥
……………………………………
ग्रामादीन्येव गौणानि भवत्यङ्गी मही मता ।
सभा शाला प्रपा रङ्गमण्डपं मन्दिरं तथा ॥ ६ ॥
प्रासाद इति विख्यातं……………

treated in separate treatises called Vāstu Śāstras. Thus the domain of Vāstu Vidyā narrowed down, and the existing Vāstu Śāstras seldom digress into discussions, except in a casual and sporadic way, on other topics contemplated in the definition. These and other cognate technics form the province of the generic subject, Śilpa Śāstra, which also has to undergo a corresponding restriction in application and significance. But, in the present work, our immediate object being a dissertation on town-planning, we are called upon only to deal with what is technically designated above as 'dharā' (ground) and incidentally with 'harmya' (building).

In India town-planning is a very ancient science Indo-Aryan traditions trace its origin to Brahmā, the Creator-Aspect of God. The sage Mānasāra (the author of the treatise of the same name) gives the following mythical genealogy of the artists: "From the four faces of the Brahmā, the creator of the universe, originated, in order, the heavenly architect Viśvakarmā, Maya, Tvashṭar, and Manu. Their four sons are called respectively Sthapati, Sūtragrāhī, Vardhakī, and Takshaka".[1] These four seem to be the apotheosized ancestors of the four classes of artists on earth. The Mayamata also

[1] Dr. Acharyya's Summary of the Mānasāra (Ch. II.). For the rank and qualifications of the engineers enumerated in the end, see Ch. 2.

ascribes the origination of the science to Pitāmaha or Brahmā and the sages that followed him. Maya only compiled and expounded the principles exactly as he got them from his predecessors including those mentioned above.[1] The treatise Viśvakarmaprakāśa is attributed in origin to the renowned divine architect Viśvakarmā.[2] The author only reproduces what was explained by Viśvakarmā for the benefit of the world. In that treatise the genesis of the science is traced to Svayambhū or Brahmā who taught it in the days of yore to the wise sage Garga. Parāśara derived it from Garga ; and Parāśara told it to Vṛhadratha

[1] Mayamatam, Ch. I, verse 12.

[2] Viśvakarmā :—Traditionally he is known as the divine architect. He is the son of Prabhāsa, one of the eight Vasus, and the creator of arts. In the matter of palaces, pleasure-gardens, orchards, houses, images and ornaments, tanks, and reservoirs, he is remembered as the engineer and the architect of the gods (Amaravardhakī) (Matsya Purāṇam, Ch. 5, *ll.* 54-6). In the Vishṇu Purāṇa (Pt. I, Ch. 15) we have: "Viśvakarmā is the inventor of thousands of crafts and arts; he is the 'vardhakī' or engineer (literally joiner) of the gods; maker of all ornaments, he is the greatest of artists or artisans. He used to construct the ærial mansions and cars (vimānas) of the gods. Men live by his arts". There is another divine architect under the name of Tvashṭar. In the Garuḍa Purāṇa he is described as the son of Viśvakarmā. But in the Vahni Purāṇa both Maya (generally known as the engineer of the Daityas) and Tvashṭar are said to be two Viśvakarmās. Again in the extracts from the Viśvakarmaprakāśa, it is evident that Viśvakarmā is a sage, a disciple of the sage Vṛhadratha, and, in the Mayamata, Maya the author is undoubtedly a sage. All these considerations make the conclusion irresistible that Viśvakarmā is a patronymic. Later on, he was deified; even to-day he is worshipped by the artisans. In Southern India, there is a class of people known as Viśvakarmās..

who taught it to Viśvakarmā, and the latter gave it to Vasudeva and to the world.[1] Beneath this mythological genealogy lie hidden certain truths : the science is so ancient in this ancient land that its origin is lost in hoary antiquity ; the traditional lore was handed down from generation to generation. Caste-guildism never allowed its extinction and saved it from oblivion. It is retained to this day, especially in Southern India where the masons and craftsmen very carefully preserve the manuscripts on the subject and are quite familiar with the principles and technical terms used in the treatises.

Of the ancient character of the science, Mr. E. B. Havell writes :—"The close connection of the geometrical system (denoted by the mystic figures Paramaśāyika, Swastika, Sarvatobhadra, etc.) with the Vedic sacrificial lore, and the position of the master-builder as a high priest or sacrificial expert, are indirect proofs of the great antiquity of

[1] *Cf.*

यदुक्तं शम्भुना पूर्व्वं वास्तुशास्त्रं पुरातनम् ॥ २ ॥
पराशरः प्राह बृहद्रथाय बृहद्रथः प्राह विश्वकर्म्मणे ।
स विश्वकर्म्मा जगतां हिताय प्रोवाच शास्त्रं बहुभेदयुक्तम् ॥ ४ ॥

Viśvakarmaprakāśa, Ch. I.

Again, at the end of the book, a colophon reads thus :—

इति प्रोक्तं वास्तुशास्त्रं पूर्व्वं गर्गाय धीमते ॥ १०८ ॥
गर्गात् पराशरः प्राप्तस्तस्मात् प्राप्तो बृहद्रथः ।

and so on.

the Indian science of town-planning; for, geometry as a science was an Indo-Aryan invention and had its origin in the complicated system of Vedic sacrifices in which it became necessary to resolve geometrical problems such as constructing a circle equal in area to a square or *vice versa*. The laying out of the Indo-Aryan village is treated in the Silpa Sāstras as the preparation of scarificial ground. I have therefore considered it justifiable to refer it historically to the Vedic period and to connect it with the camp or fortified settlement of the early Aryan invaders. There are direct references to it in Buddha's teaching."[1]

In a later volume,[2] Mr. Havell writes that subsequent investigations confirm his foregoing observations. He says: "If it be true—as the Russian scholar, Sheftdovich, asserts—that the Kassites, who took Babylon in 1766 B.C., and established a dynasty there which lasted for 600 years, were Aryans speaking Vedic Sanskrit whose chief god was Sūryya, Babylon must be regarded as a halfway house of the Aryan race in its march towards the Indus valley and some at least of the early Aryan tribes must have acquired, before they entered India, not only the high spiritual culture which is reached in the Rig Veda, but a

[1] E. B. Havell, History of the Aryan Rule in India, p. 25.

[2] Ancient and Mediæval Architecture, p. 3.

prolonged experience of the civic arts, including architecture.

"Recent German excavations on the site of Babylon show that the science of building in Vedic times had advanced much further than has hitherto been suspected."

Without assuming the somewhat suppositional assertions of the Russian scholar and launching upon disquisitions on those premises about the antiquity of Indo-Aryan town-planning, it may be safely taken that the Vedic Aryans had certainly developed a far more advanced knowledge in the science of building than a mere inchoate and crude sciolism. The plan of the towns and their denominations were identical with those of the geometrical figures that had to be, and are even now, drawn on the sacrificial altars. These figures suggested the plans and the names. It is sure that the Vedic civilisation had long ago immensely outgrown the primitive stage and still glows with innumerable and irrefragable evidences of its high water-mark. Certainly the people who could construct iron forts, plan colonnaded edifices, lay out large villages, can be credited with some scientific knowledge of the civic arts. Mr. Havell puts down the composition of the oldest of the extant Śilpa Śāstras to the 5th or 6th century A.D.[1]

[1] Ancient and Mediæval Architecture, p. 3.

But there must have been earlier compositions as is evident from the science of town-planning dwelt upon in Kauṭilya's Arthaśāstra, the date of which is generally asigned to the fourth century B.C. Moreover astronomy (including astrology) was known even to the Vedic Aryans. Astronomical works contain incidentally dissertations on Vāstu Vidyā, for the simple reason that the auspicious months, days, and moments for the foundation of a 'vāstu' are to be determined with the aid of astrology.

Macdonell and Keith give in their Vedic Index a summary of what can be culled from the Vedas about the Vedic towns (Pur, pp. 538-39) and villages (Grāma, pp. 244-5) as follows :—" Pur is a word of frequent occurrence in the Rig Veda and later, meaning 'rampart', 'fort' or 'stronghold'. Such fortifications must have been occasionally of considerable size, as one is called broad (pṛthvī) and wide (ūrvvī). Elsewhere a fort made of stone (aśmamayī) is mentioned. Sometimes strongholds of iron (āyasī) are referred to, but these are probably only metaphorical. A fort 'full of kine' (gomatī) is mentioned showing that strongholds were used to hold cattle. 'Autumnal' forts (śāradī) are named, apparently as belonging to the Dāsas; this may refer to the forts in that season being occupied against Aryan attacks or against inundations caused by overflowing rivers. Forts 'with a hundred walls' (śatabhūji) are spoken of.

"It would probably be a mistake to regard these forts as permanently occupied fortified places like the fortresses of the mediæval barony. They were probably mere places of refuge against attack, ramparts of hardened earth with palisades and a ditch (*cf.* dehi). Pischel and Geldner, however, think that they were towns with wooden walls and ditches like the Indian town of Pāṭalīputra known to Megasthenes and the Pāli texts (Mahā parinibbānasutta, p. 12). This is reasonable but hardly susceptible of proof, and it is not without significance that the word 'nagar' is of later occurrence. On the whole it is hardly likely that in early Vedic times city life was much developed. In the Epic, according to Hopkins, there are found the 'nagara' (city); 'grāma' (village); and 'ghosha' (ranch). Vedic literature hardly seems to go beyond the village; no doubt, with modifications in its later period.

"The seige of forts is mentioned in the Saṃhitās and Brāhmaṇas. According to the Ṛig Veda, fire was used.

"The primitive use of this word 'grāma' which occurs frequently from the Rig Veda onwards, appears to have been 'village'. The Vedic Indians must have dwelt in villages which were scattered over the country, some close together, some far apart, and were connected by roads. The village is regularly contrasted with the forest (araṇya) and its animals and plants with those that lived or grew wild in the woods. The villages contained cattle, horses and other domestic animals as well as men. Grain was also stored in them. In the evening the cattle regularly returned thither from the forest. The villages were probably open, though perhaps a fort (pur) might on occasion be built inside. Presumably they consisted of detached houses with enclosures, but no details are to be found in Vedic literature. Large villages (mahāgrāma) were known. The 'grāma' may be regarded as an aggregate of several families, not necessarily forming a clan but only part of a clan (viś), as is often the case at the present day."

A glance at the ancient Indian treatises on architecture shows how scientifically the Hindus, even in such early ages, studied the problems of town-planning. One may not have faith in the civic value of the mystic ceremonials and superstitious rituals, and the denominations of the interlineal chambers; one may, if he lists, even expurgate the rules and regulations which seem to him to smack more of witchcraft and ignorant faith than of knowledge and conscious utility; and after all these excisions and deletions, modern architect though he may be, yet he cannot but be impressed with the scientific knowledge, methodical treatment, detailed but systematised study displayed by Indo-Aryans in the planning of their towns and villages. The fairly high standard which the Hindus reached in the science redounds to the glory of their culture and civilisation. "The most advanced science of Europe has not yet improved upon the principles of the planning of garden cities of India based upon the Indian village plan as a unit."[1] The traditional and hereditary character of the science did not prejudice its evolution and progress. The Śilpa Śāstras lay down that every town-planning transaction should be performed with regard to its suitability, i.e., with reasons (yuktyā). A great freedom of scope was always allowed to individual character and imagination. A due regard and veneration for the past, so characteristic of Indians in all matters, served as an effective antidote to that sort of egoism which engenders the iconoclastic spirit to level down everything it cannot understand or appreciate.

Knowledge of town-planning was as extensive as it was intensive. Even the layman seems to have known something of the subject, as is evident from the descriptions of the towns that are met

[1] E. B. Havell, Ancient and Mediæval Architecture, p. 8.

with in the various literatures of India. This is further corroborated by the special treatment of the science that one frequently meets with in the Purāṇas and the astrological treatises. The Śilpa Śāstras were also written in the vernaculars of Southern India and they are still extant.

In consonance with the great attention devoted to the science and its diffusion among the people, the ancient Hindus developed a high tone of civic consciousness. Every poet seems to take pride in his beloved city and in glorifying it. The Tamil poets' enthusiasm over the elaborate descriptions of their cities, historical and architectural, proves that they were conscious of their magnificence.[1] The spirit which animated the authors of the Purāṇas to hyperbolise the dimensions, overcolour the grandeur and brilliancy, to outdecorate the ornate and florid decorations, to eulogise the lions of their cities and the actions of their heroes, after due allowance is made for the overdrawing aptitudes peculiar to old æons when imagination was not blurred by a dissecting science, can at once be recognised as the spirit of civic consciousness. "Of our two great Epics it may be said that while the pervading interests of the Mahābhārata are

[1] *Cf.* Buddhadatta's fine descriptions of Cola country quoted in the introduction of Buddhadatta's Manuals (P. T. S.); also the description of Sāgala city in Trenckner's Milinda, p. 1-2.

heroic and national, those of the Rāmāyana are mainly personal and civic. It is more than likely, indeed, that Vālmīki's poem sprang out of a deliberate wish to glorify the beloved city of Ayodhyā by painting the mythic history of its earliest sovereigns. The city, and every thing in it, fill the poet with delight. He spends himself in descriptions of its beauty on great festivals. He loses himself in the thought of its palaces, its arches, and its towers. But it is when he comes to paint Laṅkā, that we reap the finest fruit of that civic sense which Ayodhyā has developed in him. There is nothing in all Indian literature, of greater significance for the modern Indian mind than the scene in which Hanumān contends in the darkness with the woman who guards the gates saying in muffled tones, 'I am the city of Laṅkā'".[1] Such a civic sense is quite probable because the cities in ancient times were more than centres of trade and corporate life; they were the ultimate resorts of the people against hostile invasion. Settlements were scarcely possible in the open country remote from the walls of the towns or town-like villages.

The social status of the civic architect was not as low as their present descendants occupy. Viśvakarmā, the patronymic of an architect, is deified.

[1] Sister Nivedita, Civic and National Ideals, pp. 6-7.

"अहं हि नगरी लङ्का स्वयमेव प्लवङ्गम ।"

The expounders of the Vāstu Śāstras were venerable sages. The qualifications required for the different classes of architects, including knowledge of the Vedās and all other Śāstras, were very high and could only be expected of men occupying the front rank of the society. From the Mānasāra we learn that, in the ceremony of the plough and in the worship of the patron deities, the master-builder himself presented the offerings and hired Śūdras for the ploughing of the ground. The hiring of the Śūdras clearly proves that he at least belonged to a higher caste than the Śūdras ; the personal presentation of the offerings, invocation and worship of the deity without the aid of the sacerdotal class, testifies to nobility of his lineage in former times. Mayamatam plainly avers that blue blood ran in his veins (abhijātavān). It was in later times that he descended in social estimation and came to occupy a low status even among the Śūdras. This degradation must have commenced at least in the age of the Mahābhārata, for we find there Yudhishṭhira requisitioned the services of Maya, a Dānava, possibly a non-Aryan, for the construction of his council house. This could not have been possible unless the science of architecture had deteriorated among the Aryans and there was already an absence of competent experts among them. And the non-Aryans, learning the science from the Aryans, must have improved upon it. It may be that Maya represents the Southern School of architecture.

The scope of Indian town-planning comprises descriptions of markets (āpaṇa), streets and lanes, ditches, temples (devālaya), royal palaces and other buildings, i.e., housing of citizens (sarvvajana-gṛhāvāsa), arched gateways with flags hoisted upon them, sheds for drinking water (prapā), pleasure gardens (ārāmagṛha), tanks, and women of the town.[1] Though no mention is made here of the ramparts, it is superfluous to remark that their construction was one of the important functions of the civic architect. The Mānasāra and the Mayamata discuss the following cognate topics of town-planning :—(1) examination of soil (bhū-parīkshā) ; (2) selection of site (bhūmisaṃgraha) ; (3) determination of directions (dikparicchedа) ; (4) division of the grounds into squares (padavinyāsa) ; (5) the offerings (balikarmavidhāna) ; (6) the planning of villages and towns (grāmavinyāsa, nagaravinyāsa) ; (7) buildings and their different storeys (bhūmividhāna); (8) construc-

[1] Kavikalpalatā ; *vide* the word 'puram' in the Śavdakalpadruma. A special mention of the public women in the description of towns is an indirect stricture upon town-life where social bonds are in the melting pot.

पुरे वर्णनीयानि यथा ।

पुरे हट्टप्रतोलीच परिखातोरणध्वजाः ।

प्रासादाध्वप्रपारामवापीवेश्याः सतो त्वरी ॥ इति कविकल्पलता ।

tion of gateways (gopuravidhāna); (9) construction of temples (maṇḍapavidhāna); (10) construction of royal palaces (rājaveśmavidhāna). The directions given by Kṛshṇa about the planning of his capital Dvārāvatī furnish us with a list of the subjects in town-planning and the order which was followed in their constructions.[1]—"Temples were to be erected. Let there be selection of building plots and the placing and spacing of buildings. Create triangular and quadrangular 'places' at the junction of roads, or at any suitable spot. Measure up the royal roads. Ascertain the orientation of buildings. Thus ordered the Yādavas engaged for the purpose began in right earnest; selected the site; measured up the boundary lines; carried out the divisions of plots; and on an auspicious day made offerings to the presiding deities of the 'vāstu' or site. When they were thus ready to commence their work, Kṛshṇa reiterated his instructions and laid special stress upon the establishment of divine edifices. They

[1] Devī Purāṇam, Vishṇu Parva, Ch. 58. *Cf.* Viśvakarmaprakāśa Ch. 2, *ll.* 26—

प्राकारे विन्यसेदादौ वाह्यस्थान् पूजयेत्ततः ॥
परिखाश्च ततः कृत्वा तन्मध्ये च ततः पुनः ।
सव्यापसव्यमार्गेण मार्गं तस्य प्रकल्पयेत् ॥
गृहाणि वाह्यसंस्थानि कोणे कोणेषु विन्यसेत् ।
कोणस्थान् वाह्यतो गेहान् विषमान् कारयेत्ततः ॥
समे प्रदेशे मध्येतु महागेहानि विन्यसेत् ॥

carried out the orders, reserving special sites for trees."

In this volume the leading idea has been to deal with Indian town-planning from the standpoint of Indian conception of the subject. Hence the order and method of treatment adopted by indigenous traditional authorities have been followed as far as possible. It is for this reason that in some topics I have gone into details or have entered into disquisitions which the western town-planner will not be able to appreciate.[1]

[1] There are many authorities on the Vāstu Vidyā. The most renowned among them are said to number eighteen (Matsya Purāṇam, Ch. 226). Their names are :—Bhṛgu, Atri, Vaśishṭha, Viśvakarmā, Yama, Nārada, Nagnajit, Viśālāksha, Purandara, Brahmā, Kumāra, Nandīśa Śaunaka, Garga, Vāstudeva, Aniruddha, Śukra, and Vṛhashpati. Let me supplement this list with additional names taken from the Toḍarānda, attributed to the great Toḍarmal ; the names are Varāhamihira, Chyavana, Kaśyapa, Vṛddhagarga, Utpala, Māṇḍavya, Bharadvāja, Vṛddhavaśishṭha, and Lalla. Mānasāra gives the following list of the sages who are experts in architecture : Viśvakarmā, Viśa, Viśvasāra, Prabodhaka, Vṛtra, Maya, Tvashṭar, Mānabodha, Viśvabodha, Mahātantra, Vāstu vidyāpati, Ādisāra, Naya, Viśāla, Viśvakaśyapa Vāstubodha, Parāśarīyaka, Kālayūpa, Chaitya, Chitraka, Avarya, Sādhakasāra, Saṃhita, Bhānu, Indra, Lokajña, and Saura. Other notabilities in the field are Vātsyāyana, and the authors of the Purāṇas and the Tantras. But it cannot be definitely asserted that all the above personages ever dealt with town-planning ; many of them must have only expounded domestic architecture. The works of many of them are missing. A regular investigation for the manuscripts should be instituted in Southern and Western India where they are still believed to be extant.

CHAPTER II

The origin and growth of Indian cities

A city, as a concrete expression of the motive forces and ideas regulating the life of the citizens, is the noblest monument of human art and conception. In its genesis is wrapped up to a great measure the evolution of the civilization of the people who built it. This is specially true of the western world where civilization originated, evolved, and still continues to do so, in the cities. Even in India where a village, in its wider sense, s the centre of civilisation, it is no less true as we shall presently realise when we trace the origin and growth of Indian cities.

Cities may be grouped into two main divisions according as they evolved consciously or unconsciously. It cannot be definitely asserted in the history of any city that every stage of its growth from the very foundation was due to deliberate efforts to improve and expand it. Neither can the contrary proposition be seriously adduced, that at no period of a certain city did it receive any trimming from human hands. The truth perhaps lies midway between these extremes. Either it was first laid out by a certain king; then it grew and grew until the unseemly state of things called for an appropriate resetting. Or it may be where we now find a full-fledged city, there resided a patriarchal family in days of hoary antiquity. The family grew into a village; the village, possibly because of containing a market-centre, outgrew its rural dimensions and significance until it came to be a city and was, at some stage or other, rightened and improved according to the best town-planning traditions. Any locality bidding fair to grow into a town must be endowed with advantages of a market or temple, facilities of easy access and conveyance especially by water (*e.g.*, prominent trade-routes, navigable rivers or seas), a satrapy or fortress. This is true for all towns, whether in India or outside it. It may be the existence of a river or of a trade-route attracted the others. Generally in all countries it is the temples or churches that are established in the already existing towns and not the towns that are founded about them. Only in India it has been possible for a temple to throw out a city round about it.

The Śavdakalpadruma gives the following synonyms of 'puram', the Sanskrit equivalent of a city: a house (geha); a place containing a market and the like (haṭṭādi-viśishṭa-sthānam); a place of intercourse between and including many villages (vahū-grāmīya-vyavahāra-sthānam); a place of palaces or royal residence (purī); a town (nagara);

an emporium (pattanam); a local fastness (sthānīyam); a camp (kaṭakam); a crossing of great highways (paṭṭam); a commercial centre (nigama); a place on a river side (puṭabhedanam). A close study of the above synonyms will reveal the history and explain the origin and characteristics of the Indo-Aryan cities. "The cities stand always, as Kropotkin points out, at the crossings of the great highways.....The ideal city is the meeting place of shepherd and peasant, of merchant and artificer, of priest and pilgrim, of court and camp. It is the centre towards which converge streams that rise in all the quarters of the globe. It is a market-place and exchange, a focus of wealth and industry, a hall of international council, and the quadrangle of world-university."[1] The above list contains almost all the varieties of cities which had conscious origin as well as those which evolved naturally.

It should be noticed that the origin of those towns which grew independently of any deliberate planning from the beginning, can be traced to a house, a temple, a village (if it contains a market or a manufactory), or a market and to natural advantages of the locality such as an island, a river-bend, a sea-coast, a mountain valley and the like. A house, rather a patriarchal family, is the

[1] Sister Nivedita, Civic and National Ideals, p. 17.

nucleus round which developed a village as the word 'ekabhogam' (denoting a village exclusively inhabited by a single patriarch with his family and retinue) clearly demonstrates.[1] The 'pārās' of Bengal, *e.g.*, the 'pārās' of the Ghoses, the 'pārās' of the Dattas, of the Banerjees, or Mukherjees of a modern complex village, which are genealogically derived from the same patriarch, are nothing short of a village-unit. A modern village is nothing but a conglomeration of such units of different 'gotras' or primitive stocks. Similarly an Indo-Aryan city was a market-village grown to greatness. It consisted of several villages or wards, each ward being set apart for a single community exactly like a 'pārā' in a village. Like their western counterparts which "were originally nothing more than the township-mark of a Teutonic village-community", the large majority of Indian towns had their origin in villages. This is corroborated by the different grades of respective measurements of a town and of a village.[2] It will be observed that some grades of city-area more or less tally with the highest grades of a village-area. It goes to prove that

[1] *Vide* Manushyālayachandrikā, Ch. 3, śloka, 19.

एकविप्रवरागारतत्कुटुम्बसमन्वितम् ।
एकभोगं भवेद ग्रामं तद्भृत्यायतनावृतम् ॥१९

[2] *Vide* Chapter VIII.

the towns had a small beginning from a village. It may further be taken to indicate the different measurements of a single town in its different stages of development. Sir Henry Maine in his treatise on village communities says:—"The village, in becoming more populous from some cause or other, has got separated from its cultivated or common domain; the domain has been swallowed up in it; or a number of different villages have been founded close together on what was perhaps at one time unprofitable waste land, but which has become exceptionally valuable through advantages of situation. This last was the origin of the great Anglo-Indian city of Calcutta, which is really a collection of villages of very modern foundation."

I must confess that the meaning of the foregoing proposition is not quite clear. The instancing of Calcutta is surely not happy, for Calcutta was the outcome of deliberate efforts of the East India Company. It is true no doubt that many towns were established by agglutinating several adjoining villages. But Sir Henry Maine seems to be considering the unconscious growth of villages into towns. If so, then he has partially failed to indicate the motive power that worked from within to 'civilise' the rural areas. Residential villages can by no means develop, of their own accord, into towns, for they lack the contrifugal impetus. In the United Provinces and the Punjab it is still to be observed that a village is only a hamlet, called 'muhallā', a juxtaposition of several huts surrounded by a wall. Round about it is the vast expanse of paddy field It is impossible for such a hamlet to develop into a town. It is the market places surrounded by many such hamlets,—(for it is natural that hamlets should be laid out in the vicinity of a market for the many advantages which it affords or that many hamlets should organise a market in their centre)—that were the Indian towns in embryo. The word 'vahū-grāmīya-vyavahāra-sthānam' clearly establishes it. The ancient renowned town of Saptagrāma, (literally, a town consisting of seven villages), was an important emporium where merchants from remote realms gathered together for traffic. The small subdivisional towns are only expansions of the original markets (hāts or bāzārs) as the names of Cox's Bazar in Chittagong, Bagerhāt in Khulna, Rampurhāt in Birbhum unquestionably point out. It is to be noticed that it is the markets where distinctive characteristics of town life are more or less evident and which accentuate civic tendencies. It is significant that in very many towns the 'sāhāganj' or the general market is located in the centre.

But Maine's proposition stands true so far as it relates to a University town, a temple city, or a town noted for its specialities in local arts and manufactures. The famous University town of ancient Nālandā had, I presume, a humble origin in a Buddhist monastery under a revered Sthavira like Sāriputra renowned far and wide for his learning and piety. Many disciples approached him, sat at his feet, drank deep of his religious lore; some chose to remain under his inspiring influence; some after completing their training left to spread their activities in other climes. The disciples began to pour in in growing numbers. With royal or local help the monastery grew beyond its 'local habitation and name'. In course of time it developed into so well-organised a University as that of the renowned Nālandā. A 'kulapati' is a sage who trains and maintains ten thousand disciples. Hence his hermitage can be nothing short of a University town; nay, in strength of students it can favourably compare with the best residential Universities of the modern world. The great 'Naimishāraṇya' of mythological fame, where all the Purāṇas and Upapurāṇas are said to have been narrated by the sage Sauti amidst a vast congregation of inquisitive hermits listening to him with rapt and respectful attention, gives us a fair idea of an Indo-Aryan University. Navadvīp of Bengal with its Bhaṭṭapallī famous for ages as a great centre of Sanskrit learning can be likened to a University.

Moreover, the sites of great cities have often been indicated by some nascent industry—*viz.*, a mine, a bed of flint, a layer of clay useful for household utensils. In cases like these it is quite possible that villages which have specialised in any art, working upon local materials, have grown into towns. Who can say that the importance of the localities which once developed into the famous towns, of Dacca noted for its finest muslin, of Kṛshṇanagar renowned for clay-modelling, of Murshidabad distinguished for its silk-clothings, of Golkuṇḍa famous for its diamonds, of Agra known for its perfumery and marble works, was not partially derived from their excellent local manufactures which commanded a respectable market beyond the limits of the manufactories and that they were not the market-places where the artisans brought their articles for sale ? There can also be cited here many modern instances of such factory towns, to wit, Jheria and Jamshedpur.[1]

[1] *Cf.* Śilparatna, Ch. 5, śloka 34, and also Īśānaśivagurudevapaddhati, p. 327.

वने वा नगरोपान्ते नागरैस्तु जनैर्वृतम् ।
चेतारामाकरोपेतं शाखानगरमिष्यते ॥

The necessity of a trading post led to the growth of many commercial towns in India, as also in other countries. From the very earliest times it has been customary for several tribes to share a common trysting place where they held their councils, and bartered their goods in the common markets. The present Howra-Hāt, *i.e.*, Howra market, in Howra is an illustration in point. The origin of the towns of the ancient Saptagrām, modern Chittagong, and other towns situated on a sea-coast or on a river-bank, specially on the bend of a river, can be traced to marts of ancient times. The definition of a 'pattana' given in the Mayamata bears testimony to this:—"A 'pattana' is a town abounding in articles imported from other islands, alive with all classes of people, a land of commercial transactions in the shape of sale and purchase, replete with jewellery, precious stones, money, silk cloths, perfumery and the like, situated in the vicinity of a sea-coast", lying lengthwise along it.[1] Mr. Venkatarama Ayar furnishes us with an instance of such a commercial town. "Kaveripumpattinam is a very ancient city which was once a flourishing sea-port and a great centre of commerce. It is the Khabiros Emporion of the Greeks. It is also known as Pukar or the city at the mouth of the

[1] Ch. 10, *ll.* 55—7.

Kaveri. It had a splendid harbour and a lighthouse. This ancient sea-port which had an extensive commerce has ceased to be of importance owing to the silting up of the Kaveri."[1] Moreover, a trade centre like a mart is very likely to be posted on or near by the well-known trade routes of the ancient world. It was on such a trade route that the ancient town of Taxila grew up. "The valley in which the remains of Taxila lie is a singularly pleasant one, well-watered by the Haro river and its tributaries, and protected by a girdle of hills;—on the north and east by the snow-mountains of Hazra and the Murree ridge, on the south and west by the well-known Margalla spur and other lower eminences. This position on the great trade route which used to connect Hindustan with Central and Western Asia, coupled with the strength of its natural defences, the fertility of the soil, and a constant supply of good water, readily accounts for the importance of the city in early times."[2]

River sites, sea coasts, especially the mouths of rivers offer the best facilities for the origin and growth of cities, because a river is not only a means of communication with the interior of the country, a way of transport and locomotion, but it also

[1] Town-Planning in Ancient Deccan, pp. 14—15.

[2] Sir J. Marshall, Guide to Taxila, pp. 1—2.

offers an outlet unto the outer world, thus fostering and encouraging commerce. Rivers are national assets of no mean importance. Even in times of antiquity when the itinerant Aryans were spreading their civilisation and modern commercialism was out of the question, the great rivers of India offered the best routes for their spread and advance. Hence the first Indo-Aryan colonies were planted on the valleys of the Indus and the Ganges. Āryyāvarta was the country where Aryan civilisation was promulgated first and this is the part of India which was watered by the above two great river systems, *viz.*, the Indus and the Ganges. Besides, a coast belt, a river side, or a mountain valley is as easy of defence in times of war as of access in times of peace. These have also a never-failing sanitary importance. To these reasons combined with local advantages we owe the evolution of a great many Indo-Aryan settlements in the shape of riparian towns. It should be observed here that the orthodox treatises make it a rule to establish towns on the right bank of a river. Consequently all Hindu towns in India that are situated on the river lie on its right side. Hence any town in India whose location violates this rule, *e.g.* Calcutta, may be presumed to have grown up or been established under non-Hindu influence.

Looking through the hazes of the long-gone

past, we shall find a holy shrine or temple in lieu of a good many Indian cities of to-day. In India it is a truism to say that a temple was a city in the making. The word 'mandira', the Sanskrit equivalent of a shrine or temple, bears two other imports: a house, a town. "In this connection it is well worth noticing that 'Nakar', the Tamil word for the city, is used variously in ancient Tamil literature to mean a house, a temple, a palace or a castle, and a city.... The word 'Nakar' which is thus used to indicate at once a house, a palace, a temple, and a city, contains in a nutshell the chief dynamic principle of ancient town-planning, that these separate items should be so co-ordinated and each assigned such an important place in the city that the arrangement conduces to the efficiency of town life."[1] Incidentally it may be observed here that this remark of Mr. C. P. Venkatarama Ayar applies more appropriately to deliberately planned towns, than to temple cities most of which evolved unconsciously, until a king chose one to turn it into his royal seat as at Conjeeveram. More accurately interpreted, those synonyms will unfold the history of the growth of temple cities and the nature of their growth, which was always from within.

[1] Town-Planning in Ancient Deccan, p. 19. On page 21, Mr. Ayar seems to have hit upon the proper construction. *Vide infra.*

A man cannot overlook the purity of his house any more than he can ignore the sanctity of his body which must be kept purged of all impurity and uncleanliness by daily ablutions. Consequently a healthy place and sacred surroundings are the first considerations for the location of a house. For these reasons Indians are, by their traditions and scriptural precepts, desirous to erect their humble dwellings by the side of a temple which, in times of importance and renown, becomes an object of pilgrimage. A properly conducted temple ensures many concomitants. It postulates salubrious surroundings, a perennial source of water like a large lake or tank, leafy trees or luxuriant vegetation which connotes fertility of the soil. For instance, the town of Kumbhakonam in Southern India is beautified and sanctified by its very ancient Mahāmakham tank. This fine large tank has sixteen small and picturesque shrines studding its banks, four on each side. The embankments and the surrounding ground are shaded over by tall branching trees like the mango and the banian. A temple in India gains in fame not only with the ever-increasingly felt powers of benediction of its deity but also with the reputation of the hermit who carries on his meditations under the blissful influence of the deity.[1] Over and above, in ancient India a temple was not only frequented by growing bands of pilgrims, but it was a seat of learning where the hermit, a wise sage, gave his disciples a spiritual training. In very many instances, it constituted a University in miniature where learned pandits gathered in the verandah or the roofed courtyard in front and trained the scholars in literature, astronomy, holy scriptures, and other branches of learning. In process of time the importance and reputation of the temple, its deity, and its sage extended beyond the local limits. Hindus, in their old age or when they renounce the world, generally love to raise their humble cottages in places of pilgrimage and some pilgrims would therefore take their permanent abode there. With the increasing population shops were started; resting houses were erected. It may be, the place grew and grew until a king selected the site for establishing his castle. What was before a secluded place with a solitary shrine was at once made into a full-fledged city. "Thus taking the palace or temple as a starting point, houses are built around them and the city grows gradually and expands. In the case of a temple city, there were streets about the temple where the priest and

[1] *Cf.* the description of Dharmāranya and Satyamandira in the Skanda Purāna, Dharmāranya Khandas.

other servants of the temple had their residential quarters."[1] This is the story of the growth of Conjeeveram which has been quoted *in extenso* in another chapter.[2] More homely and modern instances may be cited of Tarakeswar at Burdwan, Sitakund at Chittagong, Meherkali's house near Bhingra station at Tipperah, where history is repeating itself and cities are unfolding.

It is significant that the plan of temples, especially in Southern India, corresponds to that of an Indo-Aryan village or town in its salient features. Answering to the gate-towers of the village or the town are the 'Gopuram' or the gateways of the temple. The fine alleys that lead to the temple form the prototypes of the main crossways (rājamārgāh) of the village or the city; the spacious corridors and paths encompassing the temple constitute the counterparts of the streets round the royal castle; while the girdle of wall and the 'pradakshiṇa' path or the path of circumambulation is the 'Maṅgalabīthī' or the boulevard going round the city. The pilgrims or devotees congregate in the 'maṇḍapa' of the temple which answers to the council house of the city. Every temple is well-provided with reservoirs, wells, tanks, drains,

[1] Town-Planning in Ancient Deccan, p. 21.

[2] Ch. VII.

rest rooms, study or debating halls, small supplementary temples at the corners of the compound, well provisioned with granaries, stalls, and even markets. Here and there stands erect a maṅgo or a banian tree, even within the compound, but the trees of the city are mainly respresented by the imposing and magnificent stone colonnade. Even as the royal castle is erected on the bank of a large tank round which the city grows, so in front of the temple is a small bathing ghāt into the tank the water of which is held sacred.

The plan of an Indo-Aryan town fairly reproduces on a grander scale the plan of an Indo-Aryan village. This reproduction is in conformity with the rules of Mānasāra and Mayamuni. In both we find the two central cross roads and the 'Maṅgalabīthī' or 'pradakshiṇa' path surrounding the village or the city. The same division of the ground into wards by a chess-board system of roads, the same method of distribution of the wards to people according to their profession and station in the social scale, the same type of communal temples, rendezvous under the shade of a mighty tree, communal tanks or wells, the similar towers over the gates at the four cardinal points with smaller doorways in the corner, all enclosed by a massive wall rising upon a belt of moat, we find in the village as in the city.[1] This similarity in the plan facilitated the development and extension of a village into a town, for an Indo-Aryan town is nothing but a congregation of such villages, which may be likened to the wards of a municipal corporation. A king who, attracted by its natural means of defence, by its site on the banks of a river, its material resources, or other local advantages, chose any village as a suitable site for his royal seat, could with the minimum of financial outlay, turn the village and the neighbouring ones into a great capital. It is stated that the city of Bijāpur covering an area of about two and a half square miles was made to absorb seven village sites, *viz.*, those of Gajkhanhatti, Bajkhanhatti, Chandankiri, Kyadgi, Khatarkiri, Kurburhatti and Kuzankutti.

For efficiency of administration and government, it was necessary to plant fortresses in the midst of villages which were grouped under their jurisdiction and supervision. William the Conqueror of England adopted the same policy of covering his kingdom with a net-work of strongholds in order to subjugate the refractory barons who used frequently to rise up against him. "There shall be a 'sthānīya' (a fortress of that name) in the centre of eight hundred villages, a 'droṇamukha' in the centre of

[1] *Vide* Text, Ch. VIII.

four hundred villages, a 'kharvaṭika' in the centre of two hundred villages, and a 'saṅgrahaṇa' in the midst of a collection of ten villages."[1] These military outposts favoured the growth of towns about them and the urban tendency was accelerated by the fact that the construction of the Indo-Aryan villages proceeded on the same principle as that of a fortress. The names of the towns Cuttack (Kaṭaka), Sealkot, Nagarkot, Mangalkot speak of their genesis, inasmuch as 'kaṭak' or 'kot' means a fort. Indeed even an antique house represents a fort in structure.* The predominance of defensive character in any sort of human habitation, in ancient India, be it a house, a village, or a town, is as old as the patriarchal rule in the Aryan social evolution. The word 'gotra', usually applied to denote a family descended from one of the several patriarchs, originally meant an enclosure for kine and this was the genesis of the Indo-Aryan village or town. Max Müller points out the connection between its etymological and secondary meanings thus: "In ancient times, when most wars were carried on, not to maintain the balance of power of Asia or Europe, but to take possession of good pasture, or to appropriate large herds of cattle; the hurdles grew naturally into the walls of fortresses,

[1] *Vide* Kauṭilya's Arthaśāstra, p.

the hedges became strongholds; an Anglo-Saxon *tun*, a close (German *zaun*), a town; and those who lived behind the same walls were called a 'gotra', a family, a tribe, a race."[1]

One of the most potent factors which influenced the amalgamation of several villages into a city or a capital was the political condition of ancient India. When India began to evolve politically beyond its clannish or tribal state and advantages of unity against a common enemy impressed upon the tribes the utility of hegemony under a common chief or sovereign, they made amicable efforts to round off their angularities, and the assimilation of tribal traits due to frequent intercourse hastened the hegemony. Now a clan or tribe was nothing but a family of persons descended from the same primitive stock and hence each had its own village fort. Therefore a natural consequence of consolidation of the tribal system into greater states and kingdoms was the improvement and expansion, gradual and continual, of the Indo-Aryan villages into larger cities or capitals planned in the same way as many wards of a village fitted into a larger whole. Furthermore, an Indian village community, like the Russian communes, is an autonomous political unit exercising all the functions of a state. No change in the overlordship could seriously and

[1] Chips from a German Workshop.

permanently perturb the even tenor and harmony of its career. For mutual protection or by force of arms several villages were federated together into a large state and the political organisation thus brought into existence was a democratic institution, each village community forming a unit. A king, hereditary in some cases and elected in others, who lorded over them all, raised the central village or the one most suitably situated into his royal citadel.

Though the ancient Indo-Aryan village was essentially a self-governing community, managing its own domestic concerns and only paying to a central authority the customary 'vali' or tribute due to it, the principle of co-operation for the purpose of carrying out larger public works which were beyond the means of a single village was also recognised. Not only were the village artisans liable to be called upon for their king's service in war or peace, but the villages united of their own accord to build assembly halls, pilgrims' rest houses, to perform irrigation works, to lay out and plant public parks, and to conserve the main roads of the district (*cf.* Rhys David, *Buddhist India*, p. 49). "The wonderful organisation of the Chandragupta's empire, of which Megasthenes gives us glimpses, was not the creation of the Maurian statesman, but the centralisation of the social and economic activities of the self-governing Indo-Aryan village communities. Pāṭaliputra itself was only an aggregation of Indian villages joined together by spacious parks (the sacred groves) and stately avenues."[1]

This brings us to the main reason which I have assigned elsewhere for the origin and foundation of almost all the great cities of India. They were the capitals of the different dynasties of kings holding sway in different parts of ancient India at different epochs of history. Because India was not brought under the suzereignty of one single emperor, but on the contrary, was a medley of small principali ties fighting with one another for overlordship, the military camps were turned into royal capitals. These continued to hold on for a century or a half, until they gave way under the overwhelming force of a mightier general. It was only on rare occasions that victors planted their thrones on the capitals of the vanquished; they would oftener lay out another splendid capital, perhaps on a grander scale, by the side of the fallen citadel which dwindled into a village unless its importance was sustained by any local manufactures or other special circumstances. This craze for founding new capitals was due to the constant belligerency of the states which bred suspicions about the nefari-

[1] Havell, Ancient and Mediæval Architecture, p. 24.

ous activities of a vanquished enemy. The latter, previous to the evacuation or capitulation, might in all likelihood have sunk many pitfalls, poisoned the tanks and wells, and concocted other contrivances to avenge himself and entrap the victor. But the more probable reasons seem to be that, since the towns of ancient India were all, in a sense, forts and the security of the resident king there depended upon their defensive character, the victorious king could not turn the fallen town into his capital with safety inasmuch as the vanquished foe who had been driven out was aware of the ins and outs of the fort-town and could therefore recapture it with less difficulty. Moreover, the town was already inhabited by the subjects of his fallen foe some of whom might not have forsaken the town. and might transfer their allegiance to the victor. The new king had to find quarters for his own following and subjects. Over and above, the king always tried to win the admiration and loyalty of his subjects and retinue, both old and new, and establish his superiority in regal power, by capturing their imagination with the surpassing grandeur of his capital. Hence it was almost an invariable principle emphasised by the Śilpa Śāstras that each new ruling dynasty should lay out its own capital. Thus Bhoja says: "A king residing in a city founded by his enemy or even by another king will meet death in no time."[1] This accounts for the juxtaposition of many ruined cities in close proximity to one another, as in Delhi or Taxila. Because of this constant internecine warfare, purely commercial towns or emporiums could not flourish in large numbers. Commerce had to be centralised in the royal capital under the protective ægis and patronage of the royal arms and the wealth of the country flowed into this secure haven. These circumstances combined to account for the brilliant splendour and great magnitude of a metropolis in India as compared with what may be called the country town. Indeed it can be safely asserted that in India every town of note was once a capital of some kingdom or other. The myriads of towns that stud the map of Rājputanā were at one time headquarters of various chiefs and scions of the royal families continue to reign in most of them even down to this day.

The foregoing causes and circumstances constrained the king and his following to lead what is termed 'camp life'. That is to say, he had to change his royal seat from place to place and where he settled for some years, there was built up the royal palace and the quarters of his entourage including the army and the military officers. The same circumstances operated to cause wealth and commerce,

[1] Yuktikalpataru, verse 173.

arts and literature, to follow thither and thus to develop the royal citadel into a magnificient metropolis. We all know how Uday Sing, the Rānā of Chitore, father of the great Pratāp, defeated by Mahammadan arms under Akbar, took refuge in a sequestered mountain valley where he had already excavated a magnificent lake. Now he had his royal palace built on the embankment of this lake. The subjects followed their king and what followed was the gradual evolution of the noble town of Udaypur, extolled by all travellers for its splendid plan, architectural beauty, natural setting, and imposing grandeur. It is scarcely a hyperbolical expression to say that the royal home of Jeypur presents to the view a garden of palaces. At one side of the compound, surrounding a big courtyard stand erect the Court of Judicature and all the other offices. At another courtyard stands the public Darbar House (Dewan-i-am), while at a third rises the steeple of the private Darbar palace. And in the centre of the compound, the imperial mansion Chandramahal lords it over all. At the back of this lies a large flower garden intersected with drains and embellished with fountains. The garden terminates at the shrine of Govindji, the presiding deity of the royal house. Thus we see centralised in the compound of the imperial castle all the edifices for judicial and executive functions of the state.

Finally, it is in the fitness of things that something should be said about the importance of a town-planner being conversant with the history of his town. I have to observe elsewhere that, as a preliminary to the planning of a town, the master-builder must take a historical and sociological survey of the site. It would be sheer iconoclasm if a civic architect did not respect the ancient historical relics of the place, if he pulled down and demolished everything that stood in the way of successful execution of his fanciful scheme, to advertise his own originality, and left no trace of the past with which were interwoven the traditions and sanctity of the place. It is not right and proper that the new city should be cut off from its ancient moorings, because for a healthy civic life and for the traditional sanctity of the city these historical reminiscences are essential and indispensable. It is a truism to say that the city reacted upon the life of its citizens in the same way as their culture gave the form and tone to the city. The city and citizens are indissolubly linked together. The influence of the one wove into the life and evolution of the other. Hence there must be a continuity in the growth of cities, which, in India, was from within. Put in the words of that gifted lady, Sister Ṇivedita, "The key to new conquests lies always in taking up rightly our connection with the past. The man who has no inheritance has no future (p. 67)........In the making of history it is the guiding ideas which are more important than the massing of correct details. We shall become great historians, great singers of a people's evolution, not merely in proportion as we are competent to adjudicate correctly the date of a king or battle, but rather as we are able to reveal the essential features of the past and gather from them the prophecy of the future. All historians, whether of communities or periods, have their central laws, without the recognition of which they are chaotic. Here we seek the story of the municipal ideal. Again we sit at the feet of a slowly evolving church" (p. 24).[1]

[1] Civic and National Ideals.

CHAPTER III

PRELIMINARIES TO CITY-FOUNDATION

SURVEY OF THE CITY

It is the function of the designer to find artistic expression for the requirements and tendencies of the town. His first duty then will be to keep in view the purposes for which the town is going to be laid out, then to study the political and economic conditions of the country, their relation to and effect upon city-construction, and to study the people and their requirements. The Indo-Aryan town-planner had first to determine the site with a special view to the extent to which its natural situation could best be turned into fortifications, and to allocate and distribute the towns of a kingdom on religious, political, commercial, as well as geographical considerations which go far to limit their area. It has been fully discussed elsewhere[1] how political conditions prevailing in ancient India rendered fortifications of the Indo-Aryan towns absolutely indispensable; how deserts, jungles, hills, rivers, and such like natural circumstances were utilised to defend them; and how, generally speaking, tradition fixed the curvilinear bank of

[1] *Vide* Chapter XI.

a river or the confluence of two rivers as the most auspicious site for an Aryan town.

The capital of a kingdom was as far as possible centrally situated.[1] Kauṭilya, consistently with his Machiavellian, autocratic, and imperialistic views, inculcates the necessity of a 'sthānīya' (a fortress of the same name) in the centre of eight hundred villages, a 'droṇamukha' in the centre of four hundred villages, a 'kharvaṭika' in the centre of two hundred villages, and a 'saṃgrahaṇa' in the midst of a group of ten villages. The sites of villages or towns were carefully chosen according to principles, ritualistic and sanitary, preserved in the traditions of the Indo-Aryan master-builders as well as laid down in their treatises.[2] The bank of a river or a sea-shore, the site of a lake or big tank were the most favoured and generally accepted places, so that ample bathing facilities were easily accessible. With the Hindus ablution itself is a religious rite and is an indispensable preliminary to any religious function or observance and sacrificial rites. The Devas, literally 'shining ones', who were the guardian deities of the Aryan people loved the places that by nature or artifice were provided with limpid water and pleasant

[1] Matsya Purāṇam, Ch. 217, sloka I.

राजा......मध्यमं देशमावसेत् ।

[2] *Vide* the preceding chapter.

gardens. We can cite the ancient town of Kajuraha as an instance of a town set up round a big tank. The ruins of the town can still be seen eighty-five miles to the south of the station Harapalpore on the combined lines of the G.I.P. and E.I.R. running from Jhansi to Manickpore. With the local people it still passes for a holy place of pilgrimage and they call it a 'puri' or holy city. In the heart of the ruined town lies the great tank, paved with stones along its two embankments, and by the side of the tank stands the royal palace with its back against a series of temples. The site of Udaypur, eventually the capital of the Rānās of Mewar, was first selected by the vanquished Rāṇā Uday Sing for his place of retreat and hiding because of its seclusion. But the site had this outstanding merit that it lay on the bank of that magnificent lake, Udaysāgar, which the Rānā had previously constructed after his name. It is superfluous to remark here that commercial emporiums and holy cities that owed their origins to accidents of physiography or geology, or to religious traditions, or to the sanctuary of some renowned hermit, could not be laid out on a premeditated plan with reference to the extent and symmetry of the kingdom. Their natural growth precluded any idea of deliberate planning from the very beginning. Nevertheless the town-planning traditions and instincts of the people endowed them, at various stages of their development, with certain features which stamped them with unmistakable Indo-Aryan character. When, at any intermediate stage of its growth, a town was chosen as the head-quarters of a king's representative, then it is very likely that it subsequently received a conscious planning.

Śukrāchāryya recommended a locality like the following for a capital: "The capital should be set up in a place which abounds in various trees, plants and shrubs, and is rich in cattle, birds and other animals, endowed with good sources of water and supplies of grain, adorned with pleasant forests and vegetation, that is bestirred by the movements of boats up to the seas, and is not very remote from the hills, and that is an even grounded pictureqe plain."[1] It has been a very common practice to fling out the sneering remark that ancient Indians, dominated by a Brahminical hierarchy preaching anti-social tenets of philosophy and religion, did not pay any heed to the social and

[1] Śukranītisāra, Chapter I.

नानाद्रुमलताकीर्णे पशुपक्षिगणान्विते ।
सुबहूदकधान्ये च तृणकाष्ठसुखे सदा ॥ २१३ ॥
आसिन्धुनौगमाकुले नातिदूरमहीधरे ।
सुरम्यसमभूदेशे राजधानीं प्रकल्पयेत् ॥ २१४ ॥

Cf. Yājmavalkya, *l.* 321 :—

रम्यं पशव्यमाजीव्यं जाङ्गलं देशमावसेत् ।

mundane needs of men. The foregoing excerpt conclusively refutes a charge based on ignorance. It furnishes us with a magnificent account of the ideals of material existence that should be present in the mind of a ruler of state and gives us an insight into the secular and social life that the leaders of ancient Indian society could idealise as well as realise in practice. It is significant that Śukrāchāryya lays stress upon the presence of trees and creepers. It is only recently that his occidental compeers have come to recognise the climatic, sanitary, and economic importance of forests and the evils of deforestation. The land should be fertile. The place must be rich in game and replete with animal resources. The principal avocation of Indians being agriculture, the insistence upon water and grains indicates that there should be a splendid network of rivers and water-ways to facilitate irrigation of the country outside the town. The capital should not be too remote from the sea; at least it must be situated on or near a navigable river affording easy communication with the sea. The word 'ākul' points to the busy commercial life of the city, arrivals and departures of active vessels—here boats (nau)—plying in the river. Proximity to hills ensures ample supplies of minerals, fuel, and timber. According to Śukrāchāryya a capital should lie at the foot or by the side of a mountain, but the latter must not be included within the capital. These mountains would be overtopped with fastnesses to defend the capital below. Thus Jeypore is situated on a plain at the foot of a mountain ridge on the summit of which is situated the fort of the city. But there were exceptions to this rule. The utility of trees was also recognised by the author of the Mānasāra :—"The best sort of ground should abound with milky trees, full of fruits and flowers, *e.g.*, 'khadira' (mimosa), 'kadamba' (naseclea), 'nimba' (margosa), 'champaka' (michelia), 'punnāga' (mesua), 'āmalaka' (emblica), pāṭala (bignonia), 'saptaparṇa' (echites of Linn), and some other varieties belonging to this species of trees."[1] Mayamuni suggests that it should be a plain planted with 'bilva', 'nimba', 'nirguṇḍi', 'pinḍita' 'saptaparṇa', 'sahakāra' (mangoe). It is to be noted that many of the above kinds of trees have become holy in the eyes of the Indians by virtue of their medicinal properties, and breezes from their leaves are purifying and anti-maladial. It is a recent discovery that the breezes from the nimba tree are prophylactic of malaria. The author of the Matsya Purāṇa says that the locality should be such as does not depend on casual showers for

[1] *Vide* Chapter 3.

7

cultivation and fertilisation; that is, it must be intersected with streams and canals, natural or artificial; it must be picturesque, free from reptiles, tigers, and free-booters.[1]

The Mānasāra directs the examination of the site as to its fitness from its colour, smell, taste, shape, direction, sound, and touch. The ground should be level and smooth with a declivity towards the east, producing a hard sound, with a stream running from left to right, of an agreeable odour, containing a great quantity of soil, producing water when dug to the depth of a man with his arm raised above his head, and situated in a climate of moderate temperature. The ground possessed of qualities directly opposed to those mentioned above is the worst, and that which has a mixed nature is middling."[2]

Mayamuni's test does not materially differ from that of the Mānasāra. According to the former, the ground should rise slowly towards the south and the west; *i.e.*, it must slant down towards the north and the east (*i.e.*, 'aindrottara-plabe', as the author of the Devī Purāṇa puts it). In

[1] Ch. 217, *ll.* 5,9.

अदेवमातृकं रम्यं सुरक्तजनान्वितम् ॥ ५ ॥
सरीसृपविहीनञ्च व्याघ्रतस्करवर्ज्जितम् ॥ ९ ॥

[2] Chapter 3. This test at once proves the fertility as well as the solidity of the ground.

addition to the attributes required by the latter, Mayamuni requires that the soil should be fertile enough for all varieties of seeds to sprout up in it, of uniform colour or of all colours, white, red, yellow and black, dense, cooling, pleasant to the touch, having all the varieties of taste like pungent, astringent, etc., mixed with sand to a small proportion.

The ground to be avoided, according to the Mānasāra, is that "which has the form of a circle, a semi-circle, or containing 3, 5, or 7 angles, resembling a trident or a window; which is shaped like the hinder part of a fish, or the back of an elephant or a turtle, or the face of a cow, and the like; situated opposite to any of the intermediate quarters, north-west and the like (bidiksthā); abounding with human skulls, stones, worms, ant-hills, bones, slimy earth, decayed woods, coals, dilapidated wells, subterranean pits, fragments of tiles, lime stones, husks of corn; exposed to the wafted effluvia of curd, oil, honey, dead bodies, fishes, etc.; such a space should be avoided on every account." To avoid the odium of reiteration, I mention those disqualifications which Mayamuni lays down, distinct from the Mānasāra:—" The ground that has mighty trees at its four corners, is sterile, has a large number of oceans in it or has none at all, is to be avoided"

The foregoing disqualifications of ground, leaving aside all mystic and superstitious interpretations, bespeak impurity, insanitation, sterility, insolidity, and hollowness, and irregularity of sites and plots which would effect the shape of buildings and planting of rectilinear streets and the stability of structures erected on them.[1]

Of the merits and demerits of proclivities in different directions Bhoja is of opinion that the ground should be elevated in the middle[2] and slanting towards the east and north-east. A southern declivity is responsible for all insanitariness and brings diseases ; a declivity towards the north is conducive to wealth, while a westward slope destroys peace and prosperity ; a depression of the ground in the middle conveys poverty, while a depression on the borders brings in happiness.[3] All the Śilpa Śāstras are unanimous in extoll-

[1] Mayamuni summarises the geological and physiographical qualifications of the ground in these words :—

श्वेतास्त्रक्पीतकृष्णाढ्यगजनिनदा षड्रसा चैकवर्णा
गोधान्याम्भोजगन्धोपलतुषरहितावाक्प्रतीच्युन्नता या ।
पूर्व्वोदग्वारिसारा वरसुरभिसमा शूलहीनास्थिवर्ज्जं ग
सा भूमिः सर्व्वयोग्या कणदररहिता सम्मतान्यै मुनीन्द्रैः ॥

मयमते ४थ अध्यायः ।

Translation is redundant.

[2] Elevation in the middle seems to be discouraged by Mānasāra. The ground of objection is rather unintelligible and unwarranted.

[3] Yuktikalpataru, verses 156-7. *Cf.* Nagara-rachanā-śāstra :—

ईशानपूर्व्वप्लवनो मध्यस्थानसमुन्नतः ॥
उत्तमः कीर्त्तितो देशो गृहाय नगराय च ।

ing an easterly declivity of a ground, because one obtains the full benefit of the morning sun. It is for this reason that the location of towns to the west of mountains is prohibited. For in that case the sun-rays will be obstructed by the mountains at sunrise.[1] But a northerly declivity cannot be so easily accounted for. India is situated to the north of the equator, and an inclination of the site towards the north, while lessening the incidence of the sunlight, exposes any building to the chill winds of winter. One should therefore expect that the site should be inclined towards the south. But that was not to be, say the Śilpa Śāstras. Is it to neutralise the southerly declivity of the whole of India with oceans to the south and the great Himalayas to the north? It may be remembered in this connection that to the Indians, situate as they are to the north of the equator, the north is the quarter of light, the region of the devas, the 'shining ones'. One of the reasons can be sought in the fact that the south is the quarter over which Yama, the god of death, presides. It may be that, in a hot country like India, too much exposure to the sun's rays, such as a southerly declivity would bring about, cannot be desirable, for it would make

[1] प्राच्यां निषिद्धो हि गिरिः तच्छायाप्युदये रवेः ।

Śilparatna, ch. III, śl. 33.

the buildings too hot and the soil too dry. The prevailing winds and rains in India are from the south and the west. Therefore if the ground slopes towards those directions, the houses will be dangerously exposed to every storm and shower.[1] It also may be that too much exposure to the northerly winds of the summer—which is the season of epidemics in India—would not be conducive to salubrity of the city. This apprehension of excessive exposure or the other hypotheses are so fantastic or far-fetched that they can hardly stand the test of reason. The ground of a town cannot be so slanting as to be distinctly perceptible to the eye. Sharp declivity is more or less the basis of the foregoing hypothetical explanations. Its absence in practice cuts the ground under them. Whatever the cause may be, it is patent that a declivity facilitates drainage and this has been clearly set forth in the word 'purvodak-

[1] Mr. K. V. Vaze in the July number of the *Vedic Magazine* (1922) writes :—"The ground on which a building is to be erected should not slope much nor should it slope towards the prevailing wind and rain. In India the prevailing wind and rain are from the south or west and hence the site should not slope towards the south or west. If the ground falls towards the wind and rain, it is likely to be washed off by every shower and it would not afford protection from rain and wind. The site should moreover be such as to allow of the penetration of the sun's rays into it." For this a slope towards the south would have been more favourable.

It should be noted however that, for obvious reasons, houses opening out towards the south are preferred, next to those facing the east, while houses facing north are very much discouraged.

vārisārā ' Hence, in case of southern declivity, all the filths of the town will be drained and washed into the southern ditch. In winter decomposition of any thing proceeds too slowly to affect sanitation, but heat of the summer favours decomposition. Consequently the foul vapour which the decomposed filths of the southern ditch will emit in summer will be blown into the town by the northerly winds, thus spreading plague and pestilence in the city. With a northern declivity, it will be wafted away from it. And here is the most cogent reason. Bhoja urges this very reason, when he warns against insanitariness.

In ancient India there were villages or wards in a town which were exclusively inhabited by people of the same caste. The beneficent peculiarities of the ground are said to have been different for the different castes. The Mānasāra divides the soil into four species and points out in order of superiority what is considered auspicious for residence of each of the four classes with reference to the seven qualities already alluded to, *i.e.*, colour, smell, taste, form, direction, sound, and touch. Sutradhara Maṇḍana, in his Rājavallabha, differentiates and enumerates the qualities as follows:—"The plot fit for the Brāhmaṇs is white, emanating fragrance like ghee and agreeable to the taste; that suited to the warrior class is red, smelling like blood, astringent in taste; the ground answering to the Vaiśyas is yellow, emitting a smell like sesamum oil and sour to the taste; while the ground which is black, gives out a fish-like odour, and is pungent becomes the Śūdras."[1] The details of Mayamuni on this point are fuller :—" A white square plot for the twice-born (here the Brāhmaṇs) is above all blame; moreover when rich with fig trees, and sloping towards the north it is most suitable and, if sweet and astringent, is said to be conducive to happiness. A plot whose length exceeds the breadth by $\frac{1}{8}$th part, and which is red, bitter to the taste, levelled with eastward declivity, extensive and containing 'pipul' trees, is the one most suited to the warrior class and to its all-round wealth. The ground which is auspicious for the Vaiśyas or commercial class is long $\frac{1}{6}$th as much again as it is broad, yellow, sour in taste, full of 'plaksha' trees and slanting towards the east. The tract of land which is black, pungent, possessing banian trees, sloping towards the west with a length greater than its breadth by one quarter, is recommended as good for the Śūdras and it increases their wealth and paddy."[2]

[1] Rājavallaba, Ch. I.

[2] Mr. K. V. Vaze says (*Vedic Magazine*, July, 1922) :—" In Śilpa (engineering) the terms Brāhmaṇa etc., do not mean the castes but only the first class or best etc.,—and everything *viz.* earth, stone, animals,

It should be noted that the colours of the ground answer to the colours of the respective castes, the Sanskrit term for the caste being 'varṇa', literally colour. It is said that people were originally classified into castes according to their complexions. The complexion of the Brāhmaṇs was white, emblematic of purity and holiness; that of the Kshatriyas was red, colour of the blood, symbolic of battle and martial spirit; that of the Vaiśyas was yellow, the colour of gold, emblematic of commerce; that of the Śūdras was black, the colour of the non-Aryan low class people, signifying ignorance and dirty habits. The trees have also been allotted in order of their sanctity. The tastes of the respective grounds were also appropriate and significant. The Matsya Purāṇa suggests a mystic method of determining the best building sites for the four castes. "Let a pit be sunk one cubit deep and let it be carefully besmeared over. Let a ghee-lamp of unbaked earth be placed in it, with four wicks pointing to the four cardinal directions.

trees &c., are called Brāhmaṇa &c., where it is meant to say that they are best or first class etc." A little thought upon the extract given above from the Mayamata will prove that Mr. Vaze's interpretation is not universally applicable. Besides, different storeys for different castes as laid down subsequently in the same book cannot add to or detract from the qualification of an edifice. But it is undeniable that there is great force in his contention inasmuch as it is unthinkable that the same plot or tract can be endowed, in specified quarters, with the different four-fold characteristics as contemplated in the allocation of sites to the four castes.

If the eastern wick burns brightest, then the place is suitable for the Brāhmaṇs; if the southern wick glows most, the Kshatriyas are the most suited for the place and so on. If the brilliance of the four wicks is equal, then the place is suitable for all the castes."[1]

There were many ways to ascertain the solidity of the ground. The following rule is laid down in the first section of the Kāśyapa, in the 4th chapter of the Mayamaṭa, in the 227th chapter of the Matsya Purāṇa, and in the Rājavallabha, which shows it was a universal rule: "Dig out a pit one cubit deep in the ground and again return the earth into it. If the earth more than fills up the pit, then the ground is good; if it is just sufficient then it is middling or indifferent; while if it falls short, the ground is bad. The good and indifferent varieties are acceptable, but the bad should on no account be accepted." Another way to determine the solidity as well as the fertility of the soil is as follows:—"Sink a pit one cubit deep, fill it up with water, walk away a hundred paces from it, and then come back and see. If the water stands slightly below the brim, then it is best; if the pit is empty by one quarter, then it is middling; if the pit is found only half-full, then it is worst."[2] Mayamuni's examination of the rule is slightly

[1] Ch. 227. [2] Rājavallabha.

different. He would fill up the pit with water in the evening and examine it early next morning. If there is a remnant of water in the pit, then the ground should be welcome for all purposes. If the pit is found moist and muddy, then the ground will spell ruin for human habitation, and the aridity of the pit signifies loss of grains and wealth. The *raison d'être* of the above rules can be easily inferred. These tests indicate beyond doubt that the soil of the proposed site was examined to ascertain whether it was fit for cultivation and whether good drinking water was procurable sufficiently near the surface.

Some authors of the Śilpa Śāstras have gone so far as to forbid the lower class from occupying the ground suited to the higher and *vice versa*, on pain of incurring the severest vengeance of heavens. But the principles which worked up these punctilious and superstitious distinctions were more recommendatory than mandatory. In practice, it signified little whether the ground designed for the residence of a Brāhmaṇ was square or oblong, white or red, sweet or sour, provided that the situation was convenient, the soil was fertile, and the ground was firm enough not to sink down under the weight of a superstructure. Again it is not easy to find in a single piece of land all the qualifications prescribed in the foregoing paragraphs. Indeed no place on earth is endowed with the ideal contributions of geology and physiography, and no capital or city in the world has ever been traced to possess all the gifts of hills, rivers, seas, and forests in the manner described above and also to command the vegetable and mineral resources of the country. It was enough if there was nothing to be said against the sanitation and the economic self-sufficiency of the city.

The selection of the ground over, the Sthapati (the civic architect) now turns his attention to its purification and consecration. The rites to this end prescribed both by the Mānasāra and the Mayamata are almost identical and they are these :—" In an auspicious moment the Sthapati after pious ablutions, clad in fresh garments, and adorned with garlands of flowers, in the presence of the assembled people, makes an offering of fried paddy and white flowers to the deities[1] and with invocations for the welfare and prosperity of the builder (or of the architectural enterprise he is going to undertake), he sprinkles consecrated waters in all quarters, and drives away the evil spirits that may haunt the place. Then he, guiding the oxen, draws furrows across the ground towards the east or the west, the grass and the weeds having been

[1] These are the presiding deities of the mystic diagram known as Paramaśāyika Vāstumaṇḍala. *Vide* Chapter VI.

plucked out in the first instance: 'Usually he turns the first furrow and thereafter the Sūdras hired for the purpose complete the ploughing of the ground." A new plough was specially made for the occasion. The fourth chapter of the Mānasāra deals with the construction of a plough and with ploughing. The newly-made plough was yoked to a pair of oxen, strong and without blemish, with gold and silver rings on their horns and hoofs. When the ploughing was finished, the oxen and the plough were presented to him as his perquisites, the people reverencing him as their guru. Then all kinds of seeds (generally sesasum seeds, pulse and kidney beans, *i.e.*, sacrificial grains) mixed with cow dung are sown with incantations pronounced over them. When the crops have matured and flowers are in bloom, the cows, generally the cattle of the community, together with oxen and calves, are put to graze on them and they are allowed to remain there for one or two nights: for the ground is purified by the grazing of the cattle, consecrated by their exhalations, purged of impurity by the hilarious bellowing of the oxen, cleansed and sanctified by froth flowing from the mouths of the calves, laved by bovine urine, besmeared with their ordure and chequered with slipped cud and their foot-marks. The foregoing procedures of selecting and sanctifying the ground were followed in all cases of a village, a ward, a fortress, and the like.

The Sthapati had then to go through another important function. He had to ascertain the cardinal points of the heaven by means of a gnomon. This is a procedure treated at length by writers on Hindu architecture and hence its utility and importance cannot be ignored. It was absolutely necessary that all the quarters should be distinctly and precisely ascertained and marked on the spot on which towns and their wards and buildings were to be erected, for the purpose of giving them an auspicious aspect and of preventing their being opposite to any of the intermediate points which were pronounced inauspicious. But it was not an invariable rule that the towns, at least, and, in some cases, their muhallas, should be given such an orientation, as the nature of the terrain often rendered it impossible.

The next duty of the master-builder was to fix the area of the city or village, suitable to its requirements. The books of Indo-Aryan town-planning discourse at length upon what may be the possible areas of towns and villages. Of the villages I have treated in a separate chapter and here I consider only the areas of the towns as laid down in them. The Brahmāṇḍa Purāṇa suggests that the natural fort should be eight yojanas

(1 yoyana $= 8 \times 1,000 \times 17\frac{1}{2}$ cubits) long and four yojanas broad.[1] According to Bhoja, the royal capital should be so many 'rājakshetra' square (1 rājakshetra $= 10 \times 10 \times 10 \times 10 \times 10 \times 10 \times 10 \times 10 \times 10$ cubits, here one cubit = length of the fore-arm of the particular king) as denoted by the number of the particular moment (lagna) in which the king for whom the capital was going to be built was born. Thus if a king is born at a quarter to the fourth daṇḍa when the Mesha constellation (*Aries*) is ascendant, the area of his capital should be four rājakshetras square. The astrological significance of this peculiar standard of measuring the area is explained to be that a king soon dies who lives in a town laid out in measurement with the number denoting the period of lagna pertaining to another king's birth or in a city constructed by a different king.[2] The Agni Purāṇa, on the other hand, has that the town should extend over eight or four miles square.[3] Mayamuni's detailed statements of the city area are different in different places of his book. The length of one side of a town, in his opinion, may range from 1,000 daṇḍas (1 daṇḍa=6 ft.) and the circumference

1 Ch. 8, *l*. 216.

2 परलग्नदश्नामानभिते परक्षतेऽथवा ।
नगरे योवसेद्राजा सोऽचिरान्मृत्युमाप्नुयात् ॥
युक्तिकल्पतरुः, श्लोकः १०२ ।

3 Ch. 106, verse 1.

of a town may measure four ways, varying from 2,000 to 8,000 daṇḍas, the common difference being 2,000 daṇḍas. In a different calculation he gives 768, 704, and 640 daṇḍas as the three lateral measurements respectively of good, mediocre and bad forts,[1] while the sides of the same three varieties of a town are 832, 896, 962 daṇḍas long. It is to be noted here that in both cases the common difference is 64 and the difference between the lengths of corresponding kinds of a fort and a town is also the same. Again a fort or a town may be of nine different measurements, the common difference being 16. The length may be 2, $1\frac{3}{4}$, $1\frac{1}{2}$, $1\frac{1}{4}$, $1\frac{1}{6}$, $1\frac{1}{8}$, or 1 times the breadth measured as above, or it may be as much in extent as may be desirable. Yet in another chapter he would divide towns into 78 kinds according to the lengths of a side ranging from 300 to 8,000 daṇḍas by a common addition of 100 daṇḍas. Furthermore he has innumerable townships measuring from 100 to 3,000 daṇḍas by a common addition of 10 (or 100 according to a different reading) daṇḍas. The circumference of a splendid town, he further goes on, varies 25 times from 1,600 to 4,000 daṇḍas by a common addition of 500 daṇḍas. The ratio of the other sides to these

[1] These good, mediocre, and bad kinds of fort may not mean more than that they are first, second, and third class.

is the same as laid down above.[1] Naturally these arbitrary measurements were not strictly adhered to in practice, but the measurements were varied enough to afford the master-builder ample scope for adjusting them to necessities of space and population. Indeed the conflict of measurements given for some known towns with those laid down above goes to confirm the foregoing view. Thus we find in the Rāmāyaṇa that the town of Ayodhyā was twelve yojanas in length and three yojanas in breadth and from the Harivaṃśa we come to learn that the extended and reconstructed city of Dvārakā was 12 by 8 yojanas in area.

Having marked off the peripheries as above, the master-builder had to visualise the pre-existing arteries of communication, natural and artificial, of the site with other towns of the kingdom, or with other important centres of commerce or agriculture, or with hills from which mineral resources were drawn, or with any other important place such as forts or forests with which heavy and frequent intercourse was indispensable. He had then to erect the walls and excavate the ditches and there-after to adjust the number of the city gates and their location, in conformity with this plan. The principal and essential gates were those which were situate at the four sides. His next function was to divide

[1] Mayamatam, Chs. 9—10.

the whole area within the enclosure into the mystic diagram Paramaśāyikā[1] and to determine the sites for the royal palace, council house, shrines of different deities belonging to people of different persuasions with reference to their wards; for the wells, reservoirs, markets, cremation ground, streets and lanes, gardens and orchards, blocks of houses and wards for the different communities and professions. The demarcation of all these was closely connected with the above-mentioned figures.[2] With the division of the muhallas or residential sites the duty and control of the master-builder did not end. Indo-Aryan town-planning had fixed beyond controversy the shape, area, method of planning, and distribution of various buildings of a citizen according to his caste, rank in society, position in the body-politic, and profession. The intervening space between two houses and width of streets so as to secure proper lighting and ventilation were also laid down in books of civic art. Such elaborate schemes of building operations and distribution of sites were impossible, if there was private ownership of land in the town. Śukrāchāryya says that such private ownership was not and should not be allowed in towns. Plots of ground were allotted to persons

[1] *Vide infra.*

[2] For their allocation see Chs. 5–11 of the Mayamata.

during their life-time for laying out gardens and erecting houses thereon.[1] Like the control of the modern Municipalities and Improvement Trusts, the control of the master-builder was therefore all-embracing and had to be frequently exercised.

The foregoing statements of facts may be relied upon in making the following generalisations. The sociological side of the survey carried on by the Indo-Aryan master-builder consisted in preparing maps to indicate such matters as the degree of density of population in the different parts of the town, allocation of sites for different castes and professions, distribution of residential, business, and manufacturing areas with necessary subdivisions, distribution of parks, public and other open spaces and the extent of each. If he had to improve, reconstruct, or extend an old existing town as in the case of Dvārakā, he had to take a historical survey of the shrines, buildings, or reservoirs of historical importance and traditional sanctity. And he had to project how he could best carry out his duties without violently dislocating the existing order. Such

[1] Śukranītisāra, Ch. II, *ll* 421—24.

न दद्याद द्व्यङ्गुलमपि भूमि: स्वत्वनिवर्तनम् ।
वृत्त्यर्थं कल्पयेद्वापि यावद्ग्राहस्तु जीवति ॥ २११
गृही तावद देवतार्थं विसृजेच्च सदैव हि ।
आरामार्थं गृहार्थं वा दद्यात् दृष्ट्वा कुटुम्बिनम् ॥ २१२

dislocation means unnecessary and additional financial burden or causes injustice and inconvenience to the original settlers. The history of the foundation of Madurā corroborates this.[1]

By way of geological survey, he had to ascertain the fertility and at the same time the solidity of the ground and the mineral resources that could be utilised and the building materials available. If the town was to be laid out on the bank of a river or on a sea-shore, he had to consider whether there was any probability in future of diluvion or erosion of the city and how it could be best prevented. Moreover, he had to carefully survey the general traffic, its distribution, and the relative intensity of its flow from different districts, the traffic facilities in the shape of water-ways, roads, and bridges, both proposed and desirable. He had to take into account all the existing drainage systems and water supplies and to effect necessary additions and alterations in them. Besides these, he had to take cognizance of the political situation of the country at the time and its reaction upon his own city. He had to construct his fortifications in pursuance of this military survey and to strengthen specially the strategic points of offence and defence. Maps showing the boundaries of different possessions and habitations

[1] *Vide* Venkatarama Ayyar, Madurā.

had to be prepared. Local requirements, traditional prejudices or rules affecting the desirable size or shape of building plots for various purposes and thus influencing the distribution of the streets had to be noted on the chart. Conditions as to building materials and traditional and recorded methods of building observed in the locality, the species of trees and shrubs prevalent or suitable for planting, and any other characteristics which go to make up the individuality, economic, historic, and artistic, of the town had to be carefully noted. There are no direct materials, present and discovered, to show that the Indo-Aryan master-builders were conscious of all these aspects of the science of town-planning but that they had some knowledge, however rudimentary and perfunctory, of the essentials, I have given indirect proof in this chapter and incidentally in others.

CHAPTER IV

On boundaries and approaches

The characteristic features which distinguish the towns of ancient India from the present day cities and principalities are their strong fortifications by means of circumvallation and ambient trenches. Exactly in a similar way were the ancient Greek or Roman towns, *e.g.*, Florence, Sparta, and Rome, fortified by walls and ditches. This similarity in the art of civics both in the East and the West must have originated in the similar conditions, political and social, obtaining in ancient India as well as in ancient Europe. Politically they were the times of disturbance and topsyturvydom, depradations and pillage with consequent insecurity of life and residence. Hence the ramparts and trenches constituted an integral part of oriental as well as occidental town-planning. They formed the *sine qua non* of Aryan habitation, the very breath of their life and existence; so much so that we scarcely come across a description of any town, nay of a village in ancient India which is silent about them.[1] Indeed originally a town was a fort and a fort was a town, both having

[1] *Vide* the chapter on "City as the expression of civic life."

been synonymous. In the Vedic literature the word 'pura', the modern Sanskrit synonym of a town, was used in the sense of a fort or stronghold.[1] But later on as towns grew in area these fort-towns became obsolete and were supplanted by cities containing forts within them. "Cities should be established, supported, and protected by one of the six types of forts."[2] This clearly shows that, though every city was fortified in ancient India, the city was not in all epochs, coextensive with the citadel which, in later times and in very many cases, was included within the city or was situated in some special part of it, as in the case of Jeypore, the citadel is located in its north-west corner. That the town was once a fort is further corroborated by the descriptions of Ayodhyā, Laṅkā (Ceylon), Mathurā, Dvārāvatī, Indraprastha, and other cities of ancient India which we come across in the Rāmāyaṇa, the Mahābhārata, or the Purāṇas. Many towns of Rājputanā such as Chitore were nothing but forts. Even a temple had its own girth of walls, the word 'mandira' carrying sometimes the same import as the word 'pura', the Sanskrit term for a town.

[1] *Vide* the word 'durga' in the appendix to the Śavdakalpadruma :

पुरं दुर्गमधिष्ठानं कोट्टोऽस्त्री राजधान्यपि । इति जटाधरः ।

[2] The Mahābhārata, Śāntiparva, Ch. 86, *l.* 7.

षड्विधं दुर्गमास्थाय पुराण्यथ निवेशयेत् ।

Thus it is mentioned in the Hayaśīrsha Pañcharātra that the height of walls surrounding a divine edifice should be a quarter of its height. The Śavdakalpadruma quotes the following passage from the Matsya Purāṇa (Ch. 270) dealing with the description of a temple :—" Stagnant or current, in whatever quarters of the temple, water is best. Moats and ramparts should be constructed all around it." This indicates that the divine edifices had, in some instances though not invariably, also their surrounding moats.

But the parapets and the trenches were not the only kinds of fortifications of an ancient town. Thus does Kauṭilya enumerate their different classes in his famous Arthaśāstra : "In all the quarters of the boundaries of the kingdom, defensive fortifications against any emergency of war shall be raised on the grounds rendered inapproachable by nature (daivakṛta)[1] ; water-fort (audaka) such as one of an island in the midst of a river (antardvīpa) or of a plain surrounded by low ground or morass in which water is stagnated (sthala) ; a mountain-fort (pārvata) such as one surrounded by a rocky tract (prāstara)[2] or a fort in a valley in the midst of an encircling range of hillocks

[1] Dr. Shama Shastry renders it as 'best suited for the purpose' which is wrong on the face of it.

[2] The correct reading, I suppose, should be 'prāntara'. *Vide infra* p. 75.

(guhā)[1] ; 'a desert-fort (dhānvana) such as a fort in the centre of a wild tract devoid of water and even thickets[2] or of a soil sterilized by desert-salt (iriṇa)[3] ; a forest-fort (vanadurga) such as a fort encompassed by many bogs and fens interspersed with trees and bushes (khāṁjana)[4] or one girt round by thickly set tall trees and underwoods."[5]

There are two ways of classifying fortifications. One is that put forward by Bhoja in his Yukti-kalpataru. He divides the forts under two main heads: (1) natural (akṛtrima, literally not artificial) and (2) artificial (kṛtrima). The natural fort is one which is rendered inaccessible to hostile encroaches by its very situation secured by the

[1] 'Guhā' means literally a cave and Dr. Shama Shastry erroneously takes it in its literal sense; but it has a technical significance too in which it is used here. *Vide infra*, p. 76.

[2] Dr. Shastry wrongly interprets the compound निरुदकस्तम्ब as 'devoid of water and overgrown with thickets'.

[3] Every one of the four main classes of forts is subdivided by Kauṭilya into two varieties. Dr. Shastry misses this point and his rendering of the whole passage is vitiated by this defect. Thus his translation does not make it clear that there are two species of desert-fort, 'nirudakastamva' and 'iriṇa'. His translation of the next sentence is also faulty in the similar way. *Vide infra*, p. 78.

[4] 'Khāṁjana' does not here mean 'full of wagtail' as Dr. Shastry puts it. It is used in its technical sense given above. *Vide infra*, p. 79.

[5] Arthaśāstra of Kauṭilya, Bk. II, Ch III, sec. 21.

चतुर्दिशं जनपदान्ते साम्परायिकं दैवकृतं दुर्गं कारयेत्। अन्तर्द्वीपं स्थलं वा, निम्नावरुद्धमौदकं, प्रास्तरं गुहां वा पार्व्वतं, निरुदकस्तम्बमिरिणं वा धान्वनं, खञ्जनोदकं स्तम्बगहनं वा वनदुर्गं। तेषां नदीपर्व्वतदुर्गं जनपदारक्षस्थानं, धान्वनवनदुर्गमटवीस्थानम्।

advantages of its natural defences such as deserts, rivers, and the like. In the kingdom which lacks such defensive qualifications conferred by nature, there should be established artificial forts, *i.e.*, those which are protected by ramparts surmounted by embattled parapets and girt round by large ditches. The other mode of classification is given by Mānasāra. "Forts are first divided into eight classes called Śibira, Bāhinīmukha, Sthānīya, Droṇaka,[1] Saṃviddha[2] or Vardhaka, Kolaka[3], Nigama, and Skandhāvāra.[4] There is a further sub-division[5] of these forts according to their position. They are known as mountain-fort (giridurga), forest-fort (vanadurga), water-fort (jaladurga), desert-fort (airiṇa durga),[6] god's fort (devadurga), and mixed fort (miśra durga).[7]...... All these forts are surrounded with strong walls

[1] It is the 'droṇamukha' of the Mayamata.

[2] My MSS. reads it 'saṃsiddhi'.

[3] It answers to the 'kotmakolaka' of the Mayamata.

[4] This classification, if it can be called one at all, is not based upon any advantage of natural defence, but on their situation and distribution with regard to a whole kingdom or a large capital which is defended by these fastnesses lying in its outskirts. Thus the 'nigama' is a fort lying some furlongs away from the main town defending the entr ance on the principal road leading to the latter.

[5] Strictly speaking, this is not a sub-division, but a different way of of classification according to the kinds of natural fortifications.

[6] Dr. Acharyya's reading or MSS. must be wrong. My MSS. reads it 'airiṇa'.

[7] My reading is 'mitra' corresponding to the 'sahāya' of the Śukranīti. *Vide infra.*

and ditches."[1] Mayamuni's list corresponds to this.

All the authorities base their classification upon the defensive character supplied by nature. Its various divisions are :

(1) *Mountain-fort* (giridurga or pārvata), *i.e.*, a fort secure in its mountaineous position. Situated in a sequestered place, it must have an ample supply of water in its rear in the shape of an undercurrent or fountain.[2] The road ascending to it must be narrow and difficult of ascent. It must be endowed with fertile fields yielding abundant crops and plenteous with fruit-trees.[3] It is subdivided into three classes.[4] The first is one built on the top of a mountain levelled by means of spades and shovels and sometimes provided with secret exits like subterranean tunnels. It is called 'prāntara'. It is the most auspicious of all.[5] The

[1] Mānasāra, Dr. Acharyya's Summary, Ch. X.

[2] Śukranītisāra, Ch. IV, sec. 6, *l.* 8.

'सुवारिपृष्ठोच्चधरं'' ।

[3] Kulluka's Commentary of Manu, Ch. VII, sl. 70.

गिरिदुर्गं पर्व्वतपृष्ठमतिदुरारोहं संकोचैकमार्गोपेतं अन्तर्नदीप्रस्रवणाद्युदकयुक्तं बहुसस्योत्पन्नचैववृक्षान्वितम् ।

[4] Mayamatam, Ch. X, *l.* 73.

[5] Devī Purāṇam, Ch. 72, *ll.* 115—6.

forts of Chitore and Lankā are illustrative of this type. The second species is that which is laid out on the slope of a mountain (giripārśva). The town of Bundi is an example of it. The third type is situated in a valley secluded and made inapproachable by an encircling range of mountains with natural passes like a defile. It is technically known as 'guhā'.[1] Jeypore and Udaypore may be its instances

(2) *Water-fort,*[2] *i.e.*, a fort rendered difficult of access by natural circumfluent water. It is again subdivided into two species. One is the island-fort (antar-dvīpa) : it is a fort on both sides of which rivers flow[3] or in the midst of a

[1] Devī Purāṇam, Ch. 72, *ll.* 113-4.

[2] It is variously designated as jaladurag, ambudurga, audaka or āpa.

[3] Devī Purāṇam, Ch. 72, *ll.* 104-28. Its mode of division and sub-division tally exactly with those of the Arthaśāstra.

औदकं पार्श्वं तथैव धान्वनं वनजं तथा ।
चत्वारो मूलदुर्गे तु द्विभेदाः परिकीर्त्तिताः ॥ ५३
अन्तर्द्वीपं स्थलञ्चैव गुहाप्रान्तरमेव च ।
प्रोक्तं निरुदकं सम्यगिरिणाख्यं तथैव च ॥ ५४
खाञ्जनञ्चैव विज्ञेयं स्तम्बगहनमष्टमम् ।
आपो द्विधा गता यत्र तदन्तर्द्वीपमुच्यते ॥ ५५
स्थलमुन्नतदेशः स्यादगाधसलिलावृतम् ।
जलदुर्गं द्वितीयं स्यात् तड़ागसरसोयवत् ॥ ५६

sea. This is the river-fort (nadīdurga) of Sukrāchāryya.[1] It is an insular town or fort of which modern Bombay, ancient Ceylon, Srirangam and Kaveri-pumpattinam may serve as the best examples. The other type is the land-fort (sthala-durga). It is a fort situated on a high land girt round by stagnant (as opposed to flowing) fathomless waters, or a fort in the midst of a lake or vast tank.[1] When these ambient waters are artificial, as of the ditches excavated by men, it answers to the

गिरिणामन्तरालं यद्दूरवारं सुदुर्गमम् ।
गुहाख्यं पर्व्वतं दुर्गं प्रवदन्ति मनीषिणः ॥ ५७
प्रोत्तुङ्गटङ्कविच्छिन्नं सोपचारं सुसंस्कृतम् ।
प्रान्तरं गिरिदुर्गं स्यात् सर्व्वदुर्गसुलक्षणम् ॥ ५८
वहिर्भिः सलिलं दुर्गं दृषद्वृक्षविवर्ज्जितम् ।
ज्ञेयं निरुदकं स्वम्बं सदादुर्गविधायकैः ॥ ५९
एतदेकत्वविज्ञेयमैरिणं सोषरं बुधैः ।
स्वल्पक्षारजलोपेतं द्वितीयं धान्वनं मुनेः ॥ ६०
एतावांस्तुविशेषः स्याद्धान्वनं द्विविधं पुनः ।
खाञ्जनाख्यं पुनर्ज्ञेयं सजलाधारकर्द्दमम् ॥ ६१
स्तोकवृक्षसमायुक्तं वनदुर्गं प्रकीर्त्तितम् ।
प्रोत्तुङ्गतरुसंयुक्तं सम्वाख्यं गहनं विदुः ॥ ६२

[1] Śukranītisāra, Ch. IV, sec. 6, *ll.* 1-16. Mr. S. V. Visvanatha (*Modern Review, November*, 1921) is wrong in putting it under the category of the 'mahīdurga.'

'pārikha' (*i.e.*, a fort enclosed by a belt of ditches) of Śukrāchāryya.

(3) *Desert-fort* (dhānvana), *i.e.*, a fort in the midst of a desert devoid of any water on all sides up to five yojanas.[1] 'Nirudaka' (water-less)[2] and 'airiṇa' are its principal varieties. Nirudaka is the fort encompassed by a barren tract devoid of water, trees, even of a single blade of grass.[3] It corresponds to the airiṇa of the Mayamata.[4] The second variety called airiṇa is a fort in the midst of a soil made barren by and saturated with salt or brine water. The difference between the two lies in the fact that the land enclosing the former is free from any element of salt and its barrenness might be due to sand or gravels, while the environments of the other owe their sterility to the presence of salt in them.[5] Occasionally the second

[1] Kulluka's Commentary of Manu, Ch. VII, sl. 70. It is variously termed as 'dhānvana' or 'marudurga.'

[2] Kāmandaka's subdivisions are dhānvana and airiṇa. Truly speaking he regards them as distinct types, not as two species of a genus.

[3] Devī Purāṇam, Ch. 72, *ll.* 117-8.

[4] Mayamatam, Ch. 10, *l.* 74.

[5] Devī Purāṇam, Ch. 72, *ll.* 119—21.

species is enveloped by fens full of saltish water and by thorny woods and rocks or stones.[1] In both the cases an oasis is turned into a fortified town. Many principalities in Rājputanā will fall under these heads.

(4) *Forest-fort* (vanadurga), *i.e.*, a fort defended by thick jungles on all sides up to a yojana. Its two varieties are 'khāṁjana' and 'stambha'. Khāṁjana is a fort hemmed in by fens variegated with thickets and thorny shrubs here and there, while a fort environed by a dense jungle of lofty trees and underwoods, destitute of any water, is called 'stambha'. The latter corresponds to the 'vārksha' of Manu.[2]

(5) *Earth-fort* (mahīdurga). There are three species of this, 'pārigha', 'paṅka', and 'mṛddurga'. The pārigha is a fort of which the ramparts and embattled parapets are constructed of mud, rocks or stones, and bricks. The height of its walls is double their breadth exceeding twelve cubits. The

[1] Devī Purāṇam, Ch. 72, *ll.* 122–26.

[2] Matsya Purāṇam means vanadurga by its term vārksha. *Cf.* Ch. 217, vers. 6—7.

walls must be so broad as to enable sentinels to patrol over them in times of war and are furnished with embrasures, crenalles, and windows. It answers to the mahīdurga of Manu.[1] Paṇkadurga (mire-fort) is a fort defended by a tract full of slime, mire, or quicksand.[2] Mṛddurga (mud-fort) may be a fort allied to the preceding one or it may be a fort with a girth of mud-wall[3] like that of Bharatpore.

(6) *Man-fort* (nṛdurga). Its defence lies in its strength of men. It is sub-divided into two species 'sainyadurga' and 'sahāyadurga'. Sainyadurga (soldier-fort) is an impregnable fort protected by infantry, the horse, and the elephant stationed in array as sentinels within and without it.[4] Sahāyadurga or mitradurga (ally-fort) derives its security and protection from its various allies bound by *entente*

[1] Śukranītisāra, Ch. IV, sec. 6, *l.* 4. Kulluka's commentary of Manu, Ch. 7, sl. 70.

[2] Mayamatam, Ch. 10. Is it sometimes identical with the second species of water-fort adumbrated in the Arthaśāstra ? *Vide supra.*

[3] Mahābhārata, Śāntiparva, Ch. 86, sl. 5.

[4] Kulluka's commentary of Manu, Ch. 7, sl. 70 ; and Śukranīti sāra, Ch. IV, sec. 6, *l.* 4.

cordiale to defend it in case of any emergency.[1]

(7) *Mixed fort* (miśradurga) :—Its fortifications are a combination of those of the giridurga and the vanadurga.[2]

(8) *God's fort* (daiva durga) :—It is a fort by its very nature and origin.[3] That is to say, it cannot be approached on account of its very natural circumstances. From an extract given by Messrs Ananthlwar and Raes, it is found to be a fort whose entrance and exit are guarded by gods, rākshasas (wild cannibals ?), betāls, ghosts, and evil spirits, which has been made inaccessible by hailstorm, constant typhoons, and frequent showers ; and which is protected by spells, charms, and incantations.[4] But according to Śilparatna, that fort is called divyadurga, upon whose walls

[1] Śukranītisāra, Ch. IV, sec. 6, *l.* 14. Mr. S. V. Visvanatha (*Modern Review, November*, 1921) seems to be in error in the interpretation of both these terms.

[2] Devī Purāṇam, Ch. 72, *ll.* 117-8.

[3] Mayamatam, Ch. 10, *l.* 74.

[4] Architecture of the Hindus,

ब्रह्मराक्षसवेतालभूतप्रेतग्रहैरपि ॥
शिलावर्षप्रवृष्टिभिरालोक्यावेशनिर्गमे ।
मन्त्रतन्त्रादिसामर्थ्यैकृतन्त्वदैवदुर्गकम् ॥

are installed the gods Indra, Vāsudeva, Guha, Jayanta, Vaiśravaṇa, the twin Aśvinīs, Śrīmandira and Śiva, Durgā, and Sarasvatī.[1] Except the superstitious belief that these deities sentinel the fort, there is nothing fortificatory in the arrangement. Perhaps Manu contemplates such a fort by a giri-durga resorted to by the Devas.[2] It is reckoned as a 'durga' because of the insuperable difficulty of its approaches, not that it is a resort or stronghold of men. Mount Everest may be an instance of it.

(9) *Kṛtaka* :—It is the artificial fort as distinguished from the foregoing species which are classified according to the defensive characteristics afforded by nature.

According to Śilpa Śāstras there are generally known nineteen varieties of forts.

It should be noted in the foregoing dissertation that except in the case of the 'pārigha' enumerated by Śukrāchāryya, nowhere is any reference made

1 इन्द्रश्च वासुदेवो गुहो जयन्तश्च वैश्रवणः ॥
अश्विन्यौ श्रीमन्दिरशिवौ च दुर्गा च सरस्वती चेति ।
प्राकारद्वारेषु ते यस्मिंस्तद् दिव्यदुर्गं स्यात् ॥

2 Manu, Ch. VII, sl. 72.

to the existence of any circumvallation. But all strongholds worth the name must have been invariably protected by walls.[1] Ditches were not essential as in the case of a fastness on the top of a mountain. "All forts must have unfailing stores of water, provisions, and arms, girt round by lofty gigantic trees, secured with walls, and furnished with many guarded gates."[2] The bulwarks are not alluded to because the classification of the forts is based on the fortificatory character of their natural environments. The Aryan town-planners were not slow to appreciate the utility of the local circumstances, but, on the contrary, they took advantage of the natural barriers and, with slight manipulation and modification, turned them into best fortifications where rivers and oceans, mountains and rocks, trees and bushes, deserts and swamps were made to play important parts of their own. But after all they did not favour a fort or town in the midst of a desert for the simple reason that the city in that case could with great difficulty maintain its food and water supply whether in times of peace or of war. For the sake of the best natural defence they always recommended a mountain-fort. The illustrious Hindu hero Śivājī

[1] सर्व्वँ हि दुर्गजातं सप्राकारं च सुखरचम् ॥ शिल्परत्ने पञ्चमाध्याये ३५श पङ्क्तिः ।

[2] Mayamatam, Ch. 10, *ll.* 77-8.

also had predilection for this sort of fort as he built all his strongholds on the high summits of rocky cliffs. Śukrāchāryya arranges the forts in order of merit as follows: Giri, Jala, Dhanu, Vana, Pārikha, Airiṇa, and Pārigha.[1] "Of these, water and mountain fortifications are best suited to defend populous centres, whereas desert and forest fortifications are habitations in the wilderness (aṭavīsthānam)."[2] According to the Devī Purāṇa,[3] the former should be resorted to by the civilised kings, while the barbarian hordes and wild tribes generally esconce themselves within the latter. The origin of this sort of fortification can be traced to the camp-life of the first Aryan settlers.[4]

Having dealt with the general character of fortifications, I shall now dwell upon the walls in fuller details. Even where Nature offered sufficient defence, these walls were, on rare occasions, thought unnecessary. In connection with the artificial forts the erection of ramparts and parapets were essential and the Indian town-planners were emphatic upon the point. Thus we find in the Devī Purāṇa:—"The construction of brick-built walls is indispensable in artificial forts."[5] The

[1] Śukranītisāra, Ch. IV, sec. 6, *ll.* 11-2.

[2] Arthaśāstra, Bk. II, Ch. III, sec. 21.

[3] Ch. 72.

[4] *Vide* the chapter on camp.

[5] Ch. 72, sl. 27.

ancient towns of Ayodhyā, Mathurā, Pāṭalīputra, to cite only a few instances, were encompassed by walls. That this is not a fine product of the fertile brain of the highly imaginative Aryan poets is borne out by the fact that Tamil authors also make copious references to them in their treatises. Thus, "Madurā (the capital of the Pāṇḍyas) was a fortified city."[1] Megasthenes, in his travels, also describes the timber walls of Pāṭalīputra. Some of them, *e.g.*, Ahemdabad, Delhi, retain to this day remnants in debris of their ancient circumvallation. Similarly travellers come across many towns or villages in Southern India which retain traces of their ruined walls and battlements. Firstly, mud dug out of the ditches is heaped on their banks so as to make a kuccha (mud-built) dyke round the city. The pucca wall is raised upon this 'vapra'[2] (rampart). Thus the Matsya Purāṇa lays down:[3] —"The forts should have ditches, girt with ramparts surmounted by towers on the walls." The town of Mathurā was 'chayāṭṭālaka keyūrah', that is, 'decorated with ramparts and turrets on them.'[4] Kauṭilya furnishes us with fuller details about this rampart: "At a distance of four daṇḍas (24 ft.) from the (innermost) ditch, a rampart six daṇḍas

[1] V. Kanaksavai, p. 12.

[2] *See* the word 'vapra' in the Śavdakalpadruma.

[3] Ch. 217, sl. 8.

[4] Harivaṃśa, Ch. 54.

high and twice as much broad shall be erected by heaping mud upwards and by making it square at the bottom, oval at the centre pressed by the trampling of elephants and bulls, and planted with thorny and poisonous plants in bushes. Fissures in the rampart shall be filled up with fresh earth."[1]

The number of parapets or walls upon the ramparts (vapra) was generally one, but sometimes more. Pāṭalīputra is reported to have three such walls. Tourists must have observed the eight belts of walls and ditches round the garh or fort of Rāmpāl at Dacca. Kauṭilya advises several parapets. We have in the Arthaśāstra, "Above the ramparts, parapets in odd or even numbers and with an intermediate space of from 12 to 24 hastas (cubits) from each other shall be built of bricks." I need hardly remark here that these walls were almost invariably built of bricks. The Devī Purāṇa also specifies the height of the walls ;—" The walls should be raised to nine cubits high according to rules laid down by the Muni."[2] According to Kauṭilya, "the parapets shall be raised to a height twice their breadth." The rule of the Brahmavaivarta Purāṇa is that "the maximum height should be twenty cubits and a wall loftier than that

[1] Kauṭilya, Arthaśāstra, Bk. II, Ch. III.

[2] Ch. 72, sl. 27.

is not conducive to good."[1] The reason for this, I think, is that, quite apart from economic grounds as well as considerations of defence, walls of inordinate height, planted as they were upon highly raised ramparts, would prevent the proper ventilation oj the city, at least, over the plots adjoining the ramparts and might prove detrimental to the welfare of the town. But none of the above authors gives out the principle whereby they set a limit to the height of the walls, while Śukrāchāryya wisely refrains from setting any such arbitrary limit and, on the contrary, enunciates the rule thus: "The wall of the town is to be made too high to be jumped across by robbers or enemies."[2] He further adds that "the wall (prākāra) of the town is to be uniform in depth and should have its foundation to the extent of one-half or one-third of its height and have its width one half of its height."[3]

For strengthening fortifications "the rampart should be planted," according to Kauṭilya, "with thorny and poisonous plants in bushes." The parapets were interspersed at regular intervals

[1] Brahmavaivarta Purāṇam, Śrīkṛshṇa Janmakhaṇḍa, Ch. 103.

[2] Śukranītisāra, Ch. I, *ll.* 474—6.

[3] *Ibid.*

स्वोच्छ्रायस्यार्द्धमूलोवा प्राकारः सममूलकः । २३०
तृतीयांशकमूलो वा ह्युच्छ्रायार्द्धप्रविस्तरः ।
उच्छ्रितस्तु तथा कार्य्यो दस्युभिर्नविलङ्घ्यते ॥ २३८

with towers (aṭṭālaka). Towers square throughout and with moveable staircase or ladder equal to its height shall also be constructed."[1] The wall moreover is to be provided with 'śataghnīs' (lit., hundred-killers) and 'nalikāstras' (lit., barrelled missiles), *i.e.*, guns, as well as other deadly weapons. In Vālmikī's Rāmāyaṇa we find that the city of Ayodhyā was protected by hundreds of such śataghnīs. In the ancient town of Vanchi or Karura, the capital of the Chera kingdom, now a deserted village known as Tiru Karur, on the battlements were mounted various engines to throw missiles on those who attacked the fort.[2] "The walls were always guarded by sentinels protected behind the notches (gulma).[3] Śukrāchārryya adds that they are to have a system of well-fitted windows, (corresponding to mediæval crenelles or embrasures in an embattled parapet), through which the approach of brigands or belligerents may be descried. He also insists upon a supplementary wall (pratiprākāra) lower than the main one in case of absence of any hill in the vicinity.[4]

Kauṭilya gives the minute particulars of forti-

[1] Kauṭilya, Bk. II, Ch. III. [2] Kanaksavai, p. 51.

[3] Prof. Benoy Kumar Sarkar translates 'gulma' as shrubs; but in my opinion he is wrong. Gulma means nothing but indentations into the parapets or such like hiding-places for protection of the body of fighting sentinels.

[4] Śukranītisāra, Ch. I, *l*. 479.

fication :—" In the intermediate space measuring thirty daṇḍas between two towers, there shall be formed a broad street in two compartments covered with a roof and two and a half times as long as it is broad."[1] This street seems to be intended for patrol of the sentinels, protected overhead by the roofs. The bifurcation of the street is for facilitating the double movements, forward and backward, of the guards. He goes on : " Between the tower and the broad street there shall be constructed an Indrakosha which is made up of covering pieces of wooden planks affording seats for three archers. There shall also be made a road for gods which shall measure two hastas inside (the towers ? but I think it should be Indrakosha), four times as much by the sides, and eight hastas along the parapet." The practical utility of this injunction, coming as it does from such a shrewd practical politician like Chāṇakya, is not quite clear. It only shows the religiosity of a Hindu mind which seeks some divine motive for every mundane transaction. Hence these roads appear to be meant for the presiding deities of the city who, according to the faith of their votaries, are no less wary in guarding it. There were 'charyāh' or paths to ascend the parapets (as the radical meaning connotes) which were as broad as one daṇḍa or two.

[1] Arthas'āstra, Bk II, Ch IV.

Kauṭilya proceeds:—"In an unassailable part (of the rampart) a passage for flight (pradhāvitikam) and a door for exit (nishkāradvāram) shall be made. In the centre of the parapets, there shall be constructed a deep lotus-pool; a rectangular building of four compartments, one within the other; an abode of the goddess Kumārī (Kumārīpura), having its external area one and a half times as broad as that of its innermost room; a circular building with an archway; and in accordance with available space and materials, there shall also be constructed canals (kulyā) to hold weapons and three times as long as broad. Outside the rampart passages for movements shall be closed by forming obstructions such as knee-breaker (jānubhaṁjanī), a trident, mounds of earth, pits, wreaths of thorns, instruments made like the tail of a snake, a palm-leaf, a triangle, and of a dog's teeth, rods, ditches filled with thorns and covered with sand, frying pans, and water-pools."

It may not be out of place here to notice that Megasthenes who visited Pāṭalīputra when Chandragupta was on its throne and Chāṇakya, his famous minister, identified with Kauṭilya, author of the Arthaśāstra, was at the helm of affairs of that vast empire, refers, in his accounts, to "timber walls" of Pāṭalīputra. These timber walls referred to by Megasthenes are rather mysterious inasmuchas

Kauṭilya was much against the use of wood because " fire finds a happy abode in it". Considerations of climate, economy, and æsthetics were responsible for planting and rearing up in rows " the senators of the forests " round the ramparts. Thus we find that the town of Ayodhyā was girt with a belt of śāla trees (śālamekhalā).[1]

Outside the walls and not very close to them (nātisamīpaprākārā) there were ditches surrounding the city. The number of ditches is optional, depending upon the necessity and security of the place. Thus we read in the Devī Purāṇa[2] that the number may be two, three, four, or eight as the ground requires (bhūmibaśāt). But Kauṭilya fixes the number at three ; and the three ditches are to have an intermediate space of one daṇḍa (6 ft.) from one another. The sides of the ditches were made of stones or bricks. That the ditches of Pāṭalīputra, the capital of the renowned Magadha empire, were constructed in conformity to these rules is corroborated by the account of Megasthenes. He writes that the " massive timber walls were defended by successive brick-lined moats filled with water." It may not be at all improbable that the actual number of ditches Kauṭilya saw round his principal place of activity suggested to him the

[1] Rāmāyaṇam, Ādikāṇḍa, Ch. 5, verse 12.

[2] Ch. 72, verse 28.

specified number. The king dug three moats round Mithilā—a water-moat, a mud-moat, and a dry-moat.[1]

The magnitudes of the trenches were commensurate with the defensive necessities and civic requirements such as the lie of the city ground or the erection of ramparts. The ditches of Dvārāvatī (modern Dvārakā), the capital of Srī Kṛshṇa, looked like the river Ganges.[2] Indraprastha, the new capital founded by the king Yudhishthira, was girt with ditches resembling seas by their width.[3] Śukrāchāryya lays down that "the ditch is to be constructed making the width double its depth."[4] The author of the Brahmavaivarta Purāṇa puts down hundred cubits as the suitable breadth for a ditch while the depth of ten cubits will suffice for it round an encampment.[5] Kauṭilya's details about the proportions of the ditches are fuller. According to him the three ditches round the fort are to be "fourteen, twelve, and ten daṇḍas respectively in width with depth less by one-quarter or by one-half of their width, square at their bottom, one third as wide as at their

[1] Mahā Ummagga Jātaka, translated by Rouse.

[2] Harivaṃśa, Vishṇuparva, Ch. 98, verse 11.

[3] Mahābhāratam, Ādiparva, Ch. 134, verse 30.

[4] Śukranītisāra, Ch. I, verse 240.

[5] Brahmavaivarta Purāṇam, Srīkṛshṇa Janmakhaṇḍa, Ch. 103, verse 63.

top."[1] The comparatively short breadth of Kauṭilya's trenches is due to his provision for their greater number. But the ditch round Pāṭalīputra is reported by Megasthenes to be six hundred feet broad and forty-five feet deep.

The ditches were fitted with hidden sluices or with a secret mechanism with which to regulate the current and the depth of water within them.[2] The ditches were filled with either stagnant or current water. Kauṭilya is particular about the ditches to be "filled with perennial flowing water or with water drawn from some other source." This was possible, because the ditches were connected with rivers. In case of emergency these mechanical gates could be utilised even to inundate the whole city and the surrounding plots of land.[3] It may not be inapt here to remark that the courses of Indian rivers present us with a marvellously faithful history of the growth of Indo-Aryan civilisation. Because of the riparian or littoral situation of cities, whether in India or anywhere else, flowing water was easily available. Thus the towns of

[1] Kauṭilya, Bk. II, Ch. III. The meaning of "square at the bottom" is not quite clear. The original text runs thus :—
"विस्ताराद्वगाधाः पादोनमर्द्धं वा त्रिभागमूला मूले चतुरस्राः ।"

[2] Brahmavaivarta Purāṇam, Srīkṛshṇa Janmakhaṇḍa Ch. 103, verse 64.

[3] Mahābhāratam, Śāntiparva, Ch. 69, *l.* 87.

सङ्कटद्वाराणि स्युरुच्छासार्थं पुरस्य च ॥

Pāṭalīputra, Delhi, Poona, among many others, had rivers flowing into their ditches. That the above explanation is not at all imaginary is evident from the Brahmāṇḍa Purāṇa :[1]—" The ditches were excavated with their gates connected with rivers." The Devī Purāṇa suggests that the drains of the town should clear themselves into these ditches.[2] Crocodiles, sharks, and other ferocious fishes were let off in them so that no enemy could swim across them with safety.[3] Nor were the Aryan town-planners slow to seize the slightest opportunity of making the city as picturesque as they could. In the ditches brimming with stagnant water were carefully nurtured lotus and lily plants. We read in the description of a Tamil poet that " in the broad moat surrounding the fort of Pukar, the capital of Chola kings, the waters of which were covered with beautiful flowers, the chirping of birds never ceased."[4] There was a broad belt of thorny jungle surrounding the ditch as in Bharatpur.[5] The ditches were spanned by bridges, for every gate of the town must have a bridge in front

[1] Ch. 8, *l.* 211. स्रोतसा सह तद्द्वारं निखातं पुनरेव च ।

[2] Ch. 72, *l.* 55. खातिकारचितं कार्य्यं प्रणालीभिः समन्वितम् ।
Vide also Town Planning in Ancient Deccan, pp. 61-2.

[3] Mahābhāratam, Śāntiparva, Ch. 69, *l.* 86.

आपूरयेच्च परिखां स्थाणुनक्रझषाकुलाम् । ४२

[4] V. Kanaksavai, p. 26.

[5] *Vide* Town Planning in Ancient Deccan, pp. 64-5.

of it for traffic. These bridges could be raised or lowered when occasions arose. They were, in some instances, so adjusted with mechanical devices that an enemy, once having set his feet on them, could be easily swung into the ditches. It is thus described in the Rāmāyaṇa that "at every gate of Laṅkā, the capital of Rāvana, was suspended a gigantic bridge from a mechanical structure which defended the bridge from the onset of the belligerents. It was by means of this machine that antagonists were slung into the trenches." From the peculiar nature of the Indian civic art, the utility of these ditches is manifold. They were not mere defensive works ; nor were they enjoined simply for beauty's sake. They formed not only an important part of the complex drainage system of the city, but also supplied the quantity of mud necessary for the erection of the city-walls, for filling up the low bogs and marshes of the city-ground, making the surface of the ground slant in one direction, or making it convex in accordance with the time-honoured rules of the Indo-Aryan civic art. Bharat expressly lays down that the walls are to be constructed of the mud dug out of the ditches.[1]

In alignment with the bridges stood the gopuras, or the gateways of the town in the form of pyramidal

[1] *Vide* the word 'chaya' in the Śavdakalpadruma.

towers of imposing aspect. "A turret, above the gate and starting from the top of the parapet, shall be constructed, its front resembling an aligator up to three-fourths of its height."[1] Megasthenes writes that the wall of Pāṭalīputra was equipped with 570 towers and 64 gates. This shows that there were other towers besides those over-arching the gates of the city. It may be noted here that these gopuras were a characteristic feature of the Indo-Aryan architecture so much so that they formed an integral part of almost every palatial house. The 24th chapter of the Mayamata and the 33rd chapter of the Mānasāra deal in detail with the construction of these gopuras. The towers consisted of varying storeys, their number ranging from one to fourteen. Rāmrāz, in his "Essay on Indian Architecture", furnishes us with diagrams of many such gopuras. Generally there were four main gates of the town facing the four cardinal points of the compass. Kauṭilya's Arthaśāstra, one of the oldest code of Hindu polity and sociology, mentions the designations of the four principal gates of the Aryan town or village. The northern gate was called the Brāhma Gate, that is, the gate dedicated to Brahmā, the Creator. The eastern gate was named Aindra Gate, one dedicated to Indra, the lord of the eastern quarter of the heavens, represented by the rising

[1] Kauṭily's Arthaśāstra, Bk. II, Ch. III.

Sun, for both Indra and Sun being the sons of Aditi were identified. Yama, the Lord of Death, lorded over the southern quarters, and the gate, on the south, was dedicated to him and named Yāmya Gate after him. The western gate derived its name Sainā-patya Gate from Senāpati or Kārtikeya, the commander-in-chief of the gods.[1] The author of the Agni Purāṇa christens the main gates in a different way.[2] He says that the entire plot should be divided into interlineal chambers as laid down in the case of the vāstumaṇḍal. The eastern gate should be over the chamber of the diagram dedicated to the god of the day and included within the thirty chambers occupied by the gods Īśa etc., in the present instance. The southern gate should be raised over the chamber of the vāstumaṇḍal held sacred to the Gandarvas, while the western gate of the town should be constructed over the chamber

[1] Mr. Havell, in his "History of the Aryan Rule in India," identifies the designations in this way :—"The eastern gate, the starting point of the circumambulatory rite, was dedicated to Brahmā, the Creator, represented by the rising sun. The southern gate, which symbolised the sun at noon, was dedicated to Indra, the Vedic God who ruled the firmament of the day. The western gate was dedicated to the setting sun or to Yama, Lord of Death ; and the northern gate to Senāpati or Kārtikeya, the War-god." Mr. Havell seems to be wrong here in his denomination, inasmuch-as Yama, according to Hindu traditions, is the guardian lord of the southern quarters, while Indra presides over the eastern quarters. Again it is significant that the northern parts of the city were set apart by the Indo-Aryan town-planners for the Brāhmaṇ caste and sometimes for the shrine of Brahmā.

[2] Ch. 106. *Vide* Manmatha Datta's translation.

assigned to the god of the ocean, the northern gate having been reared on the chamber dedicated to Soma. On each side of the gates the rooms should be low-roofed, extending over a considerably large area, for the gates had to bear the brunt of any frontal attack. The gates should be six cubits wide, so as to admit elephants and other large animals passing under the archways. Besides these, there were four subsidiary gates in the four corners of the city, guarded over by the deities presiding over them. In practice the number of gates varied with the area and necessity of the town. We get from Megasthenes's accounts of Pāṭalīputra that the city had sixty-four gates over-arched by lofty towers.

Mr. Havell, in his "History of the Aryan Rule in India", is responsible for the following curious and fantastic interpretation of the above appellation of the city-gates :—" The Upanishads shaped this primitive nature-symbolism into definite philosophic concepts and Vishṇu-Sūryya the All-pervading, then took the place of Indra at the zenith ; Śiva appropriated the attributes of Yama and his position in the western sky while the concept of the cosmic slumber under the name of Vishṇu-Nārāyaṇa took the place of the war-god at the nadir. It was upon this ancient symbolic rite of the Indo-Aryan village—the rite of the cosmic cross or the wheel of life—that Buddha based his doctrine of the Aryan Eight-fold Path—the new way of life which would release mankind from suffering; for, as we have seen, there were eight gates in the village walls, one in the middle of each side, and one smaller one at each corner." It is needless to remark here that the gates were fitted with unwieldy and impenetrable door-panels.

By way of illustration, it may be mentioned here that the city of Jeypore possesses seven gates. V. Kanaksavai tells us that there were four gates to the fort of Madurā surmounted by high towers. These towers were utilised by soldiers guarding the entrance of the city. The gates of the town of Jeypore have, at the top, crenelles to fire through. The gates of this city, *e.g.*, the Ajmere Gate to the south, have quadrangular areas facing them, enclosed by walls furnished with battlements through which the soldiers can point their guns at the invaders. This walled area at the Ajmere Gate can be utilised as a garrison in times of emergency and has another gate to the east, thus providing communication with the outer world.

I have already said that these gates were called "gopuras". Mr. Havell takes the word as the compound of the two words 'go' (cow) and 'pura' (town or fort), and transliterates the word as 'cow-fort'. He traces the origin of this significant name in this way :—" A broad belt of land surrounding the village (the microcosm of an Indo-Aryan city) boundaries was communal property cultivated by the villagers and the common pasture-grounds of their cattle, which were strictly guarded from wild beasts and hostile raiders by their herdsmen and the sentinels posted on the high towers or palisades over the village-gateways. Hence the latter were known as gopuras or cattle-forts, a name afterwards applied to the entrance gateways of Hindu temple enclosures which repeated the symbolism of the village plan." Though cattle played a very important part in the evolution of of Indo-Aryan civilisation and their security necessitated the pastoral Aryans to group themselves into a 'gotra' or village, which ultimately, in some cases, developed into towns, yet all these considerations cannot explain away how a gate can be identically allied with a fort. The author of the Savdakalpadruma derives the word from the root 'gup' meaning, to defend, to protect. Hence these gates were nothing but stupendous defensive structures forming an integral part of extensive fortifications of the Indo-Aryan town in the shape of embattled walls and deep trenches. Their importance in Indian town-planning cannot be over-estimated. Indeed the magnificent workmanship of gopuras, sometimes exhibiting the highest reaches of Indian architecture, presented opportunities to the Indo-Aryan architects to exercise their consummate skill and fertile imagination. The many gopuraṣ in the famous temple of Jagatśeṭh at Bṛndāvan, or in the more ancient and renowned temple of Conjeeveram, may be instanced here. The splendid art displayed in the gopuras is indeed wonderful and is a living monumental tribute to the high level of æsthetic culture and to the religious spirit of the Hindus. The main road of the Indo-Aryan town terminated in these tower-gates and the reader can conceive in his mind's eye the magnificent view presented to the eyes of a street-farer by these stately structures lording, as it were, over the whole city.

Since Indo-Aryan towns were circumscribed by walls and ditches which prevented the growth of promiscuous suburbs, it is natural that they should be given a definite shape by the town-planners of ancient India. In fact every dissertation on town-planning in any treatise dwells upon the suitability or unsuitability, auspiciousness or in-auspiciousness of different shapes. The Mayamata thus recommends five different shapes of the ramparts (*i.e.*, of the town) :[1]—(1) square (chaturasra), (2) rectangular or oblong (āyatasra), (3) roughly

[1] Ch. 10, verse 13.

circular (vṛtta), (4) elliptical (vṛttāyata), and (5) completely circular (golāvṛtta). According to the Devī Purāṇa, the towns may have these shapes :[1] —(1) quadrangular, *i.e.*, square, (2) circular, (3) triangular (tryasra), and (4) longitudinal or oblong (dīrgha). He says that in merit and auspiciousness they are, in order, best, mediocre, good, and worst. It cannot be that the Devī Purāṇa looks with disfavour a rectangular shape. It seems only to deprecate disproportionately great length of a town as compared with its breadth. Such a shape, besides presenting great difficulties to site-planning, placing and spacing of buildings, will weaken defence. The Agni Purāṇa expresses its opinion on the merits of various shapes in the following words :[2]—" A city should not be founded on plots remote from one another, nor it should be so built, as to have an angular or semi-lunar aspect (chandrārdhābha). A city resembling a 'vajrasūchī' in shape (diamond-shaped, *i.e.*, octogonal) should be regarded as inauspicious. The forepart of a city laid out or constructed in the shape of a bow (chāpābha) or 'vajranāga' should be reckoned as the most auspicious." But unlike the Agni Purāṇa, the Matsya Purāṇa highly recommends the semi-lunar shape for riparian towns. Indeed every Hindu is aware that the holy city of Benares

[1] Ch. 72, *ll.* 42—4. [2] Ch. 106, *ll* 8—10.

situate on the convex side of the Gangetic bend presents a semi-lunar aspect; while we learn on the authority of the Harivaṃśa that the town of Mathurā, standing on the bend of the river Jumna, looked like a half-moon.[1] The Matsya Purāṇa further adds that semi-lunar shape should be avoided anywhere else by those who have knowledge of the art. It approves the oblong, square, or circular shapes. According to it the triangular or drum-shaped (yava-madhya) towns are not conducive to peace and prosperity.[2] It supports even octogonal shapes like a diamond. Like the foregoing authors who deprecate the triangular shapes, Bhoja cites with approval the opinion of the Bhavishyottara Purāṇa that hardly ever should towns be shaped triangular or circular, while longitudinal or square towns are the best. By longitudinal (dīrgha) he means "extending in width to one quarter of the length of the town (pādaika-prasāra), while by 'tryasra' he means an equilateral triangle. Both concur in the view that long-shaped towns make for permanence, peace, and prosperity; while a square capital yields to the sovereign all the four fruitions (chaturvarga), Piety, Means, Desire, and Salvation. Triangular towns annihilate the three powers whereas circular ones are hot beds of

[1] Harivaṃśa, Vishṇuparva, Ch. 54, verse 56.

[2] Matsya Purāṇam, Ch. 217, *ll.* 24-8.

many endemics and pestilences.[1] On the other hand, the author of the Brahmāṇḍa Purāṇa looks with disfavour on longitudinal and fan-like forms, while, according to him, it is the inferior towns which are rotund. He highly extolls rectangular and square shapes with sides parallel to the cardinal directions of the compass.[2] The directions of the author of the Kālikā Purāṇa are particular and emphatic. He corroborates his propositions with historic and legendary illustrations. In his opinion, the shapes must be either triangular, bow-shaped (*i.e.*, semi-lunar), circular, or quadrangular, and never of any other shape. For, a drum-shaped (mṛdaṅgākṛti) town annihilates the dynasty of the reigning king, as Laṅkā, the capital of the King of the Rākshasas, being drum-shaped was conquered and left in debris. The redoubtable monarch Vali had a most formidable capital in Saunitpur and yet was forsaken by fortune, because of its shape like a fan. The pentagonal Saubha town of the king Śālva, pendent high in heavens, will also fall to the ground; while the town of Ayodhyā of the Ikshāku family, because of its shape like a bow, has earned many victories.[3] From the above it is

[1] Bhoja's Yuktikalpataru.

[2] Brahmāṇḍa Purāṇam, Ch. 8; *ll.* 218—20.

[3] Kālikā Purāṇam, Ch. 84, *ll.* 229—38.

clear that the rectangular or square shapes were the most favourable with the Indo-Aryan town-planners and were generally adopted in practice. The circular, triangular, multi-angular, or any irregular civic contours were denounced because such shapes would react upon the planning of sites and buildings, and their orientation.

The town-planners will certainly fail in their duty, if they narrow down their attention only to the construction of the city without any regard for the best arteries of its communication with the outer world. They have to mark carefully the lines of traffic flowing into the city, or the most direct thoroughfares connecting the city with the busiest and thickly populated portions of the outlying country. The above object was attained by the Indo-Aryan town-planners in many ways. First they chose the site of the capital in the centre of the kingdom. If the kingdom was divided into provinces, and the provinces into districts which consisted of some villages, it was the concern of the town-planners how to select a place in the centre of the district or province, yet on the bank of a navigable river, near the sea-shores so that water communication could be easily availed of. Indeed almost all the Indo-Aryan towns were situated on river banks or sea-shores. The author of the Sukranītisāra would not only make arrangements for these arteries of communication, but would ensure their security and protection: "Communication between the Pura and the Janapada has to be maintained by well built roads and these should be protected for the comfort and convenience of travellers. Those who molest the travellers have accordingly to be firmly put down."[1] "The village police, for instance, will have to visit the rural lanes every 'yāma' (or one hour and a half) at night."[2] And in order that the road may be safe, it is suggested also that "the sentinel should examine every egress out of and entry into a village."[3] The condition of the roads must not be neglected. Annual repairs had to be undertaken. There were series of inns or serais on the roads going from the country to the city The open highway leading from one town to another was hundred and twenty cubits wide, while the roads connecting villages were eighty cubits wide.[4]

I cannot conclude this chapter without some remarks about the practical utility of the characteristic boundaries and approaches of ancient towns. "They not only derive exceptional beauty and picture-like entity from their enclosure by

[1] Śukranītisāra, Ch. I, *ll.* 625—30.

[2] *Ibid*, *ll.* 585—6.

[3] *Ibid*, *ll.* 582—3.

[4] Devī Purāṇam, Ch. 72.

ramparts and walls, but to this enclosure was due in no small measure the careful use of every yard of building space within the wall which had led to much of their picturesque effect and which also strengthened and sharpened the solidarity of their corporate life. These also accounted for the absence of that irregular fringe of half-developed suburbs and half-spoiled country which form such a hideous and depressing girdle around modern growing towns."[1] Necessity of defence over-balanced the chances of congestion. To meet the latter contingency, settlements outside the walls were not infrequently made in times of peace. "There is always a necessity for securing some orderly line upto which the country and town may each extend and stop definitely, so avoiding the irregular margin of rubbish heaps and derelict building land which spoils the approach to almost all our towns to-day. The value of defining and limiting towns and suburbs is manifest."[2] Outside the walls and ditches lay wide belts of jungle or agricultural land, or close sequestered retreats for hermits and philosophers. These belts served as invaluable breathing places, exquisite with birds and flowers; or, provided rich game-land for pleasant hunting excursions of the king and his

[1] R. Unwin, Town Planning in Practice.

[2] *Ibid.*

suite. Again the high country roads leading to the towns, with their shading trees of luxuriant foliage planted in rows along both sides of them, afforded bracing and exhilerating walks, free from the noise and worry of street-traffic and thus secured to the citizens picturesque avenues for enjoying the charms of the country and afforded them pleasant relief from the stuffiness and aridity of town life.

CHAPTER V

Streets and their planning

One of the most important functions of a civic architect is lay-out of the streets. The roads serve two purposes: firstly, they are highways for traffic: secondly, they divide the sites for buildings. Incidentally and, as a matter of course, they have sanitary value, providing arteries of free ventilation. Hence in subservience to their primary purpose, streets should conform to the requirements of the principal currents of traffic circulation. They should be so laid out as to guarantee easy and speedy passage from one quarter of the town to another, especially to those centres of public importance to which will generally converge the mass of citizens, *e.g.*, a market, a court, a council, a bank, a university—all institutions of corporate life. Besides, upon their construction coupled with that of the buildings, depends the quantity of sunlight and ventilation the latter can receive. The width of the thoroughfares must be commensurate with and adequate for the volume of traffic through them; and the streets as well as their cross-sections should be so adjusted as to minimise the probability of collision between two or more converging currents of traffic circulation.

We have no direct materials to hand that may inform us whether the town-planning experts of ancient India understood the above principles or not. They lay down clear definite instructions about the alignment of streets and their widths; but so far as the fundamental principles underlying these instructions, or rather injunctions, are concerned, they are very reticent. This omission is in keeping with absence of any discussion of principles relating to any technical subject, peculiar not only to ancient India but to ancient times. As regards the particular topic in question, it may be said, by way of explanation, that the omission was perhaps due to absence of heavy street traffic which the modern town-planner has to take into consideration. We cannot expect the Indo-Aryan civic engineer to envisage the diverse offshoots of social evolution of dark future as reflected in the problems of modern town-planning and to provide for them in anticipation. Howbeit, the combined effect of their wonderfully harmonious and symmetric planning of the high-ways and the sites, of locating the buildings and the folks, has been to lessen and obviate the difficulties with surprising success.

It is difficult to say with any degree of certainty whether the town-planners of India had any idea of the importance of light and air in street-planning and orientated their streets accordingly, they having always enjoined the setting of streets to the four cardinal directions of the heavens. All the Smṛti Śāstras however lay down: "The purity of streets is due to wind and light of the sun and the moon."[1]

They seem to have had a clear grasp of one principle, namely, that of adjusting the width of streets to the volume of traffic through them so as to reduce the probability of congestion. Thus we read in the Devī Purāṇa:[2]—"The royal street or highway should be made as wide as ten dhanus, *i.e.*, forty cubits, so that men, horses, elephants, and vehicles can have free movement without interference and collision." Śukrāchāryya prohibits construction of small lanes such as 'vīthis' (small shopping alleys) and 'padyās' (foot-ways) in the metropolis or large cities, for they are unsuited to the place not only because they augment insanitation, but also because they are ill able to accommodate the density of passage through them. To the same end are the segregation of the slow and the quick traffic and their confinement to distinct channels of progress; for, congestion of street

[1] पन्थानश्च विशुध्यन्ति सोमसूर्य्यांशुमारुतैः ॥ ४० विष्णुसंहिता, २३श अध्यायः।

[2] Ch. 72, *ll.* 78—9.

धनूंषि दशविस्तीर्णः श्रीमान् राजपथः कृतः ॥ २९
नृवाजिरथनागानामसम्बाधसुसञ्चरः।

traffic is principally due to mixture of the two. In Kauṭilya's Arthaśāstra, Book II, Chapter IV, dealing with buildings within the fort, we find mention of roads for chariots, roads for cattle, roads for elephants, and roads for minor quadrupeds as well as for men[1] which bears testimony to appreciation and recognition of the above principle by the town-planners of ancient India. It will be too bold and presumptuous to hold that this segregation was carried out in the same thoroughfare by its longitudinal subdivision into strips allotted to different kinds of traffic as is being done in some of the more advanced capitals of the modern age. In all probability the roads were different and separate for the varying speeds classified into groups.

While on the subject of width of streets, it will not be inapt if the different widths of streets advocated by several authorities of town-planning are discussed here. Kauṭilya lays down :—" Chariot roads, royal roads, and roads leading to 'droṇamukha', 'sthānīya', country parts, and pasture grounds shall each be four daṇḍas (24 feet or 16 cubits) in width. Roads leading to 'śayonīya' (?),

[1] *Cf.* Harivaṃśa, Vishṇuparva, Ch. 38, *l.* 38 :—" Vehicular streets (rathyā), avenues (vīthi), and men's roads (nṛṇām mārgah) were constructed in the city." This classification of streets and their separate enumeration can be explained only on the hypothesis that there were distinct roads fixed for each class of passers-by.

military stations (vyūha), burial or cremation grounds, and to villages shall be eight daṇḍas in width."[1] This great width is due to the large number of people necessarily passing at the same time through these streets. "Roads to gardens, groves, and forests shall be four daṇḍas. Roads leading to elephant forests shall be two daṇḍas. Roads for chariots shall be five 'aratnis' (7½ feet). Roads for cattle shall measure four aratnis (six feet); and roads for minor quadrupeds and men two aratnis."[2] Śukrāchāryya's roads are wider: "The best royal roads (rājamārgāh) are 30 cubits wide, the average 20 cubits, while the worst royal roads are 15 cubits wide."[3] These are the main roads of towns and villages. Since the largest volume of traffic circulates through them, they are the widest: "these are used for the conveyance of marketable commodities......The 'padyā' or footpath is three cubits wide, the 'vīthi' (or shopping lanes) is five cubits wide and the 'mārga' or ordinary road is ten cubits wide whether in a town or in a village."[4] The authors of the Devī Purāṇa and the Brahmāṇḍa Purāṇa have put down exactly the same slokas (neglecting slight variations of readings) dealing with the

[1] Arthaśāstra, Bk. II, Ch. IV.
[2] *Ibid.*
[3] Śukranītisāra, Ch. I, *ll.* 520-21.
[4] *Ibid*, Ch. I, *ll.* 522-24.

measurements of roads and lanes. One must have copied the passage from another or both quote from the same authority :—" The 'deśamārgāh" (according to Brahmāṇḍa Purāṇam, 'diśāṃ mārgāh') *i.e.*, country roads should be as wide as 30 dhanus. The 'grāmamārgāh'[1] (literally village roads or roads leading to villages) should be 20 dhanus wide and the 'sīmāmārgāh'(boundary roads) ten dhanus wide. The 'rājapathāh' or royal roads

[1] M.M. Dr. Ganganath Jha (*Vide B.O.R.S.J., Vol. II, June,* 1916) says: " The highways leading from one town to another were 100 feet wide and the village roads were 60 feet wide." By the former he seems to refer to 'deśamārga', while by the latter to 'grāmamārga'. By village roads he means roads laid out in villages. This leads to an anomaly, for within the town, the principal roads were 30 feet wide and were therefore half as much wide as the roads of villages. He gives a far fetched explanation of this. With due respect to him, my humble opinion is that all his troubles are due to his wrong interpretation of the word 'grāmamārga'. As the deśamārgas were nothing but the highways of the country like the Grand Trunk Road, leading from one kingdom or principality to another, *i.e.*, joining capitals, so the grāmamārgas were the roads connecting one village with another and ultimately abutting on the deśamārgas. It should be remembered that in those days of alternating settlement and unsettlement, clusters of villages flourishing side by side, as in modern times, were non-existent or scarce. If villages lie in close proximity to one another, then the grāmamārgas identify themselves with the sīmāmārgas or the boundary roads forming lines of demarcation between them. Their exceptionally vast widths were due to the political condition of ancient India. The roads were utilised every now and then by the king or his subordinate regents or his commander-in-chief for expedition and locomotion with a vast army and suite. Indeed the origin of many of these roads can be traced to this sort of military necessity. Traces of such wide roads are however nowhere found in modern India though the bases of some may be an approximation to such breadth . Even the famous Grand Trunk Road is not so wide. *Cf.* Śukranītisāra, Ch. I, *ll.* 528-30.

should be as wide, while the branch roads (śākhārathyāh) should be four dhanus or 16 cubits wide. The breadths of lanes (uparathyāh) are three cubits, while those of bye-lanes (uparathyikā) are two cubits. The 'jaṇghāpatha'[1] (ghaṃtāpatha, according to Brahmāṇḍa Purāṇam) is four feet in breadth, and the intervening space between two houses is three feet. The drains for receiving and washing off or scouring off offals and riff-raffs are one foot wide."[2] The drains that are still extant in the ruins of Sārnāth, I may observe here, are exactly one foot wide. It is to be noted here that, according to the Devī Purāṇa, a dhanu is four cubits, while the dhanu of the Brahmāṇḍa Purāṇa measures seventeen cubits

[1] The 'jaṇghāpatha' is only a mountain pass fit for men and loaded animals, while 'ghaṃtāpatha' is a road intended for carts which are required to carry bells as a warning to passers-by. Such roads are called in the Deccan as 'ghant' and in English 'ghaunt'.

[2] Devī Purāṇam, Ch. 72, *ll.* 77—84.

चिंशद्धनूंषि विस्तीर्णो देशमार्गस्तु तैः कृतः ।
विंशद्धनुर्ग्राममार्गः सीमामार्गो दशैव तु ॥
धनूंषि दश विस्तीर्णः श्रीमान् राजपथः कृतः ।
नृवाजिरथनागानामसम्बाधः सुसञ्चरः ॥
धनूंषि चैव चत्वारि शाखारथ्यास्तु निर्म्मिताः ।
त्रिकराश्चोपरथ्यास्तु द्विकराप्युपरथ्यिका ॥
जङ्घापथश्चतुष्पादस्त्रिपादं स्याद् गृहान्तरम् ।
वृतीपादस्त्वर्द्धपादः प्राग्वंशः पादकः स्मृतः ।
अवकरः परीवाहः पादमात्रः समन्ततः ॥

Also compare Brahmāṇda Purāṇam, Ch. 8, *ll.* 227-35.

and a half.[1] In that case, while the country roads and village roads of the Devī Purāṇa are vastly wide, being 120 and 80 cubits in breadth respectively, their widths as well as the widths of the royal roads and the branch roads of the Brahmāṇḍa Purāṇa are respectively 525, 350, 175, and 70 cubits which is inconceivable and incredible. Whatever it may be, a street 40 cubits wide will be as broad as the Central Avenue or the Harrison Road, the two widest streets of Calcutta. It should be observed that the streets have widened according to the chronological order of the authorities quoted above, which demonstrates the growth of civic life and consequently, of volume of traffic with the advance of time.

The number of main thoroughfares in any city must be adequate for its area: "The king should construct as many roads as the city requires."[2] The author of the Rājavallabha gives us his own estimate of the number of chief highways that may be in a city. "The greatest city

[1] This measure of the dhanu is quite extraordinary and is opposed to its universally accepted measure which is four cubits. I think Brahmāṇḍa Purāṇam accepts this latter standard of the dhanu at least in the present case, but there must be some discrepancy in the transcription or interpretation of the original text.

[2] Śukranītisāra, Ch. I, *l.* 526 : पुरं दृष्ट्वा राजमार्गान् सुबहून् कल्पयेन्नृपः।
In my opinion the rendering of this line by Professor Benoy Kumar Sarkar is erroneous which runs as follows : "The king should lay out many roads according to the number of towns."

has seventeen thoroughfares lengthwise, and as many breadthwise ; the average city has four less, and the worst contains nine, this being the least number of longitudinal streets in a city worth the name."[1] The estimates of the Mayamata are different. " The streets running from east to west may be 12, 10, 8, 6, 4, or 2 in number and as many may be running from north to south. Or their number may be odd so that it is 11, 9, 7, 5, 3, or 1."[2]

From the above and what follows it is evident that the streets of India were arranged and planted according to what is known as the rectangular chess-board system of street-planning. That is to say that the streets were laid out in parallel rows cutting one another at right angles. Ancient town-planning, whether Greek, Roman, or Indian, has been based on the straight lines and the right angles. This is the most natural method of street-planning that suggested itself to the unsophisticated mind of the Indian civic architect, but this is also the most generally recognised one even in modern times, because the rectangle is most convenient for building block. Sister Nivedita would however trace the origin of this rectangular plan of laying out streets to the predominent occupation of Indians which is

[1] Ch. 4. [2] Ch. 10.

agriculture, *i.e.*, labour in the paddy fields. "And certainly in the Indian Jeypore, we have the rectangular plan of the rice fields reproduced with their intersecting paths."[1] I need hardly add that the streets were all straight.[2]

A remarkable feature of the towns of ancient India was the big boulevard circumscribing the city within its walls. This is the concomitant consequence of circumvallation and was common to all old towns, Indian or European, for example, the cities of Sparta and Athens. One other peculiarity is that the canonical books of the Hindu city-builders called the Śilpa Śāstras are emphatic against any structure or vāstu pointing towards the diagonal corners of the heavens. Hence all the streets ran straight from east to west and north to south. This is as it should have been, as it has been pointed out in another chapter that the contours of the city were laid out axially to the cardinal directions. Even in very ancient times, we find these directions were acted up to as illustrated in the city of Dvārāvatī which had eight large highways crossing each other at right angles, girdled round by another. Even in recent ages the city of Jeypore was laid out after a similar scheme, by a Bengali

[1] Civic and National Ideals, p. 10.

[2] Mayamatam, Ch. 10, *l.* 182. पत्तनमजुवीथीयुतं ।

Brāhmaṇ, Vidyādhar Bhattāchāryya. The plan was quite scientific and was drawn after the traditions of the Hindu city-builders. It is a chess-board plan similar to what is technically known as 'prastara'. The main streets of the city run approximately from east to west and north to south.

Indian cities were variously classified and denominated according to the number and direction of the streets and the arrangement of houses along them :—"That town is called Daṇḍaka which has only one easterly street resembling a phalanx or a staff (daṇḍa) with houses arrayed along it. If the town possesses also one northerly street intersecting the other at the centre, it is called Kartarīdaṇḍakam. If it further contains two building alleys running east-to-west (prāchīnau kuṭṭimau) at the extremities of the northerly street, then the town is known as Vāhudaṇḍakam having four gates in the four cardinal directions. If there are several sets of houses along the two sides of the northerly street with many house-lanes intervening between, it is called Kuṭikāmukhadaṇḍakam.[1] If the town is planned with three

[1] दण्डवदेका वीथी तद्दण्डकमित्यभीष्टं स्यात् ॥ ५४
उत्तरदिङ्मुखमेकं तन्मध्ये संप्रयुक्तं चेत् ।
कर्त्तरीदण्डकमुदितं प्राचीनौ कुट्टिमौ तदन्ते ॥ ५५
तद् बाहुदण्डकं स्याद् दिक्षु चतुर्द्वारसंयुक्तम् ।

east-to-west streets and three other north-to-south streets, it is termed Kalakābandhadaṇḍakam." The last four rural towns—these rather resemble the subdivisional towns in modern India—are clearly the four varieties of the daṇḍaka town. "Noted among other towns is Vedībhadrakam. It has three streets directed north and south and three vīthis or streets running to the east. These streets are separated by many residential lanes (kuṭṭimamārga), one lane intervening between every two streets. The Swastika town does not differ in plan from a Swastika village.[1] The Swastika is also a town which has six streets facing north and six others facing east, all encircled by another road and these dividing the city into residential plots (vīthipadam). The town-plan is known as Bhadrakam, if it consists of four streets running eastwise and four other running northwise. In it there are one street going round the quarters of Brahmā and three lanes to the east intervening between the

बहुकुट्टिमसंयुक्तं मध्ये वीथ्या द्विपार्श्वं तु ॥ ५६
शेषं पूर्व्ववदिष्टं कुटिकामुखदण्डकं प्रोक्तम् ।
मयमते दशमोऽध्यायः ।
प्रागुदगग्रं मार्गं कर्त्तं रीत्तसदण्डवत्तु तन्मध्ये ॥ ४२
द्वारचतुष्टययुक्तं दण्डकमिति भण्यते मुनिभिः ।
दण्डवदेका वीथी सार्व्येवं दण्डकं प्रोक्तम् ॥ ४२
मयमते नवमोऽध्यायः ।

[1] *Vide* the Chapter on the Village.

rows of houses. If the number of similarly directed streets be five and five and there be many building plots, the name of the town is Bhadramukham. Another type is Bhadrakalyāṇam ; the number of streets in it facing east and also of those facing north is six, dividing it into many building plots. The plan is known as Mahābhadram, if the number of such streets be seven and the rest as before. The town plan of Subhadra has eight streets facing the east and eight more transverse to them. The lanes which divide the building plots of this town-plan are furnished with gates and cross-bars. The Jayāṅga is the name of the town containing the imperial head-quarters. This town has a net-work of nine streets lying east to west with nine others transverse to them. It has four main gates in the four cardinal directions and four other subsidiary gates in the four corners. The lanes between the building plots are provided with portals which open out on the main streets. The experts designate the town as Vijaya in case it is divided into many building plots by lanes fitted up with gates and cross-bars to bolt them with. The number of main streets in it is ten versus ten. The imperial castle is installed in the town. Another town called Sarvatobhadra has eleven streets crossed by another set of eleven. The royal mansions are situated on any site barring the central quarters dedicated to Brahmā. In the front of the royal castle is a vast courtyard where is situated the harem. The rest should be planted according to necessity and exigencies of the situation. Its[1] street running towards the east (tat-prāg-diggata-mārga) is called Rājavīthī. The buildings of the rich range on both sides of it. Adjoining them are the quarters of the merchants. To their south are settled the weavers and to their north are established the wheel-wrights (chakriṇah, carriage-drivers ?). In their neighbourhood are quartered kindred professions. The rest is as before."[2] In fact, the above are varieties of street-planning in towns, but their difference consists in the number of principal streets and incidentally in the allocation of sites and arrangement of houses.

In the above dissertation mention is made of the doors of the roads. Such arches and gates are still visible in the lanes of Benares and Jeypore. The doors can scarcely be found, having yielded to the wear and tear of time. These doors were kept open in ordinary times and in all likelihood were bolted at night. In abnormal times such as in the event of any hostile attack or of deprada-

[1] What is this 'it' related to ? Is it the town or the Brahmā-plot or the royal house ?

[2] Mayamatam, Ch. 10.

tory incursions by brigands as frequently happened in those days of insecurity, the doors could be closed with stout and strong cross-bars and the wards could be turned into miniature strongholds. It must be remembered in this connection that the most ancient canons of town-planning forbade any doors or windows of houses opening out on the main thoroughfares. In later times this original utility and significance of the gates vanished; yet, the arches were there. The architecture of these arches was often magnificent rising to the sublime in many instances and a pedestrian could not but be impressed with the imposing spectacle confronting his eyes. His eyes would delight in feasting upon these resplendent facades.

The Mānasāra—and the Mayamata supports it in several instances—classified the towns, according to their street-planning and site-planning under eight heads :—(1) Daṇḍaka ; (2) Nandyāvarta ; (3) Sarvatobhadra ; (4) Prastara ; (5) Chaturmukha ; (6) Kārmuka ; (7) Padmaka ; (8) Swastika. The Kāmikāgama cites six more types. Their plans are exactly similar to the corresponding prototypes of villages, as the village contemplated and designed in ancient India, both in practice as well as in theory, was a miniature town or fastness. Since their characteristics have been detailed in a separate chapter, they need not be repeated here.

All these towns can be generalised into one representative type of a rectangular enclosure—only the Kārmuka and the Padmaka have different forms—with four sides facing four quarters of the heaven. The town was generally divided into four wards or sections by two large streets crossing each other at right angles at the centre.[1] These streets terminated at each end at four principal gates and the town possessed four other supplementary gates at the corners. The town was encircled within by a wide path which intervened between the walls and the outer blocks. This path went by the name of Maṅgalavīthī or the path of blessing or auspiciousness, for through this street the chariot of the presiding deity Vishṇu or Brahmā was drawn and along this path the Hindu population of the town circumambulated the town after the immemorial rite of 'pradakshiṇa'. Hence this boulevard was also known as Janavīthīkā, literally the path of men.

Denominations of the various kinds of streets in a town are as follows:—"A street that goes round the village or town is called Maṅgalavīthī which should be one to five daṇḍas wide. That which runs from east to west is called Rājapatha; that which had gates at both extremities is termed

[1] This was not the case with all towns; for, a few towns had no central streets.

Rājavīthī; that which has 'sandhis' (literally junction) is Sandhivīthī; and that which lies in a southerly direction, is named Mahākāla or Vāmana."[1] According to Mayamuni, "the streets that run straight like a staff from east to west are called Mahāpathas (broad highways). Of them the street passing through the centre (that is, the plot presided over by Brahmā) is called Brahmavīthi and this forms the navel of the network of streets. On both sides of this street and comparatively smaller than it are those streets (rest of the Mahāpathas ?) called Rājavīthī and these are fitted with gates (at the extremities). The Maṅgalavīthī and the Rathamārgas (car-streets)[2] all are 'kuṭṭimakas' (because they seem to have been paved with slabs of stone).[3] These roads if furnished with transverse doors go by the name of Nārāchapathas. The comparatively narrower streets facing towards the north and equipped with gates and bolts are called Vāmanapathas. The street that goes round the village is called Maṅgalavīthikā and the corresponding street in a capital is called Janavīthikā. But in

[1] Rāmrāz's 'Essay on Architecture'. My MSS. of the Mānasāra do not contain these lines.

[2] Are these car-streets identical with the rings of streets that encircle a town, as in Conjeeveram ? (*Vide* Ch. VII). Or, are these roads for carriage ?

[3] *Cf.* "The remains of ancient stone-paving in the principal streets" still exist in the village of Aihole in the Bijāpore district once a renowned city known as Aryyapura.

ancient authorities and in other towns, this street is technically termed as rathyā or the road along which the processional chariot (ratha) is dragged. The streets are one to five dhanus wide."[1]

Mr. E. V. Havell—and in this matter he takes the cue from Rāmrāz's excerpt—says that of the two central streets, the one running from east to west is called Rājapatha and the other running from north to south is called Mahākāla, or Vāmanapatha (the short street). In my opinion he is wrong. Firstly, it is not an invariable practice that the towns are planted longitudinally from east to west; some run north and south. In these cases the north-to-south central street cannot be called Vāmanapatha or short street. Secondly, in the case of an

[1] Mayamatam, Ch. 9, *ll.* 72—79.

प्राक्प्रत्यग्गतमार्गा ऋजुदण्डमहापथाख्यास्ते ॥ ३६
मध्यमयुक्ता वीथी ब्रह्माख्या सैव नाभिः स्यात् ।
द्वारसमेता वीथी राजाख्या च द्विपार्श्वतः क्षुद्राः ॥ ३७
सर्व्वाः कुट्टिमकाख्या मङ्गलवीथी तथैव रथमार्गम् ।
तिर्य्यग्द्वारसमेता नाराचपथा इति ख्याताः ॥ ३८
उत्तरदिङ्मुखमार्गाः क्षुद्रार्गलवामनाख्यपथाः ।
ग्रामावृता मङ्गलवीथिकाख्या पुरावृता च जनवीथिका स्यात् ।
तयोस्तु रथ्याभिहिताभिधा स्यात् पुरातनैरन्यतमेष्वथैवम् ॥ ३९ 1/2

Cf. शिल्परत्न पञ्चमाध्याये ।—
ग्रामपर्य्यन्तवीथिस्तु ख्याता मङ्गलवीथिका ॥ ६८
नगरे रथवीथी सा रथ्याख्या खर्व्वटादिषु ।

even number of streets, there cannot be one versus one central streets. Thirdly, Rāmrāz's extract does not warrant such a conclusion. And Mayamata's appellations clearly explode it. According to this authority the street that passes through Brahmā's chamber is called Brahmavīthī and all the principal roads fitted with gates and running from east to west are Rājavīthīs. Fourthly, a Rājapatha or Rājavīthī is not 'king's street', that is, the one that runs in the front of the king's palace. All the treatises, *e.g.*, Mayamatam, Arthaśāstra, Śukranītisāra deny such a compound. The proper rendering should be 'king among streets'. Pānini, the renowned grammarian, expounds the word as 'panthānām rājā', *i.e.*, king among streets. In other words, it refers to any large street. Fifthly, Vāmanapathas and Rājapathas are used in the plural number which furnishes additional proof against their singularity or uniqueness. I venture to say that Vāmanapathas are the short roads lying north to south joining two easterly parallel streets. They are the short-cuts. These short-cuts may be planted in a straight line so as to form a continuous road. The central among the northerly streets may sometimes be called Mahākālapatha. Sandhivīthīs seem to be roads which, when abut on other streets, form a triangular cross-section.

The broad central streets, the Brahmavīthī

and the Mahākālavīthī constituted the principal arteries of communication of the town with other towns and villages, thus linking them together. They were the military and commercial routes, because Indian towns and villages were generally planted at the meeting points of such high-ways. These crossings were the trysting places of caravans of traders and offered a market for disposal of their merchandise. It should be borne in mind in this connection that the towns served also as fastnesses to defend the surrounding villages under their ægis and jurisdiction. This net-work of main routes knitting together the towns and villages of the kingdom and affording easy access to them augmented the administrative efficiency of the state. Their manifold utility was patent to all and they were maintained by the co-operation of groups of villages which furnishes another example of their civic consciousness. Only the most important routes, such as the military ones, were repaired and maintained by the state, for the state was more interested in their upkeep than the villages.

This peculiarity in the situation of the Indian towns had another remarkable bearing upon Indian town-planning. As already observed, the two middle northerly and easterly streets formed the principal channels through which the main currents of importing and exporting commerce passed. India at that time had an extensive foreign trade with Arabia, Turkey, and Persia and through them with Europe. The trade routes lay through the famous passes of the North Western Frontier Provinces. Hence in normal times, the Mahākālapatha running from north to south formed the chief commercial route ; it was also the road along which the foreign invasions came. The Brahmavīthī was generally the road for inland military expeditions and inland trade. But in northern and eastern parts of India the streets exchanged their purposes. Thus we are informed that the Brahmavīthī of Chandragupta's empire was that which passed through Pāṭalīputra and right up to north-western povinces.

The fact that the two principal roads of every town and village of ancient India continued up to the main highways of the empire and thus constituted the most important channels for the ebb and flow of commerce was one of the reasons why the Hindu town-planners did not advocate diagonal streets in their town-plans. One of the functions of these diagonal streets in modern times is, to provide direct short-cuts between railway terminii or between the railway stations and the docks. It is obvious that the main streets of Indian towns adequately provided for similar through-traffic. Another reason for these radiating streets is that they afford easy and short access to important public buildings and places, such as banks or markets. But the peculiar custom of the Indian towns of centralising and judiciously allocating the public buildings at the centre, and round about it, obviated this necessity. Hence when we consider that these radial streets are responsible for ill-shaped buildings and rooms at the cross-sections—which, by the way, should be the important and picturesque edifices—and also that the main streets and the intelligent distribution of buildings splendidly served the purpose of diagonal streets of modern towns, we cannot but admire the skilful manipulation of the whole town-plan by the Indian civic architects which could only proceed from a thorough grasp of the subject.

But it must not be supposed that diagonal streets were never used. We find in the circular form of the Nandyāvarta town-plan that streets radiated from the centre of the town. But it is not definitely known if this scheme of radiating streets proceeded from any conscious understanding of the principles for which they stand. It is more likely they were the result of merely copying the configuration of the ribs of the nadyāvarta flower.[1] But the circular type of the Nandyāvarta

[1] *Vide* the Chapter on Town Expansion.

village was seldom executed in practice, for generally the village was planned after the mystic geometrical figure Nandyāvarta. Inclined streets were sometimes adopted along the outskirts as in the Swastika or multi-lateral village plans. In these, they could not be avoided.[1] But maps of many towns of ancient India, especially of Rājputanā and the Deccan, show that there are many diagonal curved streets in them. I am not sure if all of them were laid out according to orthodox town-plans or according to any pre-designed plan at all, though the town-planning traditions might have unconsciously asserted themselves in some features. Curved streets might have been there, prior to the foundation of the town and it was thought advisible not to deviate them, for natural routes best adjust themselves to the exigencies of the situation. Again many of the towns in Rājputanā and the Deccan are situated in hilly tracts where curved streets are inevitable and enhance the effectiveness of mountain vistas. Thus in the city of Vijayanagara, " instead of a flat-lying town surrounded by culti-

[1] "The word 'swastika' conventionally signifies a method of crossing the arms or legs so as to form diagonals af a square or rectangle. The plan of this type contemplates some diagonal streets dividing the vāstu into certain triangular plots. The site of the town-plan need not be marked out into a square or a rectangle. It may be of any form." (*Indian Architecture* by Messrs Ananthalwar and Reas). This new and radical interpretation of swastika-plan strikes a departure from its orthodox conception based upon the figure Swastika.

vated fields and intersected by streets regularly laid out, we find the whole site interspersed with groups of bare rocky hills or huge granite boulders, with little vegetation of any sort upon them. The ancient streets or bāzārs are placed in the villages among the hills."[1] We have at least one definite instance of a diagonal street that was deliberately conceived and laid out as a direct approach from the king's palace to another city. This was the 'Pān Supāri Bāzār' street of Vijayanagar. Even in abstract theory we find in the Garuḍa fort that central diagonal streets were advocated to be laid out connecting one corner with its opposite. As in the case of city contours where, though exact mathematical figures were recommended in the authoritative treatises on Indian town-planning, yet the territorial restrictions made irregular zigzag shapes unavoidable, so was the case with the planning of streets. They certainly were made to conform to local conditions so that, economic and æsthetic considerations were not sacrificed to the fetish of symmetry or rectilinearity in a fixed direction. It cannot be said that the curved form of these streets was due to the ignorance of the master-builders of the directions of the town-planning authorities; for there exist even to-day in Southern India numerous

[1] Archæological Survey of India, 1902-3.

descendants of these master-builders of olden times who understand and preserve the traditional lore on town-planning. Indeed they are the only persons extant who can explain the technical terms of architecture and cognate subject of town-planning. The very existence in India of the sub-castes, trade guilds in fact, is a sure guarantee that the principles of caste-profession were handed down from generation to generation.

It is not definitely known whether the streets were lined with foot-paths like the streets of a modern town. The word padyā (noticed above), literally meaning foot-fath, seems to have had a different significance and referred to only narrow roads, too narrow for vehicles plying through them. In his commentary on Āpasthambha's direction about the particular passage to be given to a murderer of a Brāhmaṇ, Horadatta, however, writes, "Some say that his passage lies along one of the two paths that border a large street (rathyā) on both sides."[1]

Special attention was devoted to the trimming of the intersections of roads. They were either triangular as when one road abuts on another or

[1] Āpasthambha Dharmasutra, Praśna 1, Paṭala 9, Khaṇḍika 24, Sutra 12. तस्य पन्था अन्तरावर्त्मनि ।

अपर आह, यत्र रथ्यादौ उभयोः पार्श्वयोर्वर्त्मनी भवतः, तत्र तयोर्मध्ये सूवकारादिपथेन सञ्चरेतेति ।

quadrangular as when two roads cross one another[1] or circular as in the case of Nandyāvarta town at the centre of which converge eight streets. These intersections were given definite shapes and were very much widened by straightening the projecting angles of the adjacent building plots. Thus we read in the Harivaṃśa that the sixteen cross-sections formed by the eight large streets of Dvārāvatī, four running transverse to the four others, were very wide.[2] On these cross-roads of the village or town were situated the council-trees or pavillions where elders of the village chatted together or laid their heads together to discuss village politics.[3] Bhuvaneswar has its great tree in the centre of the parting of three roads. The pedestals round these trees served the purpose of a dais and the trees were therefore called council-trees. On some cross roads one would find wells or fountains or water-sheds. I observed at Bharatpur one such well attached to a water-shed (*i.e.*, a house where drinking water is supplied to passers-by free of charge) made of rough-hewn stone at the junction of three roads. In some cases lamp

[1] Harivaṃśam, Vishṇuparva, Ch. 88, *l.* 17.

कल्प्यन्ताम् त्रिकचत्वराः ।

Ibid, Ch. 98, *l.* 55.

[3] *Vide* Agni Purāṇam, Ch. 65, *l.* 4.

चतुष्पथे ग्रामादौ च न शून्ये कारयेत् सभाम् ।

posts were planted. The Smṛti Śāstras enjoin lighting lamps at the cross-roads. Divine edifices were also erected at the intersections of roads. The central site of a town or a village was almost always set apart for shrines of Brahmā. The great width of the cross-sections, and the well, the chaitya, the sabhā-vṛksha (council tree),[1] or the light-post (dīpa-sthambha)[2] situated at their centres minimised the chances of collision between countergoing vehicles. In ancient India it was the custom to make a 'pradakshiṇa' (or rounding of the cross-way with the right hand turned towards it) of the cross-road[3] and this was not possible if pedestrians or conveyances did not keep to the left. Indeed great stress was laid

[1] Harivaṃśa, Vishṇuparva, Ch. 88, *l*. 131.

[2] It is difficult to say with certainty that there was any elaborate and systematic arrangement of lighting the towns of ancient India. We generally come across ritualistic injunctions upon the householder to light lamps at the cross-roads. This cannot be interpreted as a part of any lighting scheme of towns inasmuch as even village roads are included within the operation of the rule and even to-day lamps are lighted, on some special occasions, at the crossings of village roads. On festive occasions only light-posts (dīpavṛksha) were erected at regular intervals throughout the city. The Brahma Purāṇa and the Agni Purāṇa however lay down that lights should be posted in rows in the streets (rathyā) after sun-set. (दीपमालाश्च कर्त्तव्याः......रथ्याप्रदेशमा-र्गेषु...). I am not quite certain whether this rule was dictated by reasons of civics or of ceremonials and if it was followed in pratice at all.

[3] Vishṇu Purāṇa, Book III, Ch. 12, sl. 26.

अपसव्यं न गच्छेच्च देवागारचतुष्पथान् ।

upon this rule of keeping to the left. "The most convenient arrangement is to have a round space with the traffic circulating in one direction. Vehicles coming from any one road fall in with the line of traffic, circulate with it, and fall out again when they reach whatever of the other roads they wish to pass down."[1] If the custom noted above was actually followed in practice, then the vehicles in ancient India followed a clockwise motion in going round the circulation spaces at the cross-section described above. From the æsthetic point of view, a tree or a tower at the junction of roads is highly desirable. The hazy vacuity of long straight streets wearies the eye-sight as there is nothing in the front to fix the eyes upon. Contrast with this the very pleasant effect which the street causes, if it leads to some fine architectural structure or a beautiful tree. In ancient India, the junctions of roads were therefore utilised for erection of monumental buildings, such as a college, a shrine, or a monastery. At the centre of the town were sometimes erected the imperial mansions. The principal four streets radiated from this central place and they terminated at the four city gates surmounted by arches and turrets. The royal

[1] R. Unwin, Town Planning in Practice.

mansion or the sacred shrine of Brahmā had also gopuras at the four cardinal directions and the streets as a rule started from these gates. The temple or the imperial edifice was the finest building of the town and the sublimity of the vista was considerably enhanced by the picturesque gardens they contained within their compound. A pedestrian wending his way along these streets could not fail to be impressed by the delightful panorama revealed before his eyes.[1] Even the small streets and lanes had arched doors at their extremities. The Indian master-builders were very particular in bringing about this spectacular effect, for it goes a great way towards promoting the art culture of the citizens. Thus we read in the Matsya Purāṇa that the four terminii of the two main cross-streets were artistically adorned with four magnificent structures, all important from the civic point of view.[2] The principal thoroughfares were lined with trees whose sanitary and æsthetic value is obvious. "The mangoe trees and the mādhavī trees were planted at convenient spots along the streets (of Con-

[1] "At the front of the gates there should be an arbour (latāmaṇḍapa) and a garden. Every gate should be furnished with a royal chamber and also with windows. Their fronts should be decorated with ornate pictures. Bowers or maṇḍapas should be erected hard by the quarters of the armed gate-keepers." *Vide* Devī Purāṇam, Ch. 72, *ll.* 235—46.

[2] *Vide* Chapter VI.

jeeveram) and at the intersection of the streets. Indeed the city was unsurpassed for the magni ficence of its broad streets and the beautiful rows of noble avenue trees on either side."[1] The streets of the most ancient towns were lined with walls on both sides[2] and no lane or window opened on them. Later on, there was however some modification. The windows of the second storey were allowed on the road side. Small stalls for shopping were raised in rows against the walls. The height of the stall did not exceed that of the walls. I have seen a beautiful picture of such streets honey-combed with rows of shopping stalls of uniform height in the picture gallery of the Calcutta Museum.[3] Sometimes an entire profession or business or class of citizens was represented along a street which was named after it.

The buildings were not constructed in an irregular fashion and there was co-operation in alignment and structure. Thus we read in the description of Ayodhyā that the fronts of the buildings were harmoniously arranged (suniveśitaveśmāntām). We have bās-reliefs showing the general design of the frontage of buildings belong-

[1] Town Planning in Ancient Deccan.

[2] *Vide* Śilparatna, Ch. 5, *l.* 42.

पांसुचययुक्तमार्गं विधिवत् कार्य्यं हि सर्व्वत ।

[3] For the ornamental effect of the pictures on the lateral walls, *vide* Chapter XI.

ing to the Buddhistic age.. Their sculptural ornamentation and architectural workmanship are magnificent. The patriotic sculptor chiselled on the facades of the buildings splendid scenes of Buddhist mythology and culture.

Finally the streets were elevated in the middle so that they looked like the back of a tortoise and the country roads were provided with sufficient number of culverts and bridges. There were drains on both sides of the roads for passage of water.[1] The streets were sometimes paved with slabs of stones or were macadamized with broken stones and gravels. Every year they had to be repaired in this way.[2] Mr. Ayyar says that dust-bins (*purimums*) were also placed in streets, generally in the corners at the two extremities of a street. He also supplies us with a detailed description of the drainage system of the town of Vanji:—" As in other cities so also in Vanji the ditch encircled the walls of the city. The water from the palace, public halls, and private residences fell into this ditch by means of a conduit sluice known as Tumbu. The

[1] Śukranītisāra, Ch. 1, *ll.* 531-2.

कूर्म्मपृष्ठा मार्गभूमिः कार्य्याः ग्राम्यैः सुसेतुकाः ।
कुर्य्यान्मार्गान् पार्श्वखातान्निर्गमार्थं जलस्य च ॥

[2] Śukranītisāra Ch. 1, *ll.* 585-6

पङ्क्तिद्वयगतानां हि गेहानां कारयेत् तथा ।
मार्गान् सुधाश्मकैर्वा घटितान् प्रतिवत्सरम् ॥

conduit pipe discharged the water of the city into the ditch near the entrance gate where it was covered over with a stone culvert.

"By such a drainage system, the water used in private homes for domestic and bathing purposes, was conducted by pipes into the main conduit which poured its contents into the ditch. Those who could afford the expense, had separate baths specially constructed for them in such a manner that water might be filled in or let out of such baths at their pleasure. When they had finished bathing, they opened the outlet of the baths which emptied water into the drain which led to the ditch outside."[1]

It may not be out of place in this chapter to note that, like the walls ranging on both sides of the streets of the city, sometimes the streets outside the city had their own walls. In the palace-city of Rājagṛha, it is said that the roads which traversed the plain country beyond the city seem to have been protected by walls on either sides. In 1812, Buchanan was able to trace "the foundations of a double wall leading to the gap," all the way from the south gate to new Rājagṛha to the entrance of the new valley. One such road was the pilgrim's road from Sonagiri to the Son Bhāndār cave which now passes through one gap in the south wall which

[1] Town Planning in Ancient Deccan, pp. 61—2.

probably represented a south-east gate leading towards Jithian.[1]

In a tropical country like India where the prevailing wind blows either from the north or south throughout the whole year, it is reasonable that the houses should lie east to west so as to admit of free ventilation. But to receive the orient sun, the houses of the oriental countries are also directed to open out towards the east.[2]

[1] Archæological Survey of India, 1907—8.

[2] Śukranītisāra, Ch. 1, *l.* 515.

निवेशनं पुरे ग्रामे प्रागुदङ्मुखमेववा ।

CHAPTER VI

SITE-PLANNING AND FOLK-PLANNING

WHEN the principal streets called Rājapathas are laid out, the whole city area is divided by them into 'grāmas' or muhallas, *i.e.*, wards.[1] It has already been stated that street-planning was preceded by, and was therefore *generally* based upon another scheme of dividing the town or village known as Padavinyāsa. *Ordinarily* the streets lay along the lines of this division, so that the wards marked off by the principal streets were exactly identical with the blocks lined off in padavinyāsa.[2] Distribution of professions and castes as well as allotment of sites were made entirely with reference to padavinyāsa, a pada or a block being set apart for a caste or profession. The orthodox rules of the Śilpa Śāstras require that the number of 'padas' or quadrangular plots in any place should vary from one to one thousand and twenty-four,—a very large range indeed,—in accordance with its area and structural requirements. The mode of division into padas is by drawing two to thirty-three rectilinear parallel lines and as

[1] 'Grāmādīnām niveśinām' in Śukranītisāra, Ch. 1, *l.* 430.

[2] For variations, *vide* Appendix.

many transverse parallel lines. These thirty-two schemes of division are distinguished by as many different names according to the number of squares into which the whole area is partitioned out. And their names in serial order are Sakala, Pechaka, Pīṭha, Mahāpīṭha, etc., ending with the thirty-second Indrakānṭa. "The whole scheme has been arranged in such a manner that in each case the number of partitions corresponds to the square of the serial number. The eighth plot which is called Chaṇḍita or Maṇḍuka comprises a division into sixty-four squares, while by the ninth plot which bears the technical name of Paramaśāyika, the ground is divided into eighty-one squares."[1] In the case of a city or a village the mystic diagrams which are generally drawn up on the ground, thereby dividing it into appropriate numbers of plots, are Sthaṇḍila (of 49 squares), Chaṇḍita or Maṇḍuka, or Paramaśāyika.[2] For this reason and also because the plots are assigned to different presiding deities—(the authors of the Śilpa Śāstras, in folk-planning and allocation of sites or squares, refer to them in the name of their respective presiding deities)—it is essential that the scheme of dedicating the plots should be clearly understood.

[1] Dr. Acharyya's Summary of the Mānasāra.

[2] Agni Purānam, Ch. 93.

A reference to the diagrams attached hereto will explain the schemes. The adoption of the foregoing three schemes only was not, however, an invariable practice. Thus the Mayamata lays down that in the planning of villages or houses, civic experts may accept any of the schemes from the first to the tenth, *i.e.* from Sakala to Āsana.[1] Even this was not necessarily invariable as is evident from the Mayamata's plan of planting twelve east-to-west streets and an equal number of transverse ones. Indeed there was not any rigid rule on this point but the most generally recommended plan is Paramaśāyika of 81 plots.

The wards or plots were not necessarily square; their shape resembled the periphery of the town. That is to say, if the town was rectangular, the wards or plots were also rectangular and if the town had a triangular or circular contour, the wards were of irregular shape. But the latter sort of towns was rare and, only in a town situated in the midst of hillocks, such irregular shapes were allowed. As the town was generally founded on a plain site, the wards of a scientifically planned city were either square or rectangular. Now these wards

[1] *Vide* Mayamatam, Ch. 9, *l.* 110. *Cf.* Śilparatna, Ch. [illegible], *l.* 110.
सकलाद्यासनान्ते तु पदे ग्रामादि बिन्यसेत् ।

MAṆḌUKA
OR
(CHAṆḌITA)

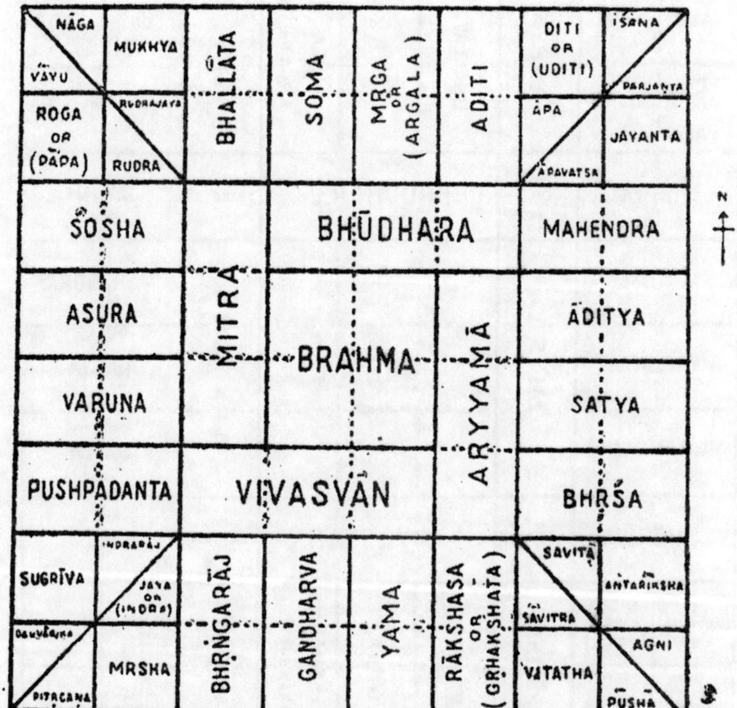

PARAMASAYIKA

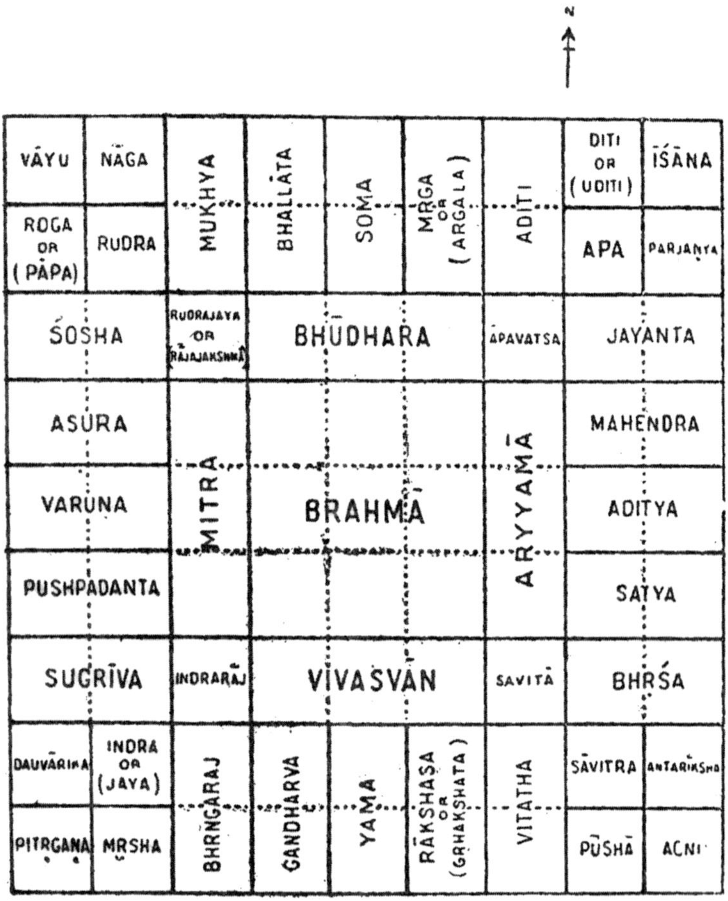

were again subdivided by a net-work of narrower and smaller streets into building blocks. All the 'grāmas' or wards were not laid out after the same pattern. Their planning was regulated by requirements of business which the residents of any ward carried on. In order to stamp the wards with individuality and diversity of character, all the wards were not divided again into the same number of building plots ; neither the building roads and lanes were planted on the same plan. All the various types of village-plans were sometimes adopted, even in a single town.

In India, considerations of efficiency in corporate life, and the principle of the Varṇāśrama Dharma developing a social stratification of the people in general and of the functionaries of the state, led to a segregation of the classes following different pursuits ; and the same caste or people of the same profession were congregated in the same ward[1] so that a uniformity of life and consequent economic efficiency and progress were secured. Every ward was set apart for a caste or trade guilt of note which enjoyed an autonomy of its own.[2] Thus if the Śūdra

[1] Śukranītisāra, Ch. I, *l.* 514.

सजातीयगृहाणां समुदायेन पङ्क्तितः ॥

[2] *Vide* Dr. R. C. Mazumdar's Corporate Life in Ancient India.

class was numerically very large, a separate block or even a separate site was allotted to it. The goldsmiths, the artisans, the perfume-dealers, the Brāhmaṇs, or the soldiers would have distinct muhallas or a detached group of blocks of their own. Even to-day in the towns or villages of Southern India the Brāhmaṇa quarter is separate and goes by the name of Agrahāram. In large cities any of the sites into which the whole city was divided by the main highways, was so large that no particular class was important and big enough to inhabit it to the full. Again in large cities such detachment of classes or castes is neither conducive to the integrity of civic life nor good for the class itself, because corporate life connotes manifold needs and responsibilities and consequently necessitates inter-dependence and inter-communication. Hence every site was divided into different blocks or plots, one being meant for each class. In a word, a site was the prototype of the whole city on a smaller scale. This admixture and congregation of classes came as a remedial measure against possible accentuation of class differences.

The above sums up the principle of folk-planning, and this folk-planning is one of the most important subjects dwelt on in the Śilpa

Śāstras.[1] It gave an individual tone to the sites; indeed folk-planning scarcely differs from site-planning. This folk-planning was designed in different fashions by different authorities, and I will give here some account of the various kinds of site-planning.

Kauṭilya designs his plan in this wise: "Demarcation of the ground inside the fort shall be made first by opening three royal roads from west to east and three from south to north.

"In the midst of the houses of the people of all the four castes and to the north from the centre of the ground inside the fort, the king's palace facing either the north or the east shall be constructed occupying one-ninth of the whole site inside the fort. Royal teachers, priests, sacrificial place, water reservoir, and ministers shall occupy sites east by north to the palace. Royal kitchens, elephant stables, and the store house shall be situated on sites east by south.

[1] It is the authors of the Śilpa Śāstras who have made their folk-planning hinge upon padavinyāsa, whereas Kauṭilya, Śukrāchāryya and the author of the Agni Purāṇa do not refer to padavinyāsa. Nowhere in their works do we come across any allusion to or description of this scheme. Their method of allocating sites and folk is therefore quite independent of padavinyāsa and the various classes and professions have been represented in their ideal towns in quarters selected only with reference to the site of the royal mansions. The latter authorities all belong to Northern India. Do we get here a glimpse of two schools, Northern and Southern ?

On the eastern side, merchants trading in scents, garlands, grains, and liquids, together with expert artisans and the people of the Kshatriya caste shall have their habitations. The treasury, the accountant's office, and various manufactories shall be situated on the sites south by east. The store house of forest produce and the arsenal shall be constructed on sites south by west.

"To the south, the superintendent of the city, of commerce, of manufactories, and of the army as well as those who trade in cooked rice, liquor, and flesh, besides prostitutes, musicians, and the people of Vaiśya caste shall live. To the west by south, stables of asses, camels, and working house. To the west by north, stables of conveyances and chariots. To the west, the artisans manufacturing worsted threads, cotton threads, bamboo-mats, skins, armours, weapons, and gloves as well as the people of Sūdra caste shall have their dwellings.

"To the north by west, shops and hospitals. To the north by east, the treasury and the stables of cows and horses. To the north, the royal tutelary deity of the city, ironsmiths, artisans working on precious stones, as well as Brāhmaṇs shall reside. In the several corners, guilds and corporations of workmen shall reside.

" In the centre of the city, the apartments of gods such as Aparājita, Apratihata, Jayanta, Vaijayanta, Śiva, Vaiśravaṇa, Aśvina (divine physicians), and Vishṇu[1] shall be situated. In the corners, the guardian deities of the ground shall be appropriately set up. ....At a distance of 100 dhanus (1 dhanu 6 feet) from the ditch (on the counterscarp side) places of worship and pilgrimage, groves and buildings shall be constructed. Guardian deities of all quarters shall also be set up in quarters appropriate to them.

" Either to the north or the east, a burial or cremation ground shall be situated; but that of the people of the highest caste shall be to the south of the city. Heretics and chaṇḍālas shall live beyond the burial grounds. Families of workmen may in any other way be provided with sites befitting their occupation and field work.

" There shall be a water-well for every ten houses."[2]

It will be manifest from the above that, in Kauṭilya's scheme, it is the streets, and not pada-vinyāsa, that divide out the city, unlike the plan

[1] Dr. Shama Śastry reads Śrī-madira-gṛha and translates it as honourable liquor house which is meaningless; and the site of a liquor-house in the midst of gods is absurd. The correct reading should be Śrī-mandira-gṛha, *i.e.*, house of Śrī-mandira or Vishṇu.

[2] Arthaśāstra, Book II, Ch. IV.

of the Śilpa Śāstras. Kauṭilya seems to have realised in his metropolis Pāṭalīputra his ideals of site-planning as set forth above.

Śukra's site-planning is different. Unlike Kauṭilya, he provides for the Sabhā or the Council house in the centre of the capital (sabhāmadhyām rājadhānīm)[1] and the royal palace in the midst of the council buidlings (rājagṛham sabhāmadhyam).[2] The court and the Śilpa-Śālā or the museum (literally, hall of arts), both are to be stationed to the north of the palace.[3] Leaving a space of hundred cubits from the palace (probably towards its north) the ministers, the clerks, the councillors, and officers should be located in detached lodges. Two hundred cubits away from the palace, either to the north or to the east, are allowed sites for the military cantonments. Śukra observes a certain order in the allocation of different classes of military barracks. First, the important personages (prakṛtayah), then the ordinary people, next the officers, then the commanders of the army, then the infantry, then the cavalry, the attendants of horses and elephants, next the guns and ordnances, the mares, the constabulary

[1] Śukranītisāra, Ch. I, *l.* 431.

[2] *Ibid, l* 435.

[3] *Ibid, l* 467.

and sentry thereafter, lastly foresters; this is the order to be followed in the location of their sites or quarters. Wealth and birth were the determining factors in the distribution of sites for dwellings of the citizens round about the royal palace. The inns and restaurants should be well protected and provided with ample supply of water. The cognate houses, their relation being determined by similarity of business or identity of caste, shall be congregated together in a row.[1] In the towns or villages, the buildings should face either the north or the east. In the market place, stalls or shops are to be placed according to the classes of commodities. The best plots along the side of the highways should be distributed with regard to the wealth and power of the residents. In this way the king should plan both the town and the grāma.[2]

The author of the Agni Purāṇa[3] has his own scheme of folk-planning. He locates the goldsmiths in the south-east corner of the town; the professional dancers and musicians, the harlots in the south; the stage-managers, the carriage-men, and the fishermen in the south-

[1] Mr. Sarkar's rendering of the line 514 is obviously incorrect.
[2] Śukranītisāra, Ch. 1, *ll.* 508—518.
[3] Ch. 106, *ll.* 12—27.

west. He gives away the western sites for the dwellings of those who deal in cars and chariots, weapons, and cutlery; the liquor merchants, the officers and employees are provided with quarters in the north-west. The northern sites are set apart for the pious people such as the Brāhmaṇs, the Yatis, and the Siddhas. Fruit stalls are situated in the north-east. This completely fills up the outermost blocks. Then in the second round in the east are given sites for the commanding officers of the army. In the south-east, the soldiers' barracks are stationed. In the south is situated the lodge of the superintendent of the women (probably the prostitutes and the court women are meant who are quartered in that direction). The archery is assigned sites in the south-west. And in the west and the north-west shall dwell ministers, the treasurers, and the artisans. The judges, the elite of the citizens, as well as the high officials belonging to the twice-born class should be assigned sites in the nortth and the north-east. Then begins the third annulus. In it, in the east are situated the Kshatriyas; in the south the Vaiśyas; in the west the Śūdras and this finishes the third circle of the sites. Within it the cavalry, the infantry, and the physicians should be situated in all directions." Nowhere in the Agni Purāṇa is it mentioned where the royal castle will be erected. But from the peculiarity of the scheme it appears that it will be located in the central part of the town surrounded by the cavalry as mentioned above. "To the east of the town," the Agni Purāṇa goes on, "should be stationed king's men in disguise. To the south the cremation ground is placed; to the west is located the pinjrapole or the cattle sheds; and to the north shall be allocated the house-plots of the husbandry." It seems that the above quarters are without the town proper. For, they cannot be adjacent to the royal compound for obvious reasons, nor is there any room for them in the outer fringe of the town which has been already disposed of. The cremation ground is generally located outside the town. Again it is not reasonable that the agriculturist who has to ply their ploughs, from day to day, in the fields lying without the town should be provided with quarters inside the town. Besides, the disguised officers will watch the approach of the enemy. For these reasons, I think, they are placed outside the town and, yet, given the protection of the town-fort. This is confirmed by the next sentence wherein it is laid down that villages will be set up in the corners without the town where Mlecchas will be quartered. There should be a symmetrical distribution of a good number of markets.

The Mayamata makes an exhaustive treatment of the proper distribution of the residential quarters interspersed with market stalls (antarāpaṇakam). It particularly deals with these inter-residential stalls and the articles sold in them.[1] It lays down: "Whether in small towns or large cities, I shall now deal with residential sites and the shops situated in their midst. Within the processional boulevard circumscribing the city are situated in rows the houses of the merchants. To the south but a little removed to the sides are given sites to the weavers; to the north are the residential plots of the wheelwrights (carters ? chakriṇām). Along the processional street are settled the various artisans and mechanics, *e.g.*, blaksmiths, or even day-labourers. Inter-residential market-stalls may be set up along the roads encircling the chambers of Brahmā and those stalls should be reserved for fruits and betel-leaves. In the quarters held sacred for the deities from Īśāna to Mahendra should be erected the stalls for fish and meat, dry articles, and vegetables. The stalls for staple foods and edibles are fixed in sites from

[1] Can it be inferred that the class of people dealing with the articles lived in the cottages adjoining the stalls ? *Vide* Chapter IX.

Mahendra to Agni; and from Agni to Gṛhakshata are raised sheds for basins and pottery. From Gṛhakshata to Niṛti should be allocated the shops for brass and bronze. The cloth shops are set up in the quarters from Pitṛs to Pushpadanta; and from the latter to Vāyu should be laid out the mart for rice and paddy. From Vāyu to Bhallāṭa quarters are meant for the drapers (tailors and cutters ?)' and those who deal in salt and oils. From that to Iśa are situated the shops for perfumeries and flowers. The above are the nine intervening shopping sheds in the outer most sites. But along the roads that are laid out within the boulevard are stationed the stalls and shops of jewels and precious stones, gold, clothes, drugs and condiments such as maṁjishṭhā, pepper, pipal, ginger, honey, ghee, oil and the like, medicines, and these in all directions. Then he makes allocation of the sites for divine edifices consecrated to various deities. In all directions are allowed all sorts of habitats. About two hundred daṇḍas to the east or to the north-east of the town the cottages for the chaṇḍalas and the washermen should be raised as in the settlement of a village. The above is the scheme of site-planning of an ordinary town. But in a port or commercial emporium such inter-residential shopping stalls are not desirable; but on the other hand to secure economic efficiency, they should be concentrated, being set up in continuous rows on either sides of the highways. In the other types of cities, every thing should be arranged with regard to the peculiar needs and interests of them."[1] The rest is to be distributed exactly as in the village.

Now the typical planning of sites in a village is described in the Mayamata in this way:—When the entire city is divided into 81, 64, or 49 plots, there is a reclassification of the divisions into zones, one within the other. The innermost zone is called Brahmā; the next annular zone is called Daivika; the third ring of plots is known as Mānusha; and the fourth annulus of plots, the outermost one, goes by the name of Paiśācha. The houses of the Brāhmaṇs lie in rows in the second and third zones. The artisans and the labouring class should be provided with quarters in the outermost zone. Here too there may be settlement of the highest three classes, if necessary and here again the deities are set up, beginning from the east. In the central quadrangle the shrine of Brahmā should be placed. In the north-east or south-east corner of this, the

[1] Mayamatam, Ch. 10, *ll* 154—83.

town-hall is located and in its north or west should be raised an edifice to Hari. To the south of the town lie the cattle sheds and to the north flower gardens. To the east or west beside the town-gate the hermitages are provided with sites. Tanks, reservoirs, and wells should be distributed all throughout the town. To the right and by the side of the Vaiśyas or trading class are stationed the houses of the Śūdras. In the east or the north, the potters are housed and the barbers as well as other craftsmen are similarly provided with housing plots in those quarters. The fishermen are to settle in the north-west and the butchers are to have sites in the west. The oilmen occupy the northern plots. A little away to the south-east or the north-west of the town or village are fixed the quarters of the architects. Further off, the washermen's hamlets are situated. A kroś (about two miles) to the east the cottages of the sweepers or methars should be set up; and the wives of the sweepers enter the villages early in the morning to clear off the nightsoil and the refuse. The cremation ground is generally located about five hundred daṇḍas to the north-east." The royal palace, according to Mayamuni, should occupy an eastern site or the quarters of Āpa and the royal buildings on the whole extend over one-seventh of the entire city.[1] The royal buildings of Jaipur are said to occupy such a proportion.

Bhoja does not make an exhaustive treatment of this subject but touches only a few salient features: The central sites, according to him, should be reserved for the nobility, the physicians, astrologers, and the pious. The extreme sites are to be apportioned to the Mlecchas or foreigners, the low class people, cruel professions, and the soldiers and the sentinels. The latter's barracks should be pitched by the side of the town-gates; the ministers counsellors should also be relegated to quarters adjoining them, for a king should not live in close proximity of his ministers, because, in that case, he runs the risk of being poisoned with sinister counsels. The quarters of the officers should be systematically distributed throughout the city. The elephant should not be stationed towards the centre nor the horse in the outskirts. Neither the infantry nor the nobility and the ministers should have their quarters very far off from the royal palace. Lest enemy spies find scope for their work, Bhoja is against installing theatres or libraries (colleges ?) within the compound of the royal buildings.

[1] Mayamatam, Chs. 9 and 29.

The general feature that is conspicuous in all the foregoing plans of allocating sites is that generally in the central part of the town all the public buildings of importance, such as the royal palace, the court, the town hall, the temple, the council house, and the like, are located, giving a stately effect to the city and centralising its corporate life. But the plan suggested in the Matsya Purāṇa, contrary to all foregoing plans, aims at decentralisation. "There should be planted four rectilinear streets. These are the two cross-streets meeting at the centre of the fort. At the end of one street should be erected the holy shrine and the royal palace should stand at the terminus of another. The court should be placed at the extremity of the third and the fourth terminates at the arched gateway of the town."[1] But for the absurdity of a gate standing at the centre of the fort, all the four structures could have been supposed to be situated at the central part at the crossing of the two streets; for, such a configuration would have as well answered the des-

[1] Matsya Purāṇam, Ch. 217, *ll.* 19-23.

चतस्रश्च तथा तत्र कार्य्यास्त्वायतवीथयः ।
एकस्मिंस्तत्र वीथ्यग्रे देववेश्म भवेद्दृढम् ॥ १०
वीथ्यग्रे च द्वितीये च राजवेश्म विधीयते ।
धर्म्माधिकरणं कार्य्यं वीथ्यग्रे च तृतीयके ॥ ११
चतुर्थे त्वथ वीथ्यग्रे गोपुरञ्च विधीयते ।

cription. As it is, the buildings cannot be otherwise than standing at the terminii of the cross-streets. The above does not indicate a serious deviation from the general scheme, in as much as the royal palace and the holy shrine are nowhere recommended to stand side by side. Barring the court, therefore, all other important public buildings are required to be located in close proximity to the royal castle. For, "to the south of the royal palace, the treasury should be placed. Further south the elephants should have their sheds facing the east or the north. The arsenal is to occupy a site to the south-east of the royal buildings, while workshops (karmaśālā) are also erected in the same quarters. Houses of the ministers, Vedic scholars, the (court) physicians, and the storehouse are provided with sites to the left of the royal mansions where also the royal priest is furnished with quarters."[1] I am inclined to suppose that the foregoing scheme sets forth the planning of the sites of the fort within the city, not that of the sites of the city itself.

I need here only refer to the various plans which the author of the Mānasāra projects in connection with the lay-out of sites in different villages. It should be remembered that the

[1] Matsya Purāṇam, Ch. 217, *ll.* 29— 36.

planning of villages tally in salient features with that of the cities in ancient India, a peculiarity nowhere to be met with in Europe. The allocation of different wards to different classes of people was also followed in Anahilavada Pattana in northern Guzrat as we read in the Kumārapālacharita of Jinamandava (A.D. 1436). The description which runs as follows refers to a period in the middle of the twelfth century: "Anahilapura was 12 kos (or 18 miles) in circuit within which were many temples and colleges, 84 chawks or squares, 84 bāzārs or market places; with mints for gold and silver coinage. Each class had its separate muhalla or quarters as had each description of merchandise, *i.e.*, hastidantas or elephants' tusks, silk purples, diamonds, pearls, etc., etc.; each had its separate chawk. There was one bazar for sarraps or money changers; one for perfumes and unguents; one for physicians; one for artisans; one for goldsmiths; one for silversmiths; there were distinct muhallas for navigators, for bards and geneologists. Eighteen varṇas or castes inhabited the city. All were happy together. The palace groaned with a multitude of separate buildings, for the armoury, for elephants, horses, and chariots, for the public accountants and officers of State . Each kind of goods had its separate maṇḍav or mart, where the duties of export, import, and sale were collected as for spices, fruits, drugs—camphor, metals and every thing costly of home or foreign growth."[1] Dr. Radha Kamal Mukherji remarks in the same paper: "The house groups, quarters or muhallas are indeed characteristic of all Indian cities. The city of Agra, for instance, is divided into so many as 212 muhallas the names of which are derived either from the caste of the inhabitants, or from some well-known building, or from a prominent resident of former days. In the cities of Bombay Presidency, each of these wards is often a separate village with its own headman, accountant, servants, and husbandsmen whose lands lie outside the city-walls. There are bāgs or gardens, temples and mosques interspersed in the central wards and the suburbs or pārās. The cloth, the grain, the fruit, and the meat markets are separate and are held in open spaces shaded with rows of nimba, kadamba and banian trees. The sāhāgunj or general market is often in the centre of the city as in Ahmednagar. Gardens are still sometimes the property of a ward and are maintained by voluntary subscriptions of the residents."[2]

[1] *Vide the Modern Review, August,* 1920.

[2] *Cf.* the description of Kaveripumpaddinam as compiled by Mr. Ayyar. He gives there a detailed account of the planning of sites and folks in the city.

CHAPTER VII

Improvement and expansion of towns

In case civic requirements outgrow the capacity of the town, that is to say, when its principal thoroughfares become too narrow or insufficient for the volume of its traffic, or when their narrowness threatens to prove deleterious to the sanitation of the buildings and hamlets overhanging and adjoining them, or when considerations of civic beauty and civic art demand the extension and the widening of the main streets, or when the town becomes too small for its population, the improvement of the town becomes imperative, even at the risk of onerous financial liabilities and of encroachments on personal properties caused by demolition of the old houses and buildings. Towards this end, of late, there has been set up in almost every important metropolis a separate board under the name of Improvement Trust which systematically carries on its improvement and extension according to the best town-planning codes. These Improvement Trusts and the like bodies are very recent institutions. Two or three decades back, a town was allowed to grow in the most haphazard way possible; lanes and roads cropped up by the side of hamlets, which conformed to no plan, while its suburbs were left uncared for in the most unsalubrious condition with the result that the sanitation of the town deteriorated with its growth and development; and the town presented a very squalid appearance. Naturally enough, this amorphous state of affairs had an adverse effect upon its traffic. It is only in recent times that the municipal authorities have begun to realise the importance and desirability, both from economic and hygienic view-points, of co-ordinated and far-sighted efforts in this direction which the art of civics requires.

In ancient times every king had his own permanent civic architect and city superintendent in his capital with their many subordinates and assistants who were wellversed in the art of planning and upkeep of cities. The civic architect, besides his other duties, looked after improvement and expansion of the town according to its requirements and the directions of the king who explained the difficulties to him. Thus we find in the Śukranītisāra[1] that the king should employ, among others, the following persons :—(1) persons versed

[1] Ch. II, *ll.* 390-396.

in the art of establishing pleasure-gardens and artificial forests (ārāma-kṛtrima-vanakāriṇah), (2) fort-architects (durgakāriṇah), (3) road-constructors (mārgakārakāh). The technical name of the dignitary who was expert in town-planning was Sthapati. The Sthapati, among his many other qualifications, must be endowed with ability to plant a town or an edifice (sthāpanārhah), knowledge of surveying (gaṇitajṁah), skill in draftsmanship (chitrajṁah), capability for reconnoitering localities (sarvadeśajṁah), mastery over the entire science of architecture and town-planning (vāstu-vidyābdhipāragah); and he should be wellversed in the holy scriptures and the Purāṇas.[1] His attributes indicate beyond

[1] Mayamatam, Ch. 5, sl. 14—24.

स्थपतिः स्थापनार्हः स्यात् सर्व्वशास्त्रविशारदः ।
न हीनाङ्गोऽतिरिक्ताङ्गो धार्म्मिकस्तु दयापरः ॥ १५
अमात्सर्य्योऽनसूयश्च तान्त्रिकः स्वभिजातवान् ।
गणितज्ञः पुराणज्ञः सत्यवादी जितेन्द्रियः ॥ १६
चित्रज्ञः सर्व्वदेशज्ञश्चान्नदश्चाप्यलुब्धकः ।
अरोगी चाप्रमादी च सप्तव्यसनवर्ज्जितः ॥ १७
सुनामा दृढबन्धुश्च वास्तुविद्याब्धिपारगः ।
स्थपतेस्तस्य शिष्यो वा सूत्रग्राही सुतोऽथवा ॥ १८
स्थपत्याज्ञानुसारी च सर्व्वकर्म्मविशारदः ।
सूत्रदण्डप्रपातज्ञो मानोन्मानप्रमाणवित् ॥ १९
शैलदार्व्विष्टकादीनां सूत्रग्राहिवशात् तु यः ।
तक्षणात् स्थूलसूक्ष्माणाम् तक्षकः स तु कीर्त्तितः ॥ २०
मृत्कर्म्मज्ञो गुणी शक्तः सर्व्वकर्म्मस्वतन्त्रकः ।
तक्षकस्तक्षितेष्वस्मिन् पर्य्युपरि युक्तितः ॥ २१

doubt that the town-planner or the Sthapati, coming as he did from a noble family, by his birth and literary attainments, was quite familiar with the cultural ideals and predilections, religious and social, of the people for whom he had to build the city. Such knowledge was an indispensable qualification of the Sthapati inasmuchas he had to bring out in the city an expression of the life of its citizens. Further it seems very probable that he had to carefully prepare a chart marking in it the boundaries, the roads, and scheme of their planting and the location of public buildings, tanks, and gardens. Next in rank to the Sthapati was the Sūtragrāhī (literally lineman or plumber) expert in surveying and drafting (rekhājṁa). He was either the son or the disciple of the Sthapati, strictly obedient to the latter. He was the superior officer (guru) over the following two. The Takshaka, the chisellor, well versed in all mechanical arts including carpentry, was the officer subordinate to the Sūtragrāhī. Under the Takshaka was placed the Vardhakī, the joiner, who was a specialist in draftsmanship and the

वृद्धिकृत् वर्द्धकिः प्रोक्तः सूत्रग्राह्यनुगः सदा ।
कर्म्मिणो निपुणाः शुद्धा बलवन्तो दयापराः ॥ २२
गुरुभक्ता सदा हृष्टाः स्थपत्याज्ञानुगाः सदा ।
तेषामेव स्थपत्याख्यो विश्वकर्मेति संस्मृतः ॥ २३

perspective and was an adept in joinery works of all sorts. All these were permanent officers under the king. In the Arthaśāstra we find, among the other duties of the city superintendent, that he had to make a daily inspection of the reservoirs of water, of roads, of the hidden passages for going out of the city, of forts, fort-walls and their defensive works. Though we do not meet with any written records about the existence of an organised board like the modern Improvement Trust and the like, yet we may, without largely drawing upon imagination, fairly presume that the permanent officials of the king such as the civic architect, the city superintendent, together with their assistants, constituted the prototype and served the purpose of the modern institutions organised with cognate objects. The elaborate way in which the treatises on Indo-Aryan town-planning allot sites and determine the areas and orientation of roads, wards, residential buildings, the royal palace, the council house, parks, and reservoirs, and secure proper lignting and ventilation by fixing the space intervening between two houses or ascertain the number of storeys and their respective heights in case of particular buildings and edifices, conclusively establish that the master-builder possessed and exercised substantial control over all building operations in the city. So elaborate and intensive indeed was the control that even absolute private ownership of land in the city was not allowed to some extent. There seems to have been several departments or divisions of functions: one was entrusted with the construction of roads; another with tanks, gardens, artificial forests, and places; the third with fortifications; and the fourth with buildings. All these departments as also the engineers, to wit, the Sthapati and others, were under the charge of a minister, called the Gṛhādyadhipati (literally, the lord of houses and the like) who held the portfolio of superintendence and planning of the city. Śukrāchāryya says that he must attend to palaces, ditches, forts, parapets, statues, weapons, tanks, wells, and reservoirs, pipes, and other engineering works.[1] Surely the foregoing are exactly those functions with which the modern Municipalities and Improvement Trusts are concerned.

[1] Śukranītisāra, Ch. II.

प्रासादं परिखां दुर्गं प्राकारं प्रतिमां तथा।

यन्त्राणि सेतुबन्धञ्च वापीं कूपं तडागकम्॥ १५९

तथा पुष्करिणीं कुण्डं जलाद्यूर्द्ध्वगतिक्रियाम्।

सुशिल्पशास्त्रतः सम्यक् सुरम्यन्तु यथा भवेत्॥ १६०

कर्त्तुं जानाति यः स एव गृहाद्यधिपतिः स्मृतः।

In the Harivaṁśa,[1] we find that Viśvakarmā[2] was the principal architect of Śrīkṛshṇa, the king of Dvārakā. The 98th Chapter of its Vishṇuparva furnishes us with an account of reconstruction of the town of Dvārakā or Dvārāvatī. When the king Śrīkṛshṇa first conceived the plan and issued instructions about the construction of Dvārāvatī, the civic architect Viśvakarmā made low obeisance to his royal pleasure with this humble remark :—" The town would not be sufficiently large for the strength of its citizens. Further extensions on a magnificent scale would have been more becoming."[3] This expert opinion was not much heeded to at that time with the result that, after lapse of a few years, Śrīkṛshṇa had to realise his shortsighted blunder and give orders for reconstruction and extension. Under the new scheme, the municipal area was doubled into eight 'yojanas' by breadth and twelve 'yojanas' by length. Though in the original city there were large streets, yet they were few in number as seems to be evident from the innumerable number of lanes in it (rathyā-koṭi-

[1] Vishṇuparva, Ch. 58.

[2] For a discussion on the word Viśvakarmā, see the Introductory.

[3] Vishṇuparva, Ch. 58, ll. 64-6.

सर्व्वमेतत् करिष्यामि यत्त्वयाभिहितं प्रभो ।
पुरीं त्वियं जनस्यास्य न पर्य्याप्ता भविष्यति ॥
भविष्यति च विस्तीर्णा हर्म्मैरस्यास्तु शोभना ।

sahasiāḍhyā). On improvement the number of large streets was therefore placed at eight. There were constructed sixteen magnificent squares at the sixteen cross-sections.[1] The town was encompassed by a large boulevard. We can visualise the magnitudinous nature of this extension and improvement by comparison with Calcutta, the second city in the British Empire. Calcutta cannot boast of more than four large longitudinal streets, viz., the Circular Road, the College Street and its continuation, the Chitpore Road,[2] and the Strand Road, while the improved city of Dvārāvatī contained six large streets including the boulevard, both longitudinally and latitudinally. Defensive weapons and missiles were set up in greater number. Gardens were symmetrically planted in hundreds and the trenches were enlarged.

It cannot be said that the above has only a mythological significance bearing out a fertile

[1] Vishṇuparva, Ch. 98.

अष्टयोजन विस्तीर्णामचलां द्वादशायताम् ।
द्विगुणोपविशां च ददर्श द्वारकां पुरीम् ॥ २७
अष्टमार्गमहारथ्यां महाषोडशचत्वराम् ।
एकमार्गपरिक्षिप्तां साक्षादुशनसा कृताम् ॥ २८

May the word 'chattvara' here refer to what is technically known as the foot-path laid out alongside the modern thoroughfares for the pedestrians to walk on ?

[2] The Chowringee Road and the Russa Road virtually form its continuation.

imagination in the author, inasmuchas, even in historical periods, we come across many such instances of deliberate civic improvement. In his history of the famous Vijayanagar, Mr. Sewell, the author, notes that one of its kings, Devaray II, raised a Jaina Temple in the city, after laying out a new street called Pān Supāri Bāzār. "It passed along the north side of the Kallama and Rangaswami temples, leaving intact the Imperial office enclosure with its lofty walls and watch towers and the elephant stables on the left, skirted the Jaina temple and another temple and passed along under the rocky hills that bound this plain (of the city) on the north till it debouched on the main road. This street would be the direct approach from the old city of Anegundi to the king's palace."[1] It should be noticed here that though this street was laid out to serve the purpose of the shortest and most direct communication between the old city and the royal palace, yet unlike those of some modern Improvement Trusts, a monotonous rectitude of the streets was not enforced at the sacrifice of historical temples, of walls as well as of other important places or rocky hills. Its course was made as straight as possible, compatible with its natural and artistic alignment.

[1] A Forgotten Empire, by Sewell, p. 78.

The above leads us to the topic of town extension. The extension of towns has not yet received as much attention from the municipal authorities as it should have. The consequence is that in suburbs history is repeating itself. The same lack of scientific plan and foresight which characterises the uncared-for growth of the modern towns and which has necessitated the inauguration of the various Town Improvement Boards with their demolishing and financially ruinous operations, disrupting the harmony and tranquillity of civic life and carrying havoc to multitudes, runs rampant, even in this scientific age, in the suburbs. No civic architect can be blind to the future possibilities of his town. "The unkempt fringe of derelict houses and rubbish heaps that so frequently surround our modern town" not only detracts from picturesqueness and organic integrity of the city but proves very detrimental to its salubrity. Over and above, such a policy of *laissez faire* with regard to the suburbs makes for financial waste inasmuchas the Improvement Trust cannot trim them to proper order without going through its demolishing functions in some measure. Such a state of affairs was well nigh impossible in the towns of ancient India, because there could not grow practically any suburb round them. The peculiar defensive works girding the ancient Indian towns in the shape of walls and ditches precluded the growth of any such clumsy outskirts about them. These walls and ditches, circumscribed sometimes by a girdle of lofty trees, combined to present the town as one isolated entity, entire and beautiful, to an ingoing visitor and contributed to the solidarity of its corporate life.

Notwithstanding their utility as impediments to growth of unsalubrious suburbs, they stood in the way of town-expansion. And this was a serious drawback of the ancient walled cities. The civic authorities, when they saw that the town was no longer capacious enough for its population, sometimes contrived to meet this difficulty by expelling the low classes of menials like the methars (night-soilers) and washermen out of the city and locating them in quarters beyond the moats. Thus the author of the Mayamata says[1] :—"A little further away from the city and surrounding it are the hamlets of all kinds of people. About two hundred daṇḍas to the east or south-east of the city are situated the huts of the chaṇḍālas and the washermen."[2]

[1] Ch. 10.

[2] It seems not altogether improbable that there was nothing more than a social, at best a sanitary significance at the back of this

This was a very simple makeshift and, at the same time, was not advocated by all. Though this externment of low class people was conducive to city-sanitation, it was hardly sufficient and not at all satisfactory. Even to-day only a very small percentage of the general population of this country lives in towns. The number of low class people, who were constrained by business to permanently reside in towns in ancient times was very meagre. The necessity for enlarging towns did not arise at those periods of Indian history when people had to flock to fortified towns and perforce to live there for protection and security. Consequently exclusion of a handful of citizens, if it was at all made to relieve congestion, was in the nature of a stop-gap rather than a permanent solution of the problem. Deliberate efforts were however made to keep down the multiplication of urban population so as to minimise congestion and put off the necessity of extension. For example, the Matsya Purāṇa lays down that a large number of people should not remain in the city or fort without any

civic externment of low class people. No attempt at relieving congestion but an inglorious hand of the caste-proud classes excommunicating the low classes—(an act which to-day has festered to the canker of untouchability in the South)—may we discern in this enforced settlement without the city-walls.

necessity or purpose.[1] In the same strain and to the same purpose is the rule of the Devī Purāṇa: "The low class people (prakṛti) should be quartered outside the city."[2] The great sage Maya, in his discourses, also endorses this view as we have seen above. It may be interesting to note here that ascetics and philosophers were made to live away from the town, probably to shun the stir and din of a town, the vortex of worldly life. Thus the Tamil poets mention that the "ascetics and philosophers also dwelt in the silent and shady groves, far away from the din and bustle of the capital."[3] These expedients could not however avail for any length of time. So the civic authorities were constrained to extend the confines of their city and the author of the Mayamata recommends extensions to the east or the south or in all directions.[4]

[1] Ch. 217, *l.* 54.

[2] Ch. 72, *l.* 52.

The word 'prakṛti' carries two imports and has been used in the same book in both the senses. Technically it signifies the eight principal departments of the State (elements of sovereignty) noticed in the Dharma Śāstras, to wit, the Crown, the Ministry, the Allies, the Treasury, the Forts, the Army, and the like; it may also mean the body of high dignitaries in charge of these departments. The ordinary meaning of the word is 'subjects of the kingdom.' In the context the word refers perhaps to those persons who had no business requiring them to take up permanent residence in the town.

[3] V. Kanaksavai, Tamil Eighteen Hundred years Ago, p. 15.

[4] Ch. 29, *ll.* 22—23.

पौराणां यदस्तु वर्द्धितुमिच्छेदभितस्तथा ॥ ११
प्रागुत्तरदिशि वृद्धिः शस्ता पारतस्तु वा न्याय्या ।

One of the methods of town-expansion has been illustrated in the case of Dvārakā. The old walls were pulled down; the existing ditches were filled up; the surrounding area was cleared and the land adjusted for foundation of the new city. In this case it was the general practice to convert the old walls and moats into a second series of streets, as in Madurā. Old streets were widened and lengthened both ways. New building quarters were delineated by new lanes and roads. New walls were erected and fresh ditches were excavated round the city. Sometimes without levelling down the existing walls, only the ditches were filled up.

A splendid opportunity for improvement and expansion of Madurā offered itself when the town, after a prosperous existence for many long years, was inundated. Excepting the ancient temple and its environments, situated as they were on an eminence, all were completely devastated with but faint traces left behind. The people who survived the great flood flocked to this elevated spot. This place was then called Naduvur or the central place, because this formed the centre of the old city thus laid waste. In process of time Naduvur grew in importance, commerce flourished, and the population increased beyond the capacity of its limited area. Extension of the city therefore became imperative in order to relieve congestion. "The ruler of the day caused a resurvey of the limits of the old city made from a study of the ancient traces with a view to preparing a fresh and comprehensive town-plan, which, while satisfying the present need of a growing population, would also make ample provision for future extensions of the city and secure in his scheme possibilities for artistic and harmonious development of the town within.

"Hence he summoned his ministers and directed them to resurvey the limits of the ancient city. The temple and the surroundings were again made the starting point of a fresh plan of reconstruction of a new city which as of old grew round the temple. And with the best available advice of his time a plan was prepared taking the temple as the starting point. The plan was drawn up afresh so as to conveniently accommodate the growing population.

"Beginning with the right side of the temple, the boundary line was formed along the natural contour, and as the measurement was completed on the left side, it enclosed a large space with the temple in the centre. Hence it was known as Alavau, *i.e.*, a circular plan, as a serpent would make if it would bring its head and tail together round an object. The full extent of the city was about nine miles. The southern gate was made the great entrance gate of the city while the smaller gate on the northern side was its exit. Thus the city grew towards the south and had the river Vaikali as a natural boundary on the north."[1]

A third method akin to the above was to reclaim a belt of land round the city and to enclose this anew by another set of walls and ditches so as to fortify the new acquisition. The low caste people were made to settle in this area making room for the high castes and the big officers within the fold of the ancient limits. But the old walls and ditches impeded the free circulation of traffic from the centre, the most important part of the ancient cities, to the limits of the reconstituted city. Only a large number of gates in the old walls and the planting of an adequate number of arteries of communication in the extensions in alignment with these gates could obviate the difficulties. This method had this advantage over its predecessor that it augmented defensive strength and involved less financial strain and hardship on the people and consequently less dissatisfaction. It is perhaps illustrated in the town of Bharatpur

[1] Town Planning in Ancient Deccan, pp. 32—4.

where traces of one ditch after another, all encircling the primeval city can still be observed, the rank and position of the settlers diminishing as we walk further and further away from the centre of the city quite in keeping with the traditional rule of ancient India regarding allocation and distribution of urban population. The present city of Delhi, called old Delhi as distinguished from new Delhi under construction, possibly furnishes us with one more example of this method of town-extension. Therein we meet with traces of a ditch about a mile from the wall of the extant city, of which fragmentary portions only remain here and there.

It is a sound principle of town-planning that buildings should continuously diminish in density as they recede from the centre so that fresh air may pass from the country into the interior of the town. What with centralisation of business in a town and what with its organic growth and development, this principle is more or less carried out in all towns inasmuchas the suburbs are only thinly inhabited and abound in many trees and gardens. It is impossible to ascertain whether this principle was recognised in ancient India, from the meagre materials that we are able to glean together, discussion of principles being a thing never to be met with in the majority of treatises on science. Yet the allocation of different citizens in order of their ranks, castes and subcastes, these diminishing in degree and order from the centre outward, and the different structures of houses peculiar to each of them, their heights and dimensions, as well as their number lessening with their distance from the centre, and also the rings of girdles encircling the city one after another with intervening plots planted with gardens and orchards, may be recalled in justification of the conjecture that this principle was fairly realised in the Indo-Aryan cities. The town of Vijayanagar is an instance in point. This city was founded in 1336 A.D. It was enlarged by Ajarao, the grandson of Bukkaraya who succeeded Harihar Deva to the throne. "This king made in the city of Vijayanagar many walls and towers and enclosed it anew. The king desiring to increase that city and make it the best in the kingdom, determined to bring it to a very large river which was at a distance of five leagues away. So he did, damming the river itself with great boulders. By means of this water they made, round about the city, a quantity of gardens and orchards and great groves of trees and vineyards and many plantations of lemons, oranges, and roses, and other trees which in this country bear good fruits."[1] Reading this in the light of detailed description of the city given by the same traveller, reproduced elsewhere,[2] one will realise how reasonable is the attempt made above to credit the ancient Indians with some acquaintance with the principle. It is to be observed here that beauty, sanitation, and usefulness of the city were considerably enhanced as a result of extension of the city executed on such a magnificent scale. It reflects great credit upon the circumspection and wisdom of the king and his civic architects. Even in these days we scarcely come across any case of such splendid scheme of town improvement carried in such magnitudinous proportions. The ancient city of Kaveripumpattinam also illustrates this method of distributing houses. "The plan was to have an outer square consisting of gardens and houses; a second square consisting of market places, workshops and so on; and smaller squares towards the centre where the more expansive houses and the palace and other public buildings were located."

In a large number of cases the method was impracticable. The majority of ancient Indian

[1] *Vide* Chronicle of Fernazo Nuniz, p. 10.

[2] *Vide* Appendix.

towns were situated on the banks of a river or on the sea-shore so that their expansion in all directions was out of question. I am inclined to think that it was due to this peculiar position that the idea originated of planting a new city in the shape of a large ward or muhallā, by the side of the old one, one of its side-moats coming in between the two and forming the one extremity of the new city. This sort of a supplementary faubourg by the side of a principal city, as illustrated in Babarkhana described below, was technically known as a Dāmaḍa. The city of Purī is supposed by competent observers to have once possessed such a sub-town the ruins of which are still traceable. In some instances the interposing moats and walls were levelled to the ground leaving an open space between the cities which were brought within the same walls and moats and the two cities looked like two detached portions of the same city. V. Kanaksavai gives extracts from the description of such a city given by the Tamil poets.[1] "Kaveripaddinam or Pukar was built on the northern bank of the Kaveri river (near its mouth) which was then a broad and deep stream into which heavily laden ships entered from the sea without slackening sail. The

[1] *Vide* Tamil Eighteen Hundred Years Ago, pp 24-5.

town was divided into two parts, one of which was called Maruvur Pakkam and adjoined the sea-coast, and the other which was situated to the west of it was called Paddini Pakkam. Between these two portions of the city was a large area of open ground, planted with trees at regular intervals, where the great market was held." The same author informs us that Paddini Pakkam contained the royal palace. Indeed it had all the elements of a complete city where all classes of people lived. Maruvur Pakkam was nothing but an emporium, a centre of trade and commerce, frequented by foreigners such as the Yavan merchants. The character of the difference between the population of the two parts shows that one was an appendage or supplement to the other, by way of an extension. The modern prototype of this ancient town may be found in Chittagong where the Double Moorings side near the mouth of the river Karnafuli constitutes the harbour of the town. It has already developed into an emporium of note. It lies to the south-west of the old town separated by a large tract of land interspersed with villages and paddy fields. These will, in course of a few years, with the growth of trade and accentuation of urban tendencies, be closetted into a single whole.

Here we cannot positively lay our finger at any deliberate scheme of extension. It may owe its inception to the natural growth of the city, to its need for a port or haven. But since both the halves of the city of Kaveripum-paddinam were defended by walls and moats, one may legimately lend more credence to the other view. Imperative necessity of defence precludes the probability of unconscious growth of the port.

Closely allied with this is the following type of a suburb. About a league away from the city of Vijayanagar stood the small town of Nagalpur connected with the main city by a "street as wide as a place of tourney, with both sides lined throughout with rows of houses and shops where they sold every thing; and all along this road were many trees that the king had commanded to be planted, so as to afford shade to those that passed along. On this road he had commanded to be erected a very beautiful temple of stone and there were other pagodas that the captains and great lords had caused to be erected."[1] This town of Nagalpur (literally a new city) served the double purpose of an extension of the main city of Vijayanagar as well as of guarding the latter,

[1] Narrative of Domingo Pæs, the Portuguese traveller; *vide* Sewell.

situated as it was at the mouth of the defile between the mountains encircling the city from a distance. A town of this nature was technically known as Vāhirikā.[1] The following instance is more probative. In the ruins of Taxila, "outside the northern wall of the Sirkap city, was a suburb, now known as Babarkhana or the Kaccha Kot from the fact that it is defined by earthen ramparts only. This suburb has a circuit of rather more than a mile and a quarter, and is enclosed on the west by a bend of the Tamra Nala, above which its fortifications rise to a height of about 40 feet. This suburb was inhabited by low class people of menial profession."[2] This is another confirmatory instance of separate provision for the low class people outside the city that we have already

[1] Both the varieties of sub-towns thrown out by a principal town, *viz*, the Ḍāmaḍa and the Vāhirikā, were also known as Śākhā-nagara (literally branch-town). The Śavdakalpadruma gives the following definition of this subsidiary town: "The town which is constructed in the vicinity or the outskirts of the main city, to accommodate its overflow population, is termed branch-town (Śākhā-nagara) from analogy with the branch of a tree."

मूलनगरेऽसम्मितस्य जनौघस्य स्थानाय मूलनगरस्य समीपे प्रान्ते वा यदन्यत् पुरं नगरान्तरं क्रियते तत् शाखानगरं मूलनगरस्य तरुस्थानीयस्य शाखेव । अभिष्यन्दिरमणमप्यत्र । स्यादभिष्यन्दिरमणं शाखानगरमित्यपि । इति त्रिकाण्डशेषः । इति तट्टीकायां भरतः ॥ अपि च । आरभ्य मूलनगराद्परं हि यत् । तदभिष्यन्दिरमणं शाखानगरमित्यपि ॥ इति शब्दरत्नावली ।

[2] A Guide to Taxila.

noticed. These branch towns bear a close resemblance to the 'colonae' of the ancient Romans which were small quasi-fortresses established for accommodating surplus population or discharged soldiers.

One other solution was suggessed by the peculiar plan of some of the ancient Indian cities. Every city was a conglomeration of wards or muhallas, each muhalla being self-contained and enclosed by walls. When extension became inevitable, it was easy to add some similar muhallas to the original number. This is suggested by the orthodox method of enlarging the diagram of interlineal chambers. If it is necessary to draw a square figure, say of nine plots deep, then the rule is to add two rows of similar plots, one to the east and another to the north of the figure of eight plots deep.[1] "The capital must have within it space for the laying out of pallīs, grāmas, kumbhas etc., *i.e.*, wards."[2] "A natural consequence of the consolidation of the Aryan tribal system into these larger states and kingdoms

[1] *Cf.* प्राच्योदीच्यैककोष्टादिसंप्रवृद्धा क्रमान्नयेत् ।
शिल्परत्ने षष्ठाध्याये २६श पंक्तिः ।

Śukranītisāra, Ch. I, *l.* 430. It should be noted here that this grāma is not a modern village. It is a technical term for a locality with certain definite measurements and corresponds to the *insulæ* of an ancient Greek town as well as to the municipal wards of a modern city.

was the gradual development of the village settlements into larger towns and cities planned on the same principles in which wards or village units, were grouped round the royal palace and the citadel."[1] When a cluster of villages was taken up and turned into a city, the intervening space between any two villages was trimmed with spacious parks (the sacred groves) and stately avenues. Mr. Havell thinks that Pāṭaliputra was nothing but an aggregation of such villages due to the centralisation of the social and economic activities of the self-governing Indo-Aryan village communities.[2] This was the way whereby the humble town of Karṇāvatī was turned into a gigantic capital of Ahmedabad by Ahmed Shah, the grandson and successor of Muzzafar Shah, the founder of the Guzrati Dynasty. This fine city which was laid out presumably according to ancient Indo-Aryan traditions was divided into 360 muhallas or wards.

The present town of Srirangam gives us the best clue to the mode of evolution and expansion of Indo-Aryan cities. The history of its development cannot be better depicted than in the words of Prof. Patrick Geddes, the famous town-planner of modern times :—" Here

[1] Havell, History of Aryan Rule in India, p. 38.
Havell, Ancient and Medieval Architecture, p. 24.

in ancient days there was a local shrine, central to the island and its villages. Some thoughtful teacher at one time, some saintly soul at another, became an influence extending beyond the island and pilgrims began to come. A little temple was raised to include the shrine and its court would be inhabited by its holy man doubtless with his disciples. Outside these gather more dwellings; first the huts of sanyasins, later more permanent, and increasingly of Brāhmaṇ character. Granaries are needed, and arise first as round huts of the old type still common as dwellings in Madras, and surviving as corn-stores in Bengal villages, though they are superseded as dwellings by rectangular plans. The whole area becomes included within a larger wall with a southward gateway,—(on the third wall from the centre). Within the enclosure and outside it also, further developments proceeded, both material and spiritual, as of increasing granaries and additional shrines. Outside arise new dwellings of large magnitude and space; in time these likewise became spiritualised in property and use; and at length transformed as well. New shrines thus appear, and here also, though probably far later, the north-east space becomes the hall of a thousand columns. The new rectangular wall is more carefully oriented than its predecessors; three gateway Gopuras are built, the largest to the eastward. There is now a clearer differentiation of temple and town, of sacred and secular; for a new street is kept clear all round the wall presumably as a Car-street, and with house-lots opposite. These are to-day of very varying breadth, suggesting that those now narrow may have arisen by division. Another wall again was raised to surround this clear rectangle of dwellings facing the Car-street next the temple wall; and this is given four gateways towards the cardinal points but these were comparatively small, in subordination to those within, and on three sides of the previous temple enclosures. But outside this a new town-extension is provided. This is again a rectangular street system parallel to the last with a fresh Car-street, and new houses on either hand and lots less deep. Evidently with city growth caste distinctions and wealth requirements being more emphasised, the lower and poorer castes are kept outside the larger gateways of this wall; and their houses cluster specially to the south and east, but not to the less spacious west. These poorer dwellings spread and subdivide from these gates on either hand, in lots of small and irregular size, and with a norrow lane running obliquely north by east, from near the east Gopuram.

"Finally comes the great completion by Tirumulu, king of builders. In the south Bazar it will be seen that existing properties were respected as they stand mostly facing northward towards the road along the south wall. But this road is norrow, so instead of wasting compensation and upsetting business (as modern municipalities and their engineers in the industrial age of lapsed planning have done, and still largely incline to do), the sensible course is taken, and also the most practical for business and communications, more seemly so, that of making new Bazar Street east and west; and of allocating new plots of larger size on each side, upon the land hitherto unoccupied. Some houses next to the wall outside also a small temple (perhaps private, perhaps for the humbler caste hitherto outside) seems to have already sprung up on the west side. The new street northward is continued with houses on either sides; but on the east the open space next the wall suffices; and also on the north, so far as existing irregular holdings allow. This new enclosure, as yet the final one, is thus kept in good proportion. Its rectangular wall is built, and the four great Gopuras, North, South, East, and West, are now begun, of course, in true alignment to their predecessors. These gateway towers are on a scale unparalleled as their megalithic beginnings show; but they remain unfinished like other works of Tirumulu owing to his untimely and tragic death and as too monumental for the means and inclinations of his successors.

"This same process of the Temple guiding and including its city developments, is even now going on, clearly and simply, at the adjacent smaller Śiva Temple town, a mile or so eastward. Outside the triple temple walls, runs the Car-street, with houses of its caste-community. A great wall, with four Gopuras, encloses the whole; and a secondary street surrounds this fourth wall, and is thus obviously included within the temple system, and so far sharing its sanctity. Here then is plainly a second Srirangam, and still in progress.

"This mode and process of growth is so essentially regular, so natural yet so reasoned, so peculiarly defined, so monumentally organised, through zone after zone of growth in succeeding centuries."[1]

It may not be out of place to observe in conclusion that in modern times when peace and

[1] *Vide the Modern Review, March,* 1919.

tranquillity reign throughout India under British hegemony and overlordship, hostile invasions and pillaging incursions are out of question, so that walls and moats,—the old fortifications,—have lost their original significance and importance. Hence in almost all ancient towns, the ditches have been allowed to be silted up beyond recognition and walls to lie in ruins with meagre traces here and there. In some cases, as in Baroda and Dabhoi, the walls have been deliberately pulled down and the ditches have been carefully filled up by the authorities. The consequence is that towns have been allowed to expand beyond their old boundaries without any plan or regulation. Thus "outside the survival of old religion and old governmental control respectively, the town has lost its unity and order, and begins to break down towards that congested slumdom, which is now so largely destroying it."

CHAPTER VIII

THE VILLAGE

Notwithstanding the uniformity of style that marked the broad features in the plans of an Indo-Aryan house, village, and town, the works on Indo-Aryan architecture, called Vāstu Vidyā (literally the science of habitation), make separate treatment of the lay-out of a village. Indeed the details about the latter subject are fuller than those about town-planning; and the civic architect is advised to utilise and adapt the self-same principles in the case of a town; of course, on a larger scale and with necessary modifications. Because, a village is a town in miniature, a variety of town (nagarabheda); the etymology of the word Trichinopallī, the name of a town in Southern India, clearly indicates it, 'pallī' being another equivalent of 'grāma,' the Sanskrit term for village.[1] The difference between a village and a town is that while the latter is artificial, the former is a natural

[1] Readers should not confuse the Indian village (grāma) with its counterpart in the West. A village in English means a collection of houses with one long street, without any public buildings etc This resembles what is known as a simple Daṇḍaka village in the Śilpa Śāstras. The measurement of a Pallī is half that of a Grāma.

unit. Hence nature plays an important role in rural life and can have wanton growth, whereas in a town which focuses and embodies the political and economic life of the people, buildings upon buildings are congregated together to accommodate maximum number of inhabitants within a minimum space, without jeopardising at the same time the city sanitation. A village may be said to be a garden interspersed with human habitations.

Mahāmahopādhyay Dr. Ganganath Jha writes :[1] —" The points of difference between a town and a village were that the town was protected by a ditch and a wall, while the village was not so protected. The town was inhabited mostly by trades-people, in addition to the king and his appurtenances, while the village was inhabited by agricultural people." As to his first point Dr. Jha is wrong, for the Śilpa Śāstras enjoin upon girth of walls and moats round the village too. Thus the Mānasāra lays down :[2] " The village should always be provided with rampart and encircling the ramparts should be excavated moats." What follows will go to

[1] House building and Sanitation in Ancient India, *J.B.O.R.S.*, vol. I.

[2] Ch. 9.

एवं ग्रामप्रकारं च तद्वहिर्वप्रसंयुतं ।
परितः परिखा बाह्ये कुर्य्याद् ग्रामेषु सर्व्वशः ॥

further corroborate my contention. Dr. Jha has however approximated to the truth in his second point; but it can not be said that villages were inhabited only by agricultural people. Many professions and ranks other than agriculture were equally represented in them.

I have already remarked that a village is a natural unit and had a natural growth. Nevertheless, Kauṭilya advises the establishment of villages throughout the kingdom for the sake of administrative efficiency. "Either by inducing foreigners to immigrate (paradeśāpavāhanena) or by causing the thickly populated centres of his own kingdom to send forth the excessive population (svadeśābhishyanda-vamanena vā), the kingdom may construct villages either on new sites or on old ruins (bhūtapūrvam abhūtapūrvam vā).

"Villages consisting each of not less than a hundred families and not more than five hundred families of agricultural people of Śūdra caste, with boundaries extending as far as a kroś (2250 yds.) or two and capable of protecting each other shall be formed. Boundaries shall be denoted by a river, a mountain, forests, bulbous plants (gṛshti), caves, artificial buildings (setubandha)[1] or by trees such as śālmalī (silk cotton

[1] The proper interpretation of 'setubandha' should be irrigational embankments or artificial dams (like causeways in some cases), so that Dr. Shama Śāstry's rendering puts a wrong meaning upon the term.

tree), śamī (acacia suma), and kshīra vṛksha milky trees)."[1]

It seems that Indian villages were also sometimes founded for military purposes. In the Ummāgga Jātaka, we find that the Rājā, previous to his starting on a military expedition, gave orders to his minister Basat:—"Go and build villages on the line of march." The minister, after accomplishing his task and completing the arrangements, informed the king: "Great king, wait not a moment on the road, but advance immediately. I have already built villages for you at intervals of seven yojanas, establishing halting places, and filled the hundreds of villages that are on the way with cloths and ornaments, food and drink. I have kept elephants, horses, and vehicles ready for you in those villages. When you go from one village to another, leave behind in each successive village the unserviceable beasts and vehicles and take others in place of them."[2] These routes of expedition constituted the

[1] Arthaśāstra, Bk. II, Ch. I. *Re* the boundary, the original text is क्रोशद्विक्रोशसीमानं ; it may be interpreted in two ways: either as refering to the boundary of a village being extended to one or two kroś or the distance between the boundaries of the neighbouring villages being one or two kroś. The latter interpretation is more probable, though Dr. Śāstry translates it in the former sense.

[2] The Ummāgga Jātaka translated by Yatawara, p. 187

great highways of the country and they also served as routes for trade and communication. It is very likely that the above mentioned villages were also utilised, subsequently to expedition, as resting places of caravans.

This brings us to the consideration of the classes that inhabited, and the fortifications that defended an Indo-Aryan village. Every devout Hindu must finish his daily ablutions and offer oblations to the deceased forefathers, before he can proceed with the day's work, at least, previous to his taking meals. Therefore a constant supply of pure water had to be secured in any locality before Hindus could settle there. It is for this reason that villages were laid out invariably in the vicinity of and round about tanks, lakes, or rivers which moreover ensured wholesome sanitation.[1] Like Kauṭilya, the Mārkaṇḍeya Purāṇa also states that a village is a settlement of peasantry, mostly of the Śūdra caste, in the centre of arable lands,[2] so that they may till their holdings without any inconvenience of traversing a long distance to get to a tank. It will be

[1] *Vide* Mayamatam, Ch. 9, *l*. 121.

[2] *See* 'grāma' in the Śavdakalpadruma.

तथा शूद्रजनप्राया सुसमृद्धकृषीवला ।

क्षेत्रोपभोगभूमध्ये वसति ग्रामसंज्ञिका ॥

erroneous however to suppose that all villages were exclusively or mostly inhabited by Śūdras. Villages there were in considerable number which were exclusively settled by each of the other three classes. Thus the Mayamata makes a detailed classification of the Brāhmaṇ villages in accordance with the numerical strength of their population :—

"There are three grades of the best class: a village settled by twelve thousand Brāhmaṇs occupies the superior grade (uttomottama); that by ten thousand Brāhmaṇs holds the middle grade (madhyama); and that by eight thousands is the inferior (adhama). The average villages are also graded into three sub-classes: a village of seven thousand vipras is the best among the mediocres (madhyamottama); that of six thousand vipras is the middling among them; while that of five thousands occupies the lowest rank. The inferior villages are also classified into three orders: the highest contains four thousand Brāhmaṇs, the middling three thousands and the lowest contains two thousand Brāhmaṇs. One thousand, seven hundred, and five hundred Brāhmaṇ inhabitants, constitute respectively the three grades among the very small (nīcha, mean or insignificant) villages. There are ten varieties of the smallest villages, rather hamlets inhabited by Brāhmaṇs ranging in number from 320 to 12."[1] The above simple villages populated by the same class of men correspond to the pallīs or wards of a modern composite village and these wards have originated through several generations of persons living side by side who derive their descent from the same ancestor. This is manifest from the meaning of the word 'ekabhoga'. This is defined to be a village in miniature inhabited by a single patriarch with his large retinue and menial staff.[2] Similarly a village of learned Brāhmaṇs is called Maṅgala (lit. auspicious), while that of noble Brāhmaṇs (viprendra) is also termed Agrahāram.[3] With the progress of civilisation and communalism, such simple villages grew, however, rare until they were replaced by composite villages where all classes of people differentiated by birth and profession peacefully led a corporate life. It is in the most backward part of the country to-day that we come across traces of those antiquated simple villages.

According to the Mānasāra and the Mayamata a village, exactly as a fort or a town, is

[1] Ch. 9, *ll.* 49—59. Also *cf.* Īśānaśivagurudebapaddhati, Kriyāpād, 25th Paṭala, sls. 42-46.

[2] Mānasāra, Ch. 9 ; Mayamatam, Ch. 9, *l.* 61.

[3] *Ibid.*

defended by a girdle of walls and moats.[1] But the lexicographer Bharata's definition of a 'grāma' or village clearly asserts that a village is devoid of them: "It is an abode of many people, such as Brāhmaṇs and others, without any wall or ditch."[2] Whether this lack of fortification in a village postulates a later stage in the social and political development of the land when peace and tranquillity reigned throughout its length and breadth, cannot be definitely ascertained at this remote period of time, especially if we presume the correctness of the cautious opinion of Macdonell that in Vedic India "the villages were probably open, though perhaps a fort (pura) might on occasion be built inside."[3] The difficulty in assuming such postulates increases when we meet with unmistakeable traces of fortifications in good many antique villages in Southern India.

The Mayamata sets forth the dimensions of the villages in two ways. According to their peripherical measurements, villages are of five kinds: the smallest village is twenty thousand daṇḍas in circumference and the contour of the

[1] Mayamatam, Ch. 9, *l* 120.
सर्व्वेषां ग्रामाणां परितः परिखा वहिश्च वप्राः ।

[2] *Vide* grāma in the Savdakalpadruma.

[3] Macdonell, Vedic Index.

biggest measures 1,00,000 daṇḍas; the perimeter of any other intermediate village can be calculated out by adding 20,000 daṇḍas to that of the preceding one. One residential block, generally inhabited by kinsmen (kutumvabhūmi), measures one-twentieth of the whole village. Lengths of villages again admit of forty varieties ranging from 500 to 20,000 daṇḍas by a common difference of 500 daṇḍas. The breadth may be 300, 500, 700, 900, 1000, 1500, or 2000 daṇḍas.[1] Mānasāra also gives several such varieties of measurements. I need hardly add here that these were rather optional; but their wide range would but give a large scope for choice.

I think it would be advisable to preface the classification of villages by recounting the salient features of a general village. "Each village is surrounded by a wall made of brick or stone. Beyond this wall there is a ditch broad and deep enough to cause serious obstructions in the event of an attack on the village. There are generally four gates at the middle of the four sides and as many at the four corners. Inside the wall, there is a large street running all round the village. There are two other large streets, each of which connects two oppo-

[1] Ch. 9, *ll.* 8—13.

site main gates. They intersect each other at the centre of the village, where a temple or a hall is generally built for the meeting of the villagers. The village is thus divided into four large blocks, each of which is again subdivided into many blocks by streets which are always straight, and which run from one end to the other of a main block. The two main streets crossing at the centre have houses only on one side facing the street. The ground floors of these houses on the main street consist of shops. The surrounding street has also houses on one side. These are mainly public buildings, such as schools, colleges, libraries, guest-houses, etc. All other streets generally have residential buildings on both sides. The houses high or low are always uniform in make. The drains (jaladhārā, lit. water passages) are made towards the sloping of the village. Tanks and ponds are dug in all the inhabited parts and located in such quarters as can conveniently be reached by a number of inhabitants. Temples of public worship as well as the public commons, gardens, and parks are similarly situated. The people of the same caste or profession are generally housed in the same quarter.....The best quarters are generally reserved for the Brāhmaṇs and the artist classes....The quarters of the Buddhist and the Jainas are described in a few lines. The habitations of chaṇḍālas as well as the places for cremation are located outside the village wall (in the north-west in particular). The temples of fearful deities such as Chāmuṇḍā are also placed outside the wall."[1]

According to their shape, and method of street-planning, folk-planning, and temple-planning, Mānasāra classifies the villages into eight types,[2] called Daṇḍaka, Sarvatobhadra, Nandyāvarta, Padmaka, Swastika, Prastara, Kārmuka, and Chaturmukha. Mayamuni bases his classification mainly upon planning of streets and his divisions are named Daṇḍaka, Swastika, Prastara, Prakīrṇaka, Nandyāvarta, Parāga, Padma, and Śrīpratishṭhita.[3] Kāmikāgama divides the villages into fifteen classes and after enumerating all the varieties named by Mānasāra and Mayamuni, cites four more, to wit, Sampatkara, Kumbhaka, Śrīvatsa, and Vaidika. I shall describe the villages now one after another by free translations from the originals as recorded in the above books. It is impossible to render all the lines into English, because in addition to their 'most barbarious Sanskrit', there are legions of

[1] Mānasāra, Dr. Acharyya's Summary, pp. 8—9.
[2] Mānasāra, Ch. 9.
[3] Ch. 9

incorrigible errors owing to ignorant amanuenses and false readings.

(1) Daṇḍaka :—Literally it means a village that resembles a phalanx or a staff. Mayamatam defines it thus :—"Its streets are straight and cross each other at right angles at the centre, running west to east and south to north. The village has four gates on four sides. Even if it has only one street (row of houses ?) yet it is also called daṇḍaka."[1] The detailed description given by Mānasāra runs thus: "The village called daṇḍaka is rectangular or square, and possesses a rampart of the same shape. It consists of one to five parallel streets (running generally from west to east) and two more streets may be planted (forming right angles) at both extremities of the above parallel streets. And a third transverse street crosses them in the middle. The width of the street varies from one to five daṇḍas. The middle-most street may be made equal to or broader than the rest. The two transverse streets at the extremeties have a single row of houses; the prin-

[1] Ch. 9 *ll.* 82—84.

[2] Three words, 'kakanī,' 'kartari,' 'kṛkarī' are used in the texts, by way of similitude, when describing two streets crossing one another at right angles. These words are of doubtful signification. Kartari may mean scissors so that its two handles crossing one another may convey the idea. Perhaps erroneous transcription has tampered with the same word.

DAṆḌAKA

cipal (central) streets are lined with a double row of houses, *i.e.*, by one on each side. Each house should be three daṇḍas broad or four or five daṇḍas broad according to reasons and suitability, and their length may be twice or thrice their breadth. The village is to be girt round by a wall or a ditch. There should be four large gates in the four cardinal directions; as many smaller ones at the several corners. To the west without the village, or in the same direction in the part presided over by Varuṇa (the king of water) or by Mitra, should be erected a shrine to Vishṇu. At the north-east quarter, either within or without the village wall, on or near the chambers held sacred to Parjjanya or Aditi, a temple should be established to Śiva. 'A shrine to Chāmuṇḍā should be built near the north gate without the wall. There should be two principal reservoirs one towards the south-west and the other towards the north-east.'[1] This is called the village Daṇḍaka especially suited to Brāhmaṇs. It may contain 12, 24, 50, 108, or 300 Brāhmaṇ families. That which is inhabited by twelve cottages of sages (munis) and is situated in the midst of forests and mountains is called āśrama or hermitage. The

[1] The lines within the inverted commas do not occur in my MSS; I have extracted them from Rāmrāz.

village situate on the bank of a river, accommodating twenty-four houses of yatis or holy mendicants, is technically termed puram. A village which contains fifty residences of those who have performed holy sacrifices (dīkshita) is a praiseworthy vāstuka or habitat. The village where there are 108 householders is called 'maṅgala.' A village possessing one hundred houses of Vikāries (Buddhists ?) is called a 'koṭa.' Or the number of Brāhmaṇ houses may be arbitrary. What is omitted in this description should be supplemented according to the Śāstras."[1] According to Kāmikāgama, the offices of the village officers and of the village Panchāyats should be located in the eastern portion of the town.

(2) Sarvatobhadra :—It is oblong or square. The village may be divided into interlineal chambers after Maṇḍuka or Sthaṇḍila. In the centre should be located the temple dedicated to the Triad—Brahmā, Vishṇu, Śiva. This may be fittingly inhabited by Brāhmaṇs, Tapasvis or those who observe austerities and perform sacrifices accompanied by great corporal sufferings (*i.e.*, anchorites), yatis or religious mendicants, Buddhists (pāshaṇḍāśramīs), Brahmachāries (celebate

[1] Mānasāra, Ch. 9.

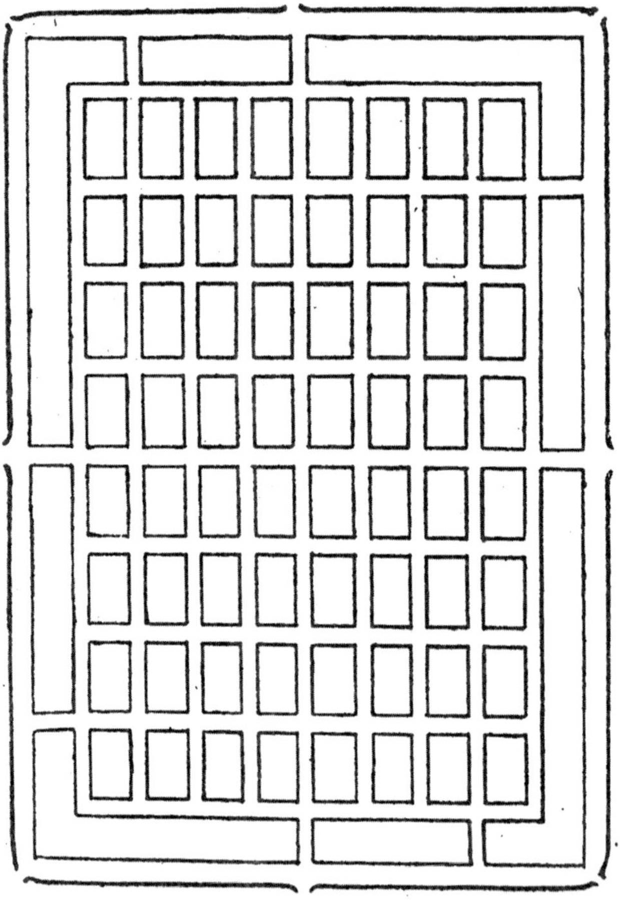

SARVATOBHADRA

students of the Vedas), or yogīs or meditators of God. The number of car-streets (rathyā) in it varies from one to five with a boulevard going round the village. The internal streets are lined with a single row of houses while a double row of houses ranges along the outer streets.[1] The streets should be so constructed as to demarcate the four annular divisions of the plot ending in the Paiśācha.[2] Here several lines occur in the original, but their readings are too faulty and their meaning too obscure for translation. "Without the walls (?) should be placed shrines of the deities who preside over and defend the several quarters of the villages. Pilgrims' pavillions, rest-houses, colleges, halls should be located at the several corners. Other divine edifices (religious halls ?) should be established in whatever quarters desirable. Towards the quarter of Agni (south-east) a water-shed should be erected. The village should be secured by a wall and a ditch, with four large gates on the sides and as many by-gates

[1] Rāmrāz gives a different version: "It has four streets of equal length on the four sides within the wall, meeting one another at right angles and two more crossing each other in the middle. Between these may be formed 3, 4, or 5 as many more streets as the extent of the village will admit on each side parallel to the middle-most street."

[2] *Vide* Chapter VI.

at the corners. The artisans and craftsmen should be assigned quarters along the boulevard (mahārathyā). The hamlets of Vaiśyas (the trading class) and Śudras (the servant class) should be allocated towards the south. In the plots between and including the two consecrated

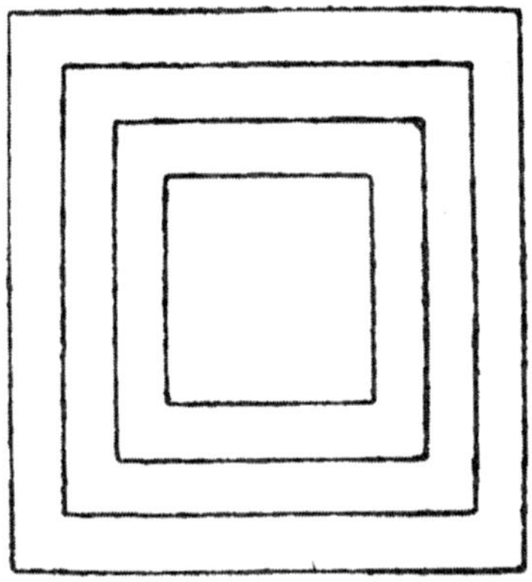

Abstract Plan of Sarvatobhadra

to Indra and Agni, *i.e.*, along the whole extreme southern side of the village should be erected in rows the houses of cowherds (gopāla) *i.e.*, agriculturists; and just outside the walls (?) to their south should be constructed the cow-sheds, guarded by pallisades. Between the chambers of Pitṛs and Varuṇa (both inclusive) *i.e.*, between the west and the south-west, the weavers and drapers are to have their quarters. A little further off are the stalls of yarn-dealers and shops of wheel-wrights. The blacksmiths are to be quartered between the chambers of Varuṇa and Vāyu (both inclusive) and further opposite to them are the fishermen and the butchers to be established. The hermits, the physicians, and the Ambashṭhas are to be assigned quarters between the plots dedicated to Vāyu and Soma. The shrine of Vishṇu may be located in their midst.[1] Over across them are the blocks of the oilsmen. Without the north-eastern gate, but by the side of the eastern wall should be erected a temple for the worship of Chāmuṇḍā, the Immanent Śakti (*i.e.*, Power) of Vishṇu and the huts of chaṇḍālas or outcastes should be further removed from it. This is the human habitation (janavāsam) beyond the pale of the village. Tanks or reservoirs should be constructed either in the south or the east or in the intermediate quarters. The master-builder should lay out the rest in conformity to the injunctions of the Śāstras.

(3) Nandyāvarta :—The dimensions of this village are the same as before. It may be square or oblong. It is divisible into as many parts as are contained in the mystic figure Chaṇḍita (also called Maṇḍuka) or Sthaṇḍila, if it is square, or in the figure Paramaśāyika, if it is oblong.

[1] Here occurs a line whose meaning is not quite clear.

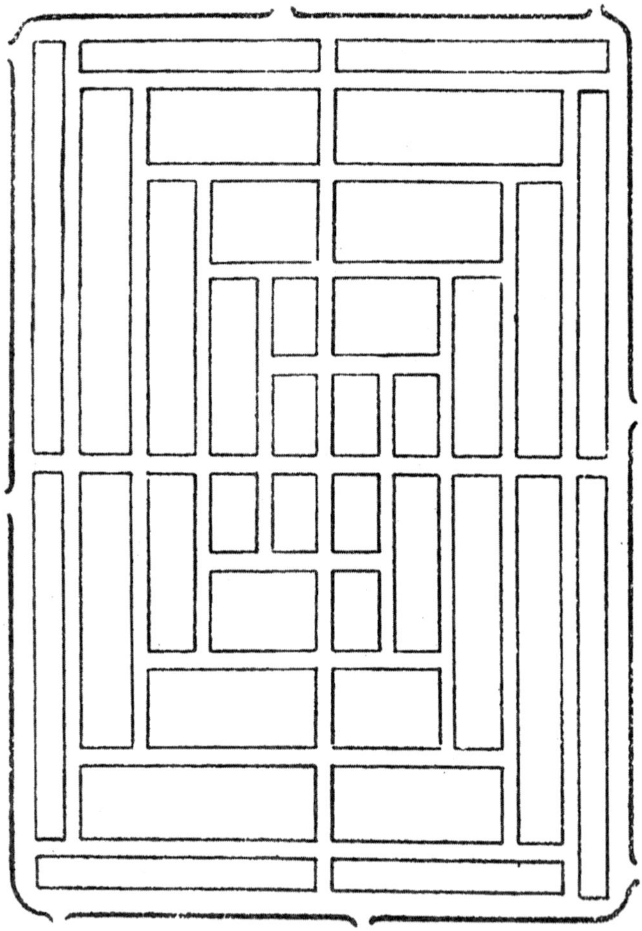

NANDYĀVARTA
(*in Manḍuka*)

NANDYĀVARTA

(in Sthaṇḍila)

The Chaṇḍita consists of 64 divisions, (being the square of eight) of which the four divisions in the centre are called Brāhmya, *i.e.*, dedicated to Brahmā. "They should be entirely appropriated to sacred purposes."[1] The twelve plots that surround the Brāhmya zone, are called Daivika, those belonging to the Devas. The next zone encircling the Daivika contains twenty divisions and is called Mānushya or that held sacred to men; and the outermost zone containing twenty-eight chambers (or plots) is named Paiśācha, that is, the one appropriated to demons. "These several rounds should be occupied by different classes in order of their superiority; *i.e.*, the Brāhmaṇs should have the Brāhmya and so with the rest."[1] The figure called Paramaśāyika contains 81 equal parts, being the square of nine, of which the central nine plots form the Brāhmya; 16 around these, the Daivika; 24 around these, the Mānushya; and the outermost 32, the Paiśācha. The figure Sthaṇḍila consists of 49 equal divisions, being the square of seven, of which the middle one is called the Brāhmya; eight around these form the Daivika; 16 around these, the Mānushya; and the outermost 24, the Paiśācha. The

[1] The lines within the inverted commas do not occur in my MSS. and I have quoted them from Rāmrāz.

village has four large streets along the sides, running in each direction at right angles. The eastern street (*i.e.*, the street in the east) beginning from the north (strictly speaking from the north-east corner) runs on to the south

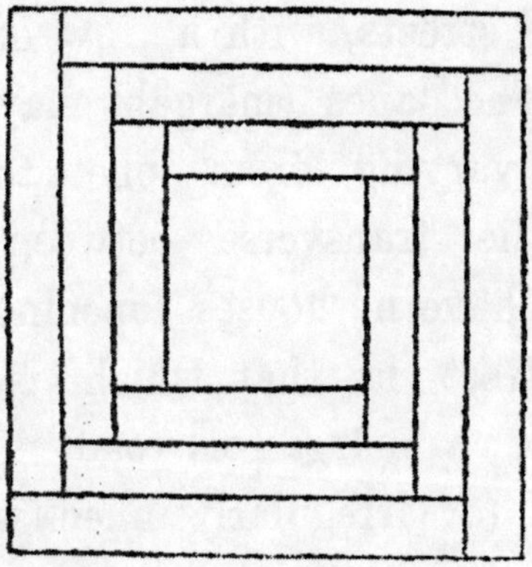

Abstraot Plan of Nandyāvarta

and projects out (to a small distance from the cross-street which intersects it); the southern street commencing from the east (*i.e.*, the eastern street at the south-east corner) runs on in a westerly direction and opens out to the west. The western street beginning from the south (*i.e.*, the southern street) runs on in a northerly direction and shoots out to the north. The northern street, running from east to west, juts forth in the east, (beyond the eastern street, at the north-east corner).[1] This plan in the lay-out of streets is like the mystic figure Nandyāvarta in the opinion of the experts. All other streets running from south to north and from east to west should follow this plan. There may be three, five, or seven such sets of streets, with a row of houses on each side. The lanes (mārgāḥ) may be planted in number varying from one to five. The lanes that lie transverse between the main roads should have no houses (opening on them).[2] A vīthī or street is that which is lined with houses, while a mārga or road is that which is devoid of (or irregularly lined with) houses. The streets of all (the villages ?) fall on the great boulevard (mahāmārga ?). The small roads should be planted at the intervals of six

[1] Rāmrāz proceeds hence with a different version not warranted by my MSS. "The number of streets in the outer compartment should be determined according to its extent, and in the compartments called Divya and Mānushya, 3 or 4 more parallel streets may be made from east to west, with as many cross ones north to south, forming as it were, so many courts or enclosures. The broad streets run through the middle of the village, from east to west and from north to south cutting one another in the middle where should be erected either a temple for Brahmā or a maṇḍapa for general meetings." Rāmrāz seems to give here a summary.

[2] The difference between a mārga and a vīthi is the same as between a road and a street, the former having discontinuous rows of houses. Or, does mārga here signify an interjacent alley between building blocks ?

or seven 'rajjus' (1 rajju = 10 daṇḍas = 60 feet). The streets should be 3, 4, or 5 daṇḍas wide, whereas in the village divided into the mystic

NANDYĀVARTA

(*Circular Plan. After Ananthalwar and Raes, Indian Architecture.*)

figure Paramaśāyika, the street round the middle-most nine divisions may be 6, 7, or 8 daṇḍas broad. The streets may be equally wide or some may be wider. The excesses in breadth over the standard street may be $\frac{1}{8}$, $\frac{3}{4}$ or $\frac{1}{2}$. The great boulevard (mahāmārga) may be as wide as the standard street or less by $\frac{1}{4}$ and the other small roads may be $\frac{3}{4}$ or $\frac{1}{2}$ as broad.

This village Nandyāvarta (literally an abode of bliss) is best suited to Brāhmaṇs. But from what follows it is clear that it is also intended for a mixed population including all the four varṇas or castes. If the village is inhabited by 58, 108, 300, 1008, 2000, or 4000 Brāhmaṇs in all the rounds Daivika, Mānushya, and Paiśācha, it is called Maṅgala (or abode of bliss). If, on the other hand, it contains also the ruling class and Vaisyas in preponderating number, then it goes by the name of Pura. Again if the predominant people be Vaiśyas and Śūdras it is called 'Agrahāram. In these human habitats (martyāpada), Brāhmaṇs are assigned quarters in the outskirts (within the wall).[1] The royal palace may be placed in any of the rounds Daiva, Mānushya, or

[1] This is against the general scheme which places the Brāhmāṇs towards the centre. Besides, the designation 'Agrahāram' of a village peopled mainly by Vaiśyas and Śūdras is contrary to recognised nomenclature, as the quarters of the Brāhmaṇs alone go by that name.

Paiśācha. But the latter round is especially fit for Vaiśyas and Śūdras. There should be planted in the Paiśācha round streets numbering from one to seven (?). The Vaiśyas should be placed in the first street on the south. The castle of the paramount emperor (chakravartty) should be established in the plot belonging to Varuṇa, while in the plot dedicated to Mitra, Jayanta, or Rudrajaya should be erected the house of an ordinary king as well as the museum (kautukālayam). The headquarters of the provincial satraps and feudatory chiefs (sāmantapramukhādi) are to be stationed in the south-west corner. The sacerdotal caste are to be provided with sites in the plots belonging to Sugrīva, Puspadanta, Dauvārika, or Rākshasa; while the plots presided over by Gandharva, Roga, or Śosha are specially fit for the twice-born classes. In the same quarters are to be stationed the brothels and theatres. The wheel-wrights have their workshops in the divisions consecrated to Nāga or Mukhya (?). Art-studios (Śilpa-śāla) and looms are located in the north, while hospitals and dispensaries are established in the plots held sacred to Aditi or Diti. The village police have their barracks in the division of Jayanta; and charity-houses are placed in those belonging to Mahendra or Satya. Arsenals are to be constructed in the plots of Vṛsha or Antarīksha. Surrounding the above quarters stand the following :—The oil-dealers have their row of stalls along the street on the north and the potters are also provided in the same quarters. The vendors of liquors and meat are relegated to the west, while the hunters and fowlers are quartered in the south. The laundry is placed in the south-east or north-west. The pillared pavillion of guests is raised in the south or in the east, while colleges or muths are given sites in the east or the west. The cobblers and the shoe-makers and others of kindred calling are located in the north. Surrounding these are to be the quarters of other craftsmen.

Then the distribution of sites is dwelt upon. On all sides of the village, as for instance, in the Ārya and other directions, even in the outskirts of it, should be designed and distributed the temples of Vishṇu and His various manifestations. In the round containing the plot of Indra, the shrine of Vishṇu is erected in the Rākshasa plot. Śrīkara is located in the east, while Nārāyaṇa in the south or north and Keśava on the north. Images of Vishṇu should be established in desirable number in the east and the north, while Nṛsiṃha should be enshrined in the south-west or the north-east. Vishṇu should face the village, while Narasimha should have his face turned away from it. Lakshmī and Nṛsiṃha should generally face the village, but in the divisions belonging to Rudra and Rudrajaya, Indra and Indrajaya, Āpa and Āpavatsa, Savindra, Īśa, Jayanta, or Parjanya, the latter should have its back turned upon the village. Śiva, either in the east or in the west should face the village and in the case of other gods, there is no such hard and fast rule as above. Within the village walls, in the plot consecrated either to Pitṛs or to Dauvārika, is to be the shrine to Subrahmaṇya; or in those quarters may be established the mote-halls of Jainas or Bauddhas. Vaināyaka's shrines may be located in all the eight directions. The temple of Sarasvatī should be constructed in the plots of Mukhya or Bhallāṭa, while that of Lakshmī in those of Aditi or Mṛga. Without and close by the gates of the village should be established the shrine of Bhairava to guard the village or it may be on the street in the parts belonging to Rākshasa or Pushpadanta. Beyond the village pallisades towards the divisions apportioned to Soma, the temple of Kālī should be located. About a kroś (roughly two miles) away from the village, either in the east, or in the north, the quarters of the Chaṇḍalas should be raised and about ten daṇḍas to the north of the village, is to be placed the cremation ground.

The village should have a girdle of wall encompassed by a ditch. The main gates of the village should be located near the four corners. The eastern gate should be opened in the quarter of Iśāna; the southern gate in that of Agni; the western gate in that of Pitṛs and the northern gate in that of Vāyu[1].....Expert authorities do not generally recommend four gates in the four cardinal directions; or two gates may be constructed in the east and the west. The four streets making up the boulevard may have openings (chāra) at their terminii. Side-gates or by-gates may be opened in the north in the plots belonging to Nāga, Mṛga, Aditi, and Diti; in the east in those of Parjanya, Antarīksha, and Pushā; in the south in those of Gandharva and Bhṛṅgarāja; and in the west on those of Sugrīva and Asura. Else, travellers' gates (janadvāram) may be constructed in the plots belonging to either Mukhya, Bhallāṭa, Mṛga, Aditi, Jayanta, Mahendra, Satya, or Bhṛśa.

Divine edifices (maṇḍapam) should be erected in the squares held sacred to Brahmā, Agni, or

[1] Here some lines follow whose reading is too faulty for any clear construction.

Mitra. Councils and town-halls (sabhāsthāna) should be established in the plots dedicated to Bhūdhara and Asura. All the above distributions and allocations are required by the authorities on Śilpa Śāstras to be made on the ground divided into the mystic figure Chaṇḍita."

The Mayamata gives the following succinct description of villages of this type: "The village has five highways running from east to west, while the number of main thoroughfares running transverse to them is variously recommended from thirteen to seventeen. It has four main gates on the four sides. Because of the peculiar orientation of its gates and numerous streets it looks like the mystic figure Nandyāvarta. Hence its significant designation."

According to Kāmikāgama, it may be circular or quadrangular.

(4) Padma or Padmaka :—Mayamatam says there are five varieties of this village. The number of easterly streets may be seven, while the number of northerly streets may vary from three to five. Or, the streets running from east to west may be six or seven, while the transverse streets may be twenty. The Kāmikāgama fixes different numbers of northerly streets varying from seven to twenty-nine, while

PADMAKA[1]

[1] तद्देशेऽथ तथा स्थाप्यं मण्डपं वा सभा नयेत् (?) ।
तद्बहिः पूर्व्ववीथीषु पद्मेरावर्त्तकेषु च ।
चतुष्पथषट् सप्त चाष्टकं वाथ वीथिका ॥
मध्य ह्रदं विना कुर्य्यात् चतुर्द्दिक्षु चारकल्पकं । मानसारे नवमोऽध्यायः ।

The plan given above is a departure from the one suggested by Rāmrāz and others. But the very name Padmaka and the word 'आवर्त्तकेषु (circular) occurring in the above extract embolden me to it places the number of cross streets at seven. Mānasāra's details are: Its length and breadth are made equal, while the enclosing walls are circular. Or, the village and its walls may be quadrangular, sexagonal, or octagonal. The village ground should be divided into the mystic figure Sthaṇḍila or Chaṇḍita. The divine edifice and the council house should be erected in the central plot. Round about this plot should be planted streets numbering four to eight and they are lined with houses. There should be gates in four cardinal directions. The rest is identical with the above-mentioned Nandyāvarta.

(5) Swastika :—The lay-out of streets contemplated by Mayamuni in this village is as follows: The eastern street beginning from the north-east projects out to the south; the southern street begins to run from the south-east towards the west; the western street runs in northerly direction commencing from the south-west; the northern street beginning to run from the north-west shoots out in the eastern direction.

Mānasāra's particulars are exhaustive: Lengths and breadths of the village may be arbitrarily pro-

suggest the above plan as the right one answering the description. If my interpretation is correct of which I am not quite certain for want of a more reliable manuscript or text—then here is a town-plan consisting of oblique street.

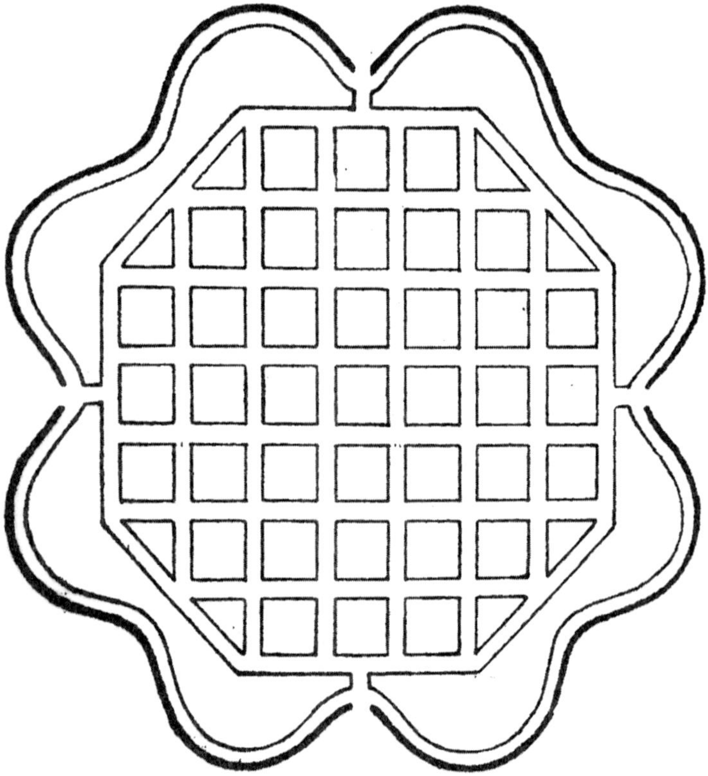

PADMAKA
(*in Sthaṇḍila*)

portional, and the ground should be divided into the mystic figure Paramaśāyika. Streets in it should be planted up to the extremity of the Paiśācha round. The streets should be planted in conformity with the figure Swastika. There should be two streets passing through the centre of the village, one running from west to east and the other cross-street running from south to north cutting the former in the middle and the rest of the highways should emanate from one or other of the four branches of these two cross-roads. The (northern-most) easterly street runs from the north to the north-east; the eastern-most southerly street beginning from the east terminates in the south-east; the southern-most westerly street starting from the south abut on the south-west; the western-most northerly street setting out from the west ends in the north-west. The above four streets starting from the extremities of the four (*i.e.*, two) cross-roads are directed clock-wise round the village and together with the latter, from the figure Swastika by four plough-like (⌐-like) streets each bent respectively at right angles at the four cardinal points of the compass; thus each of these plough-shaped streets has two extremities one at the farthest point of the cross-road and another at the corner and each of them has two

SWASTIKA

openings one on the sides and the other at the angular points.

In the first quadrant having the plots of Brahmā, Soma, Íśāna, and Āditya at the angles, the parallel streets run from west to east; in the second quadrant within the corner-plots of Brahmā, Āditya, Agni, and Yama, the parallel streets run from north to south; in the third quadrant enclosed by the corner-chambers belonging to Brahmā, Yama, Nirti and Varuṇa the parallel streets run from east to west; in the fourth quadrant formed by the corners occupied by Brahmā, Varuṇa, Vāyu, and Soma, the parallel streets run from south to north. These streets have rows of houses on one side only. At both the extremities of these streets there are building blocks on a smaller scale. The surrounding boulevard too is lined with a double row of houses. Ramparts should defend the village and a ditch is to enclose these ramparts. There are eight main doors, four at the extremities of the cross-roads and the remaining four at the terminii of the four branches of the figure Swastika. There may be eight other supplementary doors, constructed on the plots belonging to Bhṛśa and Antarīksha, Bhṛṅgarāja and Mṛsha, Śosha and Roga, Aditi and Diti. The principal doors are designed like a plough, furnished with double door-panels. Here and there are the turrets over the walls fitted with varieties of missiles to be utilised in times of battle.

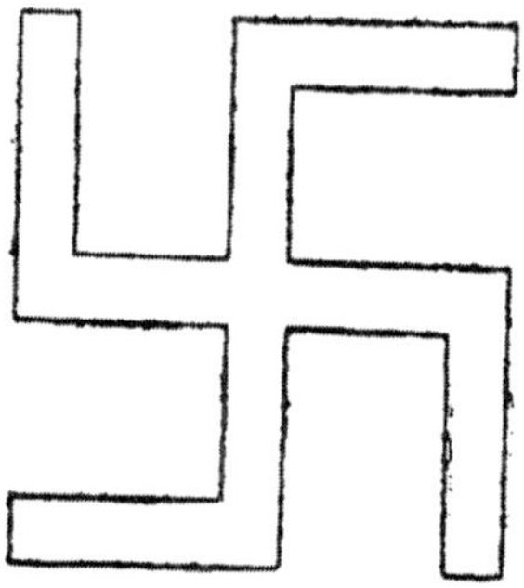

Mystic Figure Swastika

Full of various classes of people the Swastika is fit for habitation of kings and should be adopted in the Sthānīya (or local fastness or town). The royal palace may be erected in the four cardinal directions or at the corners or in the centre. When erected in the four cardinal quarters, it should be placed, without the central plot presided over by Brahmā, at the four plots, Aryyamā and others. There seems to be a classification of this type of village under different denominations, to wit, Āgata, Saṃgraha, Vijaya, and Sthānīya, according to the method of allocation of the royal palace. In the Āgata the palace may be situated on the plot belonging to Varuṇa, Āditya or Indrarāja; in the Saṃgrāma, it may be located on the plot consecrated either to Yama or Soma; in the Vijaya, it may be set up on the plot held sacred to either Soma or Vivasvān; in the Sthāṇīya, it may be assigned a site in the plot belonging to either Mitra, Varuṇa or Aryyamā.

In the Sthānīya and the other three, the temple of Vishṇu should respectively be erected on the plots presided over by Mitra, Varuṇa, Vivasvān, and Mahendra. The plots of Indra and Indrajaya, Rudra and Rudrajaya, or Āpa and Āpavatsa, Iśāna and Jayanta, should be alloted for the shrines to Īśa facing away from the village. The Buddhist temple should be established on the plot of Vāyu and the monastery of the Jainas should be erected on the south-west plot of Ṇiṛti. There should be four gates on the four sides and the temple to Bhairava should be raised beside them. The temple of Durgā and Ganapati should be established in the four directions or in the four intermediate directions, while the six-faced God should be located in the plot belonging to Sugrīva; the temple of the fever-god in that of Agni or Pushā; the temple of Bhāratī (Goddess of Learning) in the plot consecrated to Āditya; the temple of Bhūteśa (the Lord of

Beings) in the plot belonging to Sauraka or Mukhya. The temples of Vishṇu and Rudra may be suitably distributed. Human habitations should be laid out round about these divine edifices. The outermost road is lined with a single row of houses, while the other streets have a double row of houses. The above is the list of the internal divinities, while there is no fixed number of the external ones. The phallic emblem of Pāśupata may be set up within the village and, according to the Vaikhānasa, the remaining phalluses too may be established within it. The temple of Chāmundā is to be placed away to the north or the east of the village, facing the north. Without the village, to its east, north, west or south-west, the maṇḍapam of Senālokanāyaka (?) is to be established.

The rest is identical with the preceding types.

(6) Prastara :—Etymologically it means a village resembling a couch. Mayamuni says it is intersected by three streets running from east to west and by several transverse roads numbering from three to seven.

Mānasāra's description of the village is too crude and the MSS. I have access to is too

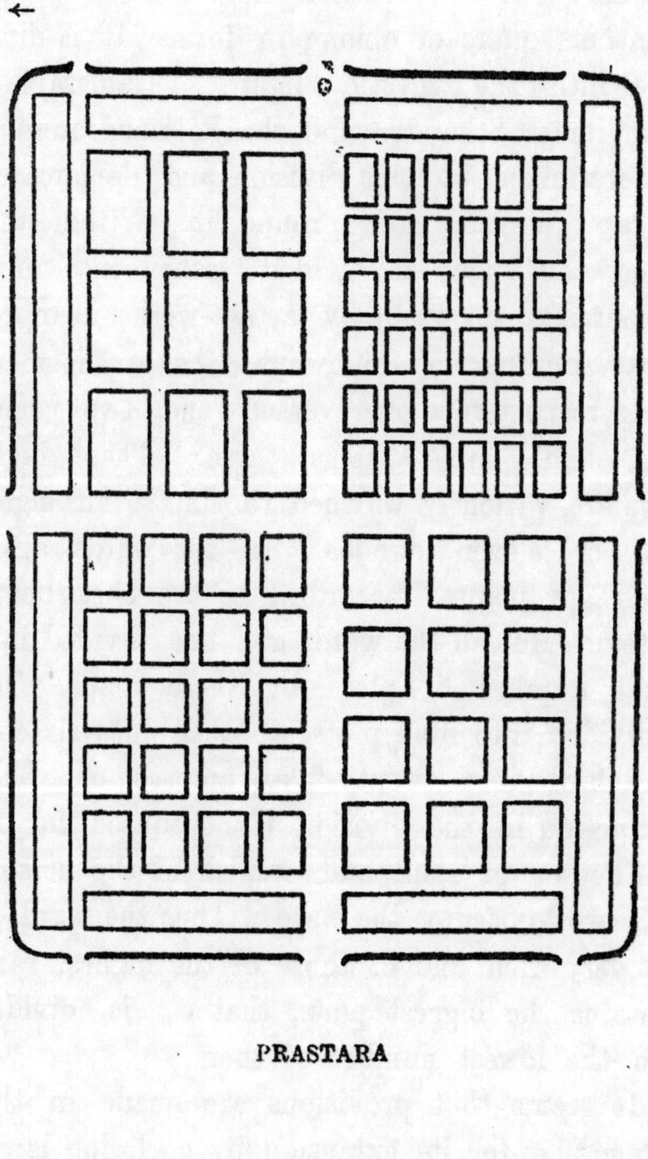

PRASTARA

erroneous for a literal rendering of it. What follows is a free but substantially correct summary of the description. The village is either square or oblong in form. It is divisible into the mystic figure Paramaśāyika, Chaṇḍita or Sthaṇḍila and the Paiśācha annulus is determined by this division and demarcated by a boulevard going round it. Within this round the space is divided either into four, nine or sixteen wards by a net-work of appropriate number of highways, the arrangement being respectively one versus one, two versus two, and three versus three. These highways are variously widened to six, seven, eight, nine, or eleven daṇḍas. In the wards again roads are planted according to the chess-board system. But all the wards are not divided into equal number of plots by these roads. One is divided into nine plots, another into sixteen, the third into twenty-five, and so on. This distinction in the division is accounted for by the degree of rank and wealth of the persons that are to occupy the ward. Thus the ward of the very rich and of those of the highest rank contains the biggest plots, that is, is divided into the lowest number of them.

It seems that provisions are made in this village plan for its extension by enclosing larger areas with fresh walls. There may be even eight or twelve such exogenous enclosures. The shape of every such enclosure should be identical with that of the original village.

Even in modern times arrangements like the above are made in all important town-extensions where there are assigned separate sites for houses, colleges, and bungalows in certain prescribed dimensions for each class.

In the north of the village is quartered the Vaiśya class and in the borders called the Paiśācha plot, all the artisans and craftsmen. Accommodation for the royal palace, shrines, courts, hospitals, colleges, and other buildings is made in the same way as in the Sarvatobhadra plan. The village is enclosed by walls and ditches with four principal gates on the sides and four subsidiary ones in the corners. The number of gates may also be twelve or more.

(7) Kārmuka :—It literally means a bow. Its shape is semi-circular or semi-elliptical, like a bow and hence its name. The towns of the varieties of Paṭṭana, Kheṭa or Kharvaṭa are planned after this. The Paṭṭana has a preponderance of Vaiśyas; the Kheṭa is generally inhabited by traders and labourers; while the Kharvaṭa is inhabited by lower classes of people. The

KĀRMUKA[1]

[1] रथ्या श्वेकवैक (?) स्यात् पश्चिमोदग्गर्त तथा ॥
दक्षिणे पूर्व्वके रथ्या उत्तरे पूर्व्वकेऽपि वा ।
दक्षिणे पश्चिमे वापि रथ्या चैवनमाहुधः ॥
तद्वये वीथी मात्मेतु कार्मुकं तकारवत् पृथक् ।

Kārmukha plan is generally suited to a riparian site or a sea-shore. There are two car-streets (both quadrangular ?) and one principal road. If the bow faces the west, one of the car-streets runs (along the circumference of the semi-circle) from south to east and the other from north to east. But if the village faces north then the former street runs from west to south. The other principal (straight) street runs from north to south (in the former case) or from east to west (in the latter case), thus the three streets forming the figure of a bow. The number of transverse streets may be one to five. Houses range on both sides of them. There may be additional radial roads. Divine edifices should be distributed as before. The gates of the village may be as many as desirable and its circumvallation is optional. The temple of Vishṇu or Śiva should be raised at the juncture of its two cross streets. The temple of Iśa or Saṅkara may be erected in the middle of the right side.

(8) Chaturmukha :—It is square or oblong

एतद्विमिचतुःपञ्च वीथीरेवं प्रकल्पयेत् ॥
एथ्यासव्वँ द्विपथं तिर्यङ्मार्गे यथेच्छया ।
चतुर्दिक्षु प्राक्प्राक्षैः चेत्तवत् पदविन्यसेत् ॥ मानसारे नवमोऽध्यायः ।
Here it is clearly directed that the streets should be oblique (तिर्यक्) and resemble the letter ग like a bow.

lying east-to-west-wise, so that its walls are also of similar shape. There are four great car-streets on the four sides. Two large streets crossing at right angles in the centre divide the whole site into four square blocks or wards and the principal four gates are raised over the terminuses of these two highways and there may be constructed supplementary doors as in the former cases. Each of the four wards is again planted with four (comparatively) smaller roads crossed by the same number of them. Rudra and his attendant deities should be installed within the village. The Brāhmaṇs should be assigned sites as in the Padmaka plan. If the village be chiefly populated with the trading class, then it is called Kolakoshṭha. According to some, the twice born class should fill up the four wards. The south-eastern ward is to be inhabited by the Brāhmaṇs; the south-western block by the ruling class; the north-western, even the north-eastern ward too, by the trading class. The Śūdras or the artisans and labourer class are relegated to the extreme borders, namely, the Paiśācha block. The shrines of Vishṇu, Rudra, and other divinities should be planted as in the preceding ones. What has been omitted in this description should be supplemented from the plans of the foregoing villages. Residential

←

CHATURMUKHA

blocks (Narāyaṇa)[1] should not be constructed on the car-streets; else, it will provoke perdition.

(9) Prakīrṇaka:—According to Mayamuni there are five varieties of this type. The number of easterly roads is fixed at four, while that of the transverse, that is, northerly roads, varies from eight to twelve respectively in either of the five plans. According to the Kāmikāgama, the number of northerly streets varies from four to seventeen; and yet it fixes the number of various plans at five like the Mayamata. Prakīrṇaka really means a 'chāmara', a fan made with big *chowries* (hairy tails) of yaks fastened to a handle.

(10) Parāga:—This village, according to Mayamuni, possesses six easterly streets and eighteen to twenty-two northerly ones. The Kāmikāgama, on the other hand, would lay out in it six to twenty-three northerly streets confining the gradual increment to unity and six cross-roads facing east. It is a small village but cob-webbed with such a large number of streets that facilities of traffic and locomotion are comparatively largest and easiest in it as the name implies.

[1] Does 'narāyaṇa' mean passages of men, *i.e.* foot-paths intended for pedestrian traffic?

(11) Śrīpratishṭhita :—Mayamuni defines it to be a village consisting of eight principal highways facing the east and of northerly streets numbering twenty-eight to thirty-two. The Kāmikāgama, while prescribing the same number of east-to-west streets, varies the northerly streets from eight to thirty-six, probably with common addition of four, thus bringing the number of varieties down to eight. The radical significance of the name is that Śrī, the Goddess of Fortune, is established and permanently secured in it.

(12) Sampatkāra :—This and the following three are varieties of villages especially noted in the Kāmikāgama. It consists of five streets running from east to west crossed by twenty-one transverse streets. The etymological meaning of the name indicates that it is very auspicious and secures wealth and prosperity.

(13) Kumbhakam :—Its shape is like a pitcher as the word denotes. It is either circular or polygonal. The number of streets in it is many and they run parallel to the contour.

(14 & 15) Śrīvatsa and Vaidika :—In both these types, there is no limitation to the number of streets but in the latter, it is obligatory that

each street should be lined with houses on both sides. In this plan, the houses are allowed to be built up in more storeys than one.

The descriptions of the last seven villages vouchsafed to us in the Mayamata or in the Kāmikāgama are very meagre, but one feature to be marked in all of them is that the number of northerly streets in all the types far exceed that of the easterly streets. This means that the villages were elongated east to west and east-to-west streets are longer so that winds could not blow up clouds of dust, while the buildings were open to free ventilation which in India generally runs from north to south or south to north.

It should be borne in mind that the villages in question were quite different from the existing villages of Bengal. These are results of unconscious spread of human habitation, in the wake of increasing population, into soil which was originally overgrown with woods and thickets. There is no vestige of conscious planning in the Bengal villages. But the villages under consideration were something like towns in miniature. There was the same juxtaposition of house blocks raised in rows; the same sort of folk-planning as in the town. Hence while in Bengal a garden-village will be out of question, every village here being a settlement amidst trees and woods, in the villages of ancient India—prototypes of which are still visible in Southern India and in some parts of Northern India—it was thought possible to lay out what is known as a garden-village exactly like a garden-city. Mr. Venkatarama Ayyar furnishes us with a picture of such a garden-village, corroborating his general description by many examples from the Deccan. He says that such garden-villages were planted round a temple either of Śiva or of Vishṇu or other holy Divinity commanding parochial, and not unoften extra-parochial, reverence and influence. This exogenous lay-out exactly answers to that of a temple-city or a garden-city. "The temple may be ever so modest a structure; but it must have a tank adjoining it; and also a flower-garden and an open space about it. And the practice of building houses abutting round such an open square or in front of the tank adjoining the temple is very useful from a hygienic point of view, for admitting fresh air and light to each and every home.

"Thus came into existence a number of villages each with a central temple and a tank and a garden adjoining it. Streets were then formed round the temples and the houses were built for the use of those temple servants to whom it was an advantage to live near their place of work. And likewise, rows of houses grew in well-ordered plan on all sides of the tank. And as fresh temples were constructed, villages grew in the same manner on the model of the older villages. And so on, villages and cities with temples and public baths were studded throughout the length and breadth of Southern India." Mr. Ayyar illustrates his description with instances of South Indian villages. It should be observed that the villages, from their nucleus,—the shrine—to their full-fledged state, were not laid out at once on a deliberate plan, but in their exogenous evolution traditional town-planning instincts inherent in the people asserted themselves with remarkable precision and expression. In all probability the village Viśvakarmās had a large hand in the planning of the temple as well as in the development of the village by lay-out of successive house-blocks.

CHAPTER IX

OF BUILDINGS AND BUILDING BYE-LAWS

Though construction of buildings does not come within the province of a town-planner and forms a separate subject by itself, yet civic and domestic engineering sciences are so correlated together that it is necessary that the town-planning authorities should exercise some control over the construction and arrangement of buildings in their bearings upon the proper lay-out of a city. Such co-operation between the civic and the domestic architects goes to maintain harmony and methodicity among the rows of houses in the same quarter and to preserve proper sanitation. A sense of the whole ward or city must dominate the individual building so as to bring out its organic entity. Hence there must be some co-ordination in the construction of the several structures; these are the constituents of an organic whole, the city. This cannot be left to the civic sense of the individual house-holder or the building engineer. A superior controlling agency to enforce the rules formulated and enacted for this purpose is sometimes a necessary and useful establishment.

In ancient India this sense of civic integrity gave rise to many salutary and noteworthy building bye-laws. I propose to consider them here one after another, emphasising their importance from the standpoint of civic arts.

(1) First lay out the town and then only plan the houses. Violation of this rule portends and brings evil.[1]

This simple rule has a far deeper and wider connotation than what appears at first sight. It means that an unconscious growth of houses one beside another, leaving insufficient space for streets and other civic factors and upsetting the arrangement of castes and professions, does not make a good city. This rule lays stress upon systematic and comprehensive lay-out of a city —its walls, its streets and lanes, the distribution of sites and buildings in proper order.

(2) First plant the trees and erect the premises thereafter: otherwise they will not look graceful and seemly.[2]

[1] Viśvakarmaprakāśa, Ch. 2, *ll.* 206-7.

नगरं विन्यसेदादौ पश्चाद्गेहानि विन्यसेत् ॥ १०३,
अन्यथा यदि कुर्व्वाणस्तदा न शुभमादिशेत् ।

[2] Viśvakarmaprakāśa, Ch. 2, *ll.* 208-9.

आदौ वृक्षाणि विन्यस्य पश्चाद्गृहाणि विन्यसेत् ॥ १०४
अन्यथा यदि कुर्य्यात्तु तद् गृहन्नैव शोभनम् ।

The trees generally recommended are aśvattha (*ficus religiosa*), banian (*ficus indica*), udumbara (*ficus racemosa*), plaksha (*ficus tusida*), the red flower tree, the tree exuding milk (kshīra vṛksha), the rubber tree (*manihol glazionii*), banana, and flower plants. The prominent among this list, it will be observed, because of their mighty magnitudes and bulky proportions in their full growth affording shade to the jaded and scorched wayfarers, are too big for domestic orchards; they are meant for the parks and promenades of a city, its avenues and broad streets. If the order and arrangement proposed above are inverted, then difficulties will arise in selecting suitable sites for these trees and their arbitrary location may ultimately prove detrimental to the proper lighting and ventilation of the neighbouring premises. The nimba (*azadirachta indica*), the bæl (*ægle marmelos*) are generally recommended for domestic orchards because of their anti-malarial properties.

(3) The houses of Brāhmaṇs should be chatuhśālā ;, that is; they must occupy the four sides of a quadrangle which is an open space in the centre. Sālā means a long structure of one span only. The houses of Kshatriyas should be triśālā, *i.e.*, occupying the three sides of the rectangular plot. The houses of Vaiśyas should

be dviśālā, *i.e.*, forming the two sides of the plot, while those of Śūdras should be ekaśālā.[1]

Their facades are only important to us, for the triśālā and the dviśālā can be so adjusted as to accommodate an open space in their front along the road which can be laid out as a flower garden. Thus if all the houses on one or both sides of a street recede in the middle as a triśālā or a dviśālā contemplates, we get gardens by the roadside. We have no definite materials at hand to infer that such gardens existed in ancient India. Certainly there were the open spaces; and the branching blocks of the buildings abutting on the streets relieve the monotony of a wall-like front of the thick-set structures or of the long rows of gardens that otherwise would have been the result.

(4) The imperial palaces should be raised to eleven storeys; the buildings of Brāhmaṇs to nine storeys; those of the ordinary kings to seven storeys; the buildings of the provincial satraps (sāmanta) to five storeys; Vaiśyas and the soldier class (Kshatriyas ?) should have four-storeyed buildings and Śūdras should have their

[1] Viśvakarmaprakāśa, Ch. 2, *ll* 252-3.

ब्राह्मणानां चतुःशालं क्षत्रियाणां त्रिशालकम् ।

द्विशालं स्यात्तु वैश्यानां शूद्राणामेकशालकम् ॥ १२६।२

houses one to three storeys high.[1] Mānasāra would determine the storeys in a different way and according to him the lower classes must on no account construct houses of more than a single storey. This assortment of the number of storeys under the different schools should not be disturbed.[2] The Vṛhat Saṃhitā lays down that no building should be more than hundred cubits high.[3]

It is immaterial for our present purpose which authority recommends what number of storeys for the different classes of people. It is enough that there is the definite number of storeys for the definite classes and that they vary. Sound town-planning requires that there must be some correspondence and proportion between the width of a street and the height of the buildings rising along it. Buildings of disproportionately excessive height obstruct light and ventilation. Now in ancient India folkplanning set up an inter-relation between

[1] Mayamatam, Ch. 29, *ll.* 159-64 ; *vide* also Ch. 11, *ll.* 44-50.

सकलक्षितिपेन्द्राणामेकादशतलं भवेत् ।
नवभूमिर्द्विजातीनां नृपाणां सप्तभूमकम् ॥ ८०
षट्तलं मण्डलीकानां पञ्चभूमावराजते ।
वैश्यानां तु चतुर्भौमं योधसेनेशयोरपि ॥ ८१
एकादित्रितलान्तं च शूद्राणां प्रतिविधीयते ।
सामन्तप्रमुखादीनां कारयेत् पञ्चभूमकम् ॥ ८२

[2] Mayamatam, Ch. 11, *l.* 52.

[3] Ch. 53, *l.* 32 ; *vide* also Viśvakarmavidyāprakāśam, *l.* 72

the site, the breadth of a street planted therein, and the rank of the residents in that quarter. This rule worked out in such a way that the high class people were assigned premises along the wide thoroughfares, while the low class people were relegated to the comparatively narrow roads, so that in all structures along the street the number of storeys was the same. If we remember this in connection with the above mentioned bye-laws, it is obvious that a definite proportion between the width of streets and the heights of buildings was arranged for in practice. The height of the walls of the buildings should not be too small or too great.[1]

(5) As far as possible the height of buildings in the same street should correspond, that is to say, one should not be lower and another higher.[2]

It is obvious that absence of a uniformity in the height of buildings on the same street detracts from the beauty of the street.

(6) A deviation from the fixed measurements of lengths, breadths, and heights of the respec-

[1] *Vide* Nārada Saṃhitā, Ch. 29, *ll.* 111-112.
नात्युच्छ्रितं नातिनीचं कुड्योत्सेधं यथारुचि ।
गृहोपरि गृहादीनामेवं सर्व्वत्र चिन्तयेत् ।। ५६

[2] Viśvakarmaprakāśa, Ch. 2, *ll.* 25 5-6..
शालादिभिर्न कर्त्तव्यं न कुर्यात्तुङ्गनिम्नकम् ।
समा शाला ततः कुर्यात् समं प्राकारमेव च ।

tive buildings of the different classes of people is not conducive to good and should not be made.[1]

This means and ensures an all-round uniformity of the buildings on the same street, for only a particular class was allowed residence in the same street. This rule and the preceding one also require that heights of the various storeys of the different buildings should correspond. Haphazard irregular heights of the storeys of the buildings are distressing to the eye. It is only a system, a regularity even in the variations that augments artistic beauty. Even the same style of architecture was followed in their broad features in the construction of buildings along the same thoroughfare. Since the wide streets separated the wards and these were assigned to the different classes of people, the buildings on both sides of a highway might not be constructed on the same scale, thus making a diversity in uniformity. The latter scheme was only possible in those later-day cities where the wards were not fortified with a circumvallation.

(7) The houses should be furnished with

[1] Vṛhat Saṃhitā, Ch. 53, *ll.* 29-30; Viśvakarmavidyāprakāśam, *l.* 60.

हीनाधिकं समानादशुभकरं वास्तु सर्व्वेषाम् ॥ ३०

verandahs (alinda)[1]; and with flight of steps[2] leading down from the high plinth of the verandahs and stone-couches. A 'vedikā' or raised seat should be constructed on each side of the door.[2]

"Life in the clear air and under the cloudless skies of India, is necessarily passed much in the open air. The street is a kind of club."[3]

(8) Outside the house and touching it there should be planted a foot-path (vīthikā), like the two paved foot-paths on either sides of the main thoroughfares of a modern city which should be as wide as one-third of the breadth of the house.[4] The foot-walk formed an indispensable part of the house. Mānasāra clearly lays down that there should be raised foot-paths on both sides of the streets.[5]

[1] Vṛhat Saṃhitā, Ch. 53, l. 65; Viśvakarmavidyāprakāśam, l. 72; Viśvakarmaprakāśa, Ch. 2, l. 306; and Mayamatam, Ch. 30, l. 221. This indicates that the rule was widely appreciated and generally observed.

[2] Mānasāra, Ch. 38.

[3] Sister Nivedita, Civic and National Ideals, p. 15.

[4] Vṛhat Saṃhitā, Ch. 53, l. 39; Viśvakarmaprakāśa, Ch. 2, l. 307; Viśvakarmavidyāprakāśa, l. 77; and Mayamatam, Ch. 25, l. 73. So many authorities' emphasis upon the same rule testifies to its wide appreciation.

[5] शालाविभागतुल्या कर्त्तव्या वीथिका बहिर्भवनात् ॥ २८।४२

वीथीनां पार्श्वयोर्द्वे वेदिकायोरन्तकृतं।

(9) All the houses should face the royal roads and at their backs there should be vīthīs or narrow lanes to allow passage for removal of offals and night-soil.

The first part of this bye-law forms an interesting study in the evolution of civic architecture with reference to construction of buildings. For in many ancient treatises and even in old buildings extant now, we find that the doors never opened on the roads. The credit of this improvement upon older styles is due to Śukrāchāryya.[1]

(10) "The front, middle and back doors of a private dwelling house should be so designed as to be on the same level and in the same straight line with one another. Let the outer door be placed, not exactly in the middle of the facade but a little moved to one side. The general practice is this: If the front of the house be ten paces in length, the entrance should be between five paces on the right and four on the left."[2]

[1] Śukranītisāra, Ch. 1, *ll.* 533-4.

राजमार्गमुखानि स्युर्गृहाणि सकलान्यपि ।
गृहपृष्ठे सदा वीथिर्मलनिर्हरणस्थलम् ॥ २६७

[2] Mānasāra. Rāmrāz's Essay on Architecture. *Cf.* Dr. Ganganath Jha; "House building and Sanitation in ancient India", *J.B.O.R.S.* Vol. 11. Pt: 11: "Every house should have doors on all four sides, but no two doors should be exactly opposite each other" His reference is difficult to be traced.

(11) "Not encroaching upon what belongs to others, new houses may be constructed. From each house a water-course of sufficient slope three pādas or one and a half aratnis long shall be so constructed that water shall either flow from it in a continuous line or fall from it into the drain. Violation of this rule shall be punished with a fine of fifty-four panas.

"Between any two houses, or between the extended portions of any two houses, the intervening space shall be four pādas or three pādas (feet).[1] The upper storey shall be provided with a small but high window. If a neighbouring house is obstructed by it, the window should be closed. The owners of houses may construct their houses in any other way they collectively like; but they shall avoid what is injurious. Violation of this rule shall be punished with the first amercement. The same punishment shall be meted out for causing annoyance by constructing doors or windows facing those of others' houses except when these houses are separated by the King's road or the high road."[2]

This reservation of an intervening space

[1] Vāyu Purāṇām, Ch. 8, *l.* 241; and Bhavishya Purāṇam and Brahmāṇḍa Purāṇam

[2] Arthaśāstra, Bk. III, Ch. 8.

between any two houses of the same owner or two neighbouring tenements of different owners is conducive to sanitation.

The foregoing bye-laws prove the existence of co-operation in the construction of buildings. I cannot conclude this chapter without reproducing the description of an ancient city given by John Marshall in order to show that the above rules were more or less observed in actual practice. "The city of Sirkap (in the ruins of Taxila) shows several large blocks of dwellings, separated one from the other by narrow side streets. Although the plans of these houses exhibit considerable variety, they were all based on the same principles. The unit of their design is the open quadrangle surrounded by chambers (chatuhśālā) and this unit is repeated two, three, four or more times according to the amount of accommodation required by the occupants, the small rooms fronting on the street being usually reserved for shops. The walls are constructed either of rough rubble or of diaper masonry."[1]

[1] A Guide to Taxila, by John Marshall, pp. 70-1.

CHAPTER X

OF CENTRES AND ENCLOSED PLACES

In ancient towns, the importance of centres from the standpoint of citizenship and public life could not be overestimated. "So much more of that life was carried out in the open air, so much more of the intercourse and exchange of ideas was effected by speech in the market place, in the days when the printing and the newspaper were unknown, that it is very difficult for us who gather the news of all the world at our breakfast table and transact the main part of our business by letter or by telephone to realise, for instance, the importance of the agora in the life of a Greek city or of the forum in that of the Roman town."[1] This pregnant remark of Mr. Unwin aptly applies also to the pillared pavilion in the centre, the council-tree, the temple, or the royal palace so conspicuously bossed up in ancient Indian towns. It was their remarkably distinctive characteristic that in the central place of the town or village were grouped the shrine of the presiding deity, the royal house, the court, the council, the quarters of the ministers and the commanders of the army, the treasury and other important public buildings. Though

[1] Town Planning in Practice.

this centralisation of public buildings was the outcome less of any town-planning principle than of the socio-political philosophy and the circumstances that were upperhand at the time, yet their indirect effect upon the plan of the towns or the villages was singularly happy. The effect of public buildings is lost if they are scattered indiscriminately throughout the city. Not only is public life disintegrated in some measure, but dissipation of corporate life and waste of useful time and energy on the part of the citizens are its inevitable consequences. On the other hand, an overzealous desire to concentrate civic life in the heart of the town, causing a sort of atrophy and stagnation in other quarters is too palpably suicidal to require any special comment. Subsidiary centres of public life, ensuring facilities for proper exercise of corporate functions in the different wards, should therefore be provided for in the city. It cannot be gainsaid that in the town-plans elaborated in the Śilpa Śāstras and in the actual illustrations we come across in the old towns existing to this day, as well as in literature studded with pen-pictures of ancient towns, both these principal and secondary centres are found to have been carefully organised. Every Indo-Aryan city comprised many centres and enclosed places; they were their lungs and afforded open spaces of free and pure breathing, relieving the stuffy and congested life of the citizens. The following lines give succinct sketches of some of them.

The royal palace and other public buildings[1]

"The palace is to be in the midst of the council buildings, must have stables for elephants, horses and cattle, is to be well adorned with spacious tanks, wells and water pumps, is to have sides of equal length in all directions and is to be high southwards and low northwards. The palace is to have walls guarded by sentinels equipped with arms and weapons and defended by strong machines, should have three courtyards and four beautiful gates in four directions. The king should furnish the palace with various houses, tents, rooms and halls."[2] " In the central portion or *akanakar* was situated the palace of the king. Separate baths were improvised here for the exclusive use of the queen and other ladies of the household. Some of these baths were artificial reservoirs of water which could be filled and emptied at will. There were also artificial mounds of stone and sand where the members of the royal family spent some time.

[1] *Vide* Chapter VI in this connection.

[2] *Vide* the same Chapter for the location of other public buildings. Also see Śukranītisāra, Ch. 1, *ll.* 435—7, 440—1, 444.

"The parks by the side of the palace contained deers and other games. Such parks were guarded by soldiers and were closed to the public. There were other tanks and flower gardens which were also reserved for the exclusive use of the queen and other princesses. Platforms were raised at convenient places in these parks and gardens. In making arrangement for the amenities of the royal household, the kings combined usefulness with beauty and taste. One of such artificial features planned near the palace in ancient times, is the Samudram, a beautiful sheet of water near Tanjore said to have been dug out to give an idea of the ocean to the ladies of the royal family."[1] Another such object of beauty was an artificial mound or hillock on which various flower plants and trees were carefully reared. Many gorgeous fancy birds, *e.g.*, the peacock, used to perch there and the hill was used for pleasure walk. One has only to visit the cities starring the whole of Rajputana or the cities of Southern India to realise the almost fastidious grandeur and picturesqueness of this scientific combination of the garden of Government buildings and the gardens of trees and flowers, tanks or lakes, and mounds. In the capital of Bijapur, "the most interesting spot of

[1] Venkatarama Ayyar, p. 177—8.

all is the citadel; for within the small and almost circular enclosure, were the palaces and private apartments of the king and his family, various public buildings such as the civic and criminal courts, the military and revenue offices and treasury, interspersed with courts and gardens, fountains, cisterns and running water."[1] To bring out prominently the personality of this charming centre, it was separated from the rest of the city by planting large wide streets around it and also radiating from it. Centres should be as widely visible as possible. This would suggest the choice of some hill-top, and undoubtedly it is desirable to choose the summit of some rising ground. It is for this reason that " as a rule, the palaces in Rajputana are situated on rocky eminences jutting into or overhanging lakes or artificial pieces of water, which are always pleasing accompaniment to buildings of any sort in that climate; and the way they are fitted into the rocks or seem to grow out of them leads to the most picturesque combinations. Sometimes their bases are fortified with round towers or bastions, on whose terraces the palace stands;

[1] For richer and more varied descriptions, see Ferguson's History of Indian Architecture and also the History of Bijapur Architecture. I have also dwelt upon this subject on various occasions in this treatise to illustrate different topics.

and even when this is not the case, the basement is generally built solid to a considerable height, in a manner that gives a most pleasing effect of the solidity to the whole."[1]

Temples

The temple of the tutelary—hence the principal—deity of the city is another important centre. It is the Brahmapīṭha installed in the Brahmasthāna, the square in the centre. The whole compound of the temple is divided into various courts. Mānasāra recommends five such: the innermost court is called antarmaṇḍala ; the second antarnīhāra ; the third madhyanīhāra ; the fourth prākāra ; the fifth and the last is known as mahāmaryādā or the extreme boundary where the gopuras are constructed. Around the shrine of the principal divinity the temples of the attendant deities are to be erected. " At the eight cardinal points of the innermost or the first court, the temples of a group of eight deities are built. Groups of sixteen and thirty-two deities are located in the second and third courts respectively."[2] Even the temples of the Bauddhas and the Jainas were sometimes included in the com-

[1] Ferguson, History etc.

[2] Mānasāra, Chs. 31 & 32, Dr. Acharyya's Summary.

pound. The compound bristled with numerous maṇḍapas for such purposes as bath, bed, assembly, horses, musicians, dancing girls, cows,[1] stores and the like. There were also tanks and gardens within the compound. Outside the walls of this temple-group were laid out on a rectangular plan, four broad streets to demarcate its individuality and other streets abutted on these, thus emphasising the importance of the centre. I have detailed on council-tree and pillared pavilion that were reared round it in various other connections.

The Aśrama, Maṭha and the College

The 'āśrama' (hermitage) or the 'maṭha' (monastery) was another important centre in the civic life of ancient India. Though sometimes it was relegated to a sequestered part of the forest lying in the outskirts of the city, yet in many cases it was accorded an honoured location within it. It consisted of many buildings constructed for various purposes such as the debating hall and reading rooms, the quarters of the students and the professoriate. There were also a tank, a flower garden and a shrine of the tutelary deity within the compound. It was a university of the modern type. The famous Nālandā Vihāra

[1] Mānasāra, Chs. 31 & 32, Dr. Acharyya's Summary.

and the maṭha of Taxila are illustrations in point. Even the house of a Brāhmaṇ Paṇḍit was a college in miniature, because he had not only to coach his students free, but also to provide them with board and lodge in his house.

Public Halls

Other minor centres were the serais, the theatres, and the markets. The Mahābhārata (Ch. 69 of the Śāntiparva) cites the following centres—a market, a field for athletics, a hall of the nobility, a pleasure garden, a garden, the assembly of officials, and the council. I need not repeat that serais were placed at the cross-sections of highways. Tanks were attached to them. There were also special halls exclusively meant for ascetics. "The public rest-houses or choultries were constructed either by the state or by private citizens in the town. It was usual to construct a 'chattram' on some good locality with ample open space around it."[1] In the markets lanes were carefully laid out. No carriage, even that of the king, was allowed admission into them. Mr. Ayyar furnishes us with a description of the market of Kaveripumppattinam; "The central market was situated in a wide open area between the two im-

[1] Venkatarama Ayyar, p. 140.

portant divisions of the city. Each stall floated a flag bearing the name of the article sold therein. The stumps of freshly cut trees were planted in front of these stalls, that they might afford a cool shade and breeze. The sun-shade in front of these stalls was raised on these stumps so that they served the double purpose of serving as support for the roof in front of the stalls while providing fresh air in a busy place. As each stall had thus a tree in front of it, the market presented the lively appearance of a park. In the centre of the area set apart for the market and where the main streets intersected, there was a temple dedicated to the Guardian Deity of the city. Here was a temple with a tree and a shrine."[1] There were also town-halls (sabhā or nagara-mandira). These centres and places are signified by the word *manram* in Tamil literature, which means " a public hall, a public place of worship, a place of public resort, public walk or maidan, a law-court with the guardian deity of Justice installed therein, a public bath or park." Any ward allotted to men of a particular caste or profession contained a hall where the confraternity or the guild of these persons periodically met to debate and transact

[1] Venkatarama Ayyar, p. 90.

corporate business. These constituted supplementary local centres.

Of what are called technically 'places' or 'enclosed places' in the modern town-planning science, there were many in ancient towns not only in India but also in other countries as well, inasmuchas congestion of cities was not so intense then as at present and tanks had to be provided for to supply water. Much attention was paid to their maintenance and distribution. It has already been noticed that each shrine of the city was associated with 'tīrthams' or bathing tanks. "There should be at least two tanks or reservoirs in a city or a village, one of which would be in the south-west."[1] According to the Silparatna,[2] there should be abundance of tanks and reservoirs judiciously distributed in all the wards, whereas pleasure-gardens should be allocated in the north. Gardens were laid out on their banks; and lily, lotus and other flowering plants were reared up in the water, thus enhancing the charm of the place. A small alley called khsudra-vāhya-vīthi was planted round the tank so that people could breathe fresh air and enjoy a pleasant walk in the

[1] Rāmrāz, Essay on Architecture, p. 41.

[2] *Vide* Ch. 5, *l.* 140.

भ्रस्तं सर्व्वत्र वाप्यादि ह्युत्तरे पुष्पवाटिका ।

morning and evening. In many villages and towns large tanks for the purpose of fresh drinking water were excavated in their centre. Besides public tanks, there were private tanks too. Moreover deep wells were sunk here and there with flights of steps leading into them. Over and above the gardens trimmed as adjuncts to the tanks, there were also gardens and parks, all excellent open spaces, with no tanks attached to them. The remarkable features of these gardens and the enclosed tanks were the cool 'gūḍhagṛha' or 'samudra-gṛha' (used in summer) *i.e.*, a secluded or shaded room, may be subterranean, a shower-bath room (called dhārā-gṛha or dhārā-yantra-gṛha), a fountain, a bower, a cradle (dolā) swinging from the branch of a tree." There were also constructed vedikās or pīṭhikās, that is, altars or raised pedestals where the walkers could take their seat and enjoy rest and friendly chats. There were also raised water-sheds (prapā) for distribution of pure drinking water and they were placed at the junctions of roads. It is interesting to note that in ancient cities sites were also assigned for ladies' parks.[1] There were also public play grounds (krīḍā-sthāna). There were open spaces where horses and elephants were trained for military purposes. The cross-sections of roads were

[1] The Rāmāyana, Ayodhyā Kāṇḍa, Canto 71, verse 22.

widened and arranged into triangular plots and quadrangular squares.

These centres and enclosed places were evenly distributed. Every ward or residential quarter was endowed with them to relieve congestion and to ensure ventilation of fresh air and proper light. So much importance was attached to these centres and places and so much attention was devoted to their proper management, that hardly any city is met with in ancient Indian literature, *e.g.*, the Purāṇas and the two Epics, which fails to glorify them. A description of the city is identified with the description of these. Indeed the authors seem to take pride in their prominent edification and this bears testimony to appreciation of their civic importance.

CHAPTER XI

INDIVIDUALITY OF INDO-ARYAN TOWNS

The deadening monotony caused by drilling all town-plans of a country into a similar type or pattern and its evil effects are too obvious. Such uniformity not only spells a lack of lively imagination on the part of the civic architect, but also a disregard of all the local circumstances regulating style and shape of the city-structure and the materials available, as well as the peculiar purposes for which the city stands. And it also hampers the natural lay-out of the city to the best advantage and, at the same time, with minimum troubles and expenses. Individuality of cities is so spontaneous and natural that every city is unconsciously but unmistakably stamped with it and conscious efforts only emphasise this individuality.

The site of the city—a river laving its feet and gurgling beside it, the high summit of a mountain commanding panoramic vistas, or a dreary wilderness—contributes much to the growth of this individuality. Again there were cities wreathed round with girdles of several broad ditches and wild woods. We further meet with charming description of lofty walls, strong ramparts with bastions and buttresses, watch-towers and embrasures, a belt of lofty trees, in all of which was displayed skill of architecture and civic engineering. These, coupled with the style and shape of the cities, square or rectangular, circular or elliptic, lotus-like or bow-shaped, could not but impress any traveller with the diversity of character of the Indo-Aryan towns. To crown all, there were the sublime and gorgeous gopuras or pyramidal towers surrounding the great city-gates —their storeys varying from one to fourteen, their structure at once fantastic and diversified.

Local building materials endowed the ancient towns with certain peculiarities of colour and workmanship. In these days of superabundant facilities for carriage and transport building materials can be easily conveyed from one end of the country to the other and blind uniformity is often the result. In the city of Sirkap, the walls of the buildings were constructed either of rough rubble or of diaper masonry which came into fashion at the beginning of the Kushan period ; and both the inner and outer faces were covered with lime and plaster to which traces of painting are still found adhering. In the city of Conjeeveram red bricks were used in the building of houses. None can fail to notice the reddish or white stone walls and floors of the buildings in the towns of Rajputana such as Jaipur, whereas the houses in Southern India were generally made of wood and those in Burma made of teak and bamboo. "In earlier times, the superstructure at least of the dwellings was either of wood-work or brick-work. In either case it was often covered, both internally and externally, with fine chunam plaster work, and brilliantly painted, in fresco, with figures or patterns."[1] I have myself marked such picturesque paintings on the walls of the buildings ranging on the streets of Jaipur. Certain special characteristics also arise from the nature of the local natural scenery, life of the citizens, as well as from the character of the industries prevalent in the locality.

In the Vāstu Śāstras, towns are classified according to their characteristics. The following are the free renderings of the descriptions given in Mānasāra (Ch. 10) and Mayamatam (Ch. 10).

(1) Nagara :[2]—A nagara or an ordinary town

[1] *Vide* Rhys Davids, Buddhist India, p. 68.

[2] दिक्षु चतुर्द्वारयुतं गोपुरयुक्तं तु सालाढ्यम् ।
क्रयविक्रयकैर्युक्तं सर्व्वजनावाससङ्कीर्णम् ॥ २०
सर्व्वसुरालयसहितम् नगरमिदम् केवलं प्रोक्तम् ।
मयमते दशमोऽध्यायः ।
जनैःपरिवृतं द्रव्यक्रयविक्रयकादिभिः ॥
अनेकजातिसंयुक्तं कर्म्मकारैः समन्वितम् ।
सर्व्वदेवतसंयुक्तं नगरं चाभिधीयते ॥
मानसारे नवमोऽध्यायः ।

has four gates in the four cardinal quarters surmounted by pyramidal towers. It is full of thick-set buildings; it is a place of brisk traffic, sale and purchase of merchandise, congested with all classes and ranks of people. Artisans settled there busily ply their tools. The place is sanctified by shrines dedicated to all deities, Brahmā, Vishṇu, Śiva and the like. In other words it is a place of inland trade and the headquarter of the district. I need hardly add that for military defence, the towns were generally well fortified. Their dimensions, according to Mānasāra, vary from 100 × 200 daṇḍas upwards.

(2) Rājadhānī:—Mayamatam furnishes us with a description of a royal capital with its imperial castle. It has a belt of walls and ramparts circumscribed by ditches. Further away from the ditches are encamped the military outposts to watch the approach of the enemy. Within the walls and along its western and northern sides are rows of residential quarters, while in the east and the south are quartered the royal army and officers. It has lofty gopuras with many garlands adorning it. Within the metropolis there are shrines dedicated to various deities. Of brothels there are many. Gardens are evenly laid out in it. The elephant, the horse, the infantry, and the military officers and all classes of men

put up in it.[1] It possesses many gates, principal and subsidiary. Sukrāchāryya's description of a capital runs as follows :—"It is to have the beautiful shape of a half-moon, a circle, or a square, is to be surrounded by walls and ditches and must contain sites for grāmas or other divisions. It is to have the Sabhā or Council Hall in the centre, must ever be provided with wells, tanks and pools; it is to be furnished with four gates in the four directions. It must have good roads and parks planted in rows, and well-constructed taverns, temples and serais for travellers."[2]

(3) Paṭṭana :—It is a large commercial port, situated on the bank of a river or sea. It is frequented by traders from distant lands (dvīpāntarāgata, deśāntarāgata) coming on commercial missions. Merchandise is imported in large quantities. All classes of men, especially the trader

[1] प्रत्यगुदग्दिशि गहना परितः शाखा बहिः सपांसुचया ॥ २१
परितः परिखा बाह्ये शिबिरयुतानेकमुखरथ्या ।
पूर्व्वायां दक्षिणतश्चाभिमुखा राजवश्मयुक्ता ॥ २२
उन्नतगोपुरयुक्ता नानाविधमालिकोपेता ।
सर्व्वसुरालयसहिता नानापणिकान्विता बहुद्वारा ॥ २३
हस्त्यश्वरथपदातिबहुमुख्या सर्व्वजनयुक्ता ।
हारीपक्षारयुताभ्यन्तरतोऽनेकजनवासा ॥ २४
या नृपवेश्मसमेता सा कथिता राजधानीति ।

मयमते दशमोऽध्यायः ।

[2] Mr. B. K. Sarkar's Translation.

class called Vaiśyas, are settled there and brisk commercial transactions are constantly carried on. It is replete with jewels, wealth, silk, perfumery and other articles.[1]

(4) Durga :—A fort or a fortified town. It must have a unfailing stock of forage and provisions, a perennial source of water and should be strongly equipped with weapons and arsenals. It is girt round by brick-built walls at least twelve cubits high with many watch-towers and military outposts. It is surrounded by ditches overgrown across with thick jungles. The approaches to the fort are at once difficult and well guarded. Its gates are embellished with massive towers tapering

[1] द्वीपान्तरागतवस्तुभिरभियुक्तं सर्व्वजनसङ्कुलम् ।
क्रयविक्रयकैर्युक्तं रत्नधनक्षौमगन्धवस्त्वाढ्यम् ॥ २८
सागरवेलाभ्याशे तदनुगतायामि पत्तनं प्रोक्तं ।

मयमते दशमोऽध्यायः ।

क्रयविक्रयसंयुक्तमब्धितीरसमाश्रितं ।
देशान्तरागतजनैर्नानाजातिभिरन्वितम् ॥
पत्तनं तत् समाख्यातं वैश्यैरध्युषितं तु यत् ।

मानसारे नवमोऽध्यायः ।

पत्तनसंज्ञं तदत् पोतान्वितवारिधितटोपेतम् । १७२

मनुष्यालयचन्द्रिका ।

पत्तनं शकटैर्गम्यं घाटिकैर्नौभिरेव च ।
नौभिरेव तु यद्गम्यं पट्टनं तत्प्रचक्षते ॥

इति रायसेंधीय सूत्रव्याख्याने—प २०६ कौटिल्यार्थशास्त्रे
पण्डितश्यामशास्त्रिधृतवचनम् ।

This leads us to suppose that there is a distinction between 'pattana' and 'paṭṭan a'.

high and furnished with secret flight of stairs. The pair of doors had four iron or wooden bars to bolt with and were thick-set with large pointed nails. The sizes of the gates should be in proportion to the dimensions of the buildings and towns. The fort bustles with many classes of men. Camps were pitched round it. The royal quarters and the barracks of the army are situated within the fort. It must possess a large storage of paddy, oil, salt, medicine, iron, fuel, etc.[1]

There is a fort known as Suparṇa Durga or Garuḍa fort. The general plan of this is like the

[1] पञ्चषगव्यात्रमञ्चं ह्यतिविपुलोत्तुङ्गघनसालम् ।
सर्व्वं हि दुर्गशालं सप्राकारं त्वनेकमुखरचम् । ३९
बहिरुदकं रहितवनं छन्नपथं दुष्प्रवेशं च ।
गोपुरमण्डपयुक्तं सोपानच्छन्नमच्छन्नम् ॥ ४०
द्विकवाटचतुष्परिखार्गलहस्तोन्नतेन्द्रकोलयुतम् ।
स्थूणमध्यमालयमिश्रकसहितं सगूढसोपानम् ॥ ४१
द्वाराणि मण्डपसभाशालाकाराणि कार्य्याणि ।
द्वादश शालाकाराश्चतुरं वृत्तं तदायतं च पुनः ॥ ४२
चक्रं वृत्तं कौक्कुटमिह कुम्भं नागवृत्तं च ।
अष्टचतुरं त्रिकोणमष्टास्रं नेमिखण्डं च ॥ ४३
प्राकारस्येष्टकया द्वादशहस्तोच्छ्रिताद्धीनाः ॥
उत्सेधार्द्धं विशाला मूले भित्तिः ससञ्चारा ॥ ४४
सर्व्वस्याभ्यन्तरतः पांसुचयोपर्य्यनेकशन्वयुतम् ।
परितः परिखोपेतं पांसुचये संहताट्टालम् ॥ ४५
परितः शिबिरोपेतं नानाजनवाससंकीर्णम् ।
नृपभवनसमीपेतं हस्त्यश्वरथपदातिबहुमुख्यम् ॥ ४६
धान्यैस्तैलैः क्षारैः सलवणभैषज्य गन्धविषम् ।
लोहाङ्गारस्नायुविषाणवेणिन्धनैर्युक्तम् ॥ ४७

Padmaka type of village, but the main roads run from north-west to south-east instead of west to east and is slightly more elongated in that direction. The cross-road runs from south-west to north-east. The temple is located in the north-west and the royal palace in the south-east. There are only two entrances in the fort at the north-east and south-east corners. There is no particular rule that such a fort shall be surrounded by a moat. No Saiva or Sākta shrine should be built within the fort premises. Shrines to Nāgarāja or Serpent God may be located within the fort. But if there be no Vishṇu temple built there, a temple to Garuḍa should invariably be erected and the usual processions carried out. The evil consequences of departure from the traditional rule of temple or town orientation are staved off in this plan by virtue of what is called Garuḍa mantra or Garuḍa symbol adopted in it. The king residing in such a fort shall bear a flag staff carrying the figure of Garuḍa.[1]

(5) Kheṭa :—It is a small town situate on the plain near a river, or in a forest by the side

त्वक्चर्मकाष्ठयुक्तं सवल्कलं सारदारुयुतम् ।
दुर्गं दुर्गममुक्तं दुर्लङ्घ्यं दुरवगाहं च ॥ ४८

मयमते नवमोऽध्यायः ।

[1] *Vide* Indian Architecture by Ananthalwar and Raes.

of hillocks. It is girt round with a mud-wall. It lies in the midst of villages[1] having facilities of communication by land or water. The main population of the town consists of Śūdras or labouring class. Such a town if thrown out by local industries, such as mining, is known as Sākhānagara.[1] According to its area it is classified into three varieties whose breadths respectively are 256, 320, 384 daṇḍas, while their lengths are 2, $1\frac{3}{4}$, $1\frac{1}{2}$, $1\frac{1}{4}$, $1\frac{1}{6}$, $1\frac{1}{8}$ times or equal to their breadths.

(6) Kharvaṭa :—Exactly similar to a Kheṭa is the town called Kharvaṭa defended with a girdle of wall. Its walls are not massive enough. It is a town lying in the rāshṭra or country side.[1] It is from here that the neighbouring town gets its daily supply of foodstuff and other articles of consumption. According to Kauṭilya it is situated in the centre of two hundred villages. The three measures breadth-wise of its three classes respectively are 448, 512 and 576 daṇḍas,

[1] Śilparatna, Ch. 5, *ll*. 28, 67—8 .

ग्रामयोः खेटकं मध्ये राष्ट्रमध्ये तु खर्व्वटम् ॥ १४
वने वा नगरोपान्ते नागरैस्तु जनैर्वृतम् ।
क्षेत्रारामाकरोपेतं शाखानगरमिष्यते ॥ २४

Cf.

यद्रैरधिष्ठितं यन्नद्यचलावेष्टितं तु तत् खेटम् ॥ २६

Mayamatam.

'प्रांशुप्राकारनिबद्धखेटं' ॥

the ratio of the lengths to the breadths being the same as in the case of the Kheṭa. It is a town bigger and hence more prominent than the Kheṭa.[1]

(7) (i) Śivira :—It is a military encampment of a king out on an expedition of fresh conquest and annexation, within his own kingdom or in the dominion of another king, where soldiers and officers are busy with preparations before commencing hostilities.[2] I have given elsewhere a detailed description of Śivira.

(ii) On a par with the Śivira is the Senāmukha. It is like a military base, rear station where the military staff carry on their duties away from the battle field. Hence it is well guarded and always lively with bustle of active officers. In times of yore when kings used to be at the head of every military expedition, the royal camp was also stationed in this Senāmukha. It may also

[1] परितः पर्व्वतयुक्तं खर्व्वटकं सर्व्वजनसहितम् ।

Mayamatam, Ch 10, *l*. 53.

"शुद्धकमाकारं वेष्टितं खर्व्वटं" ।

[2] परनृपदेशसमीपे युद्धारम्भक्रियोपेतम् ।। २९

सेनासेनापतियुतमिदमुदितं शिविरमिति च वरैः ।

Mayamatam, Ch 10, *ll*. 58-9.

परराष्ट्रे स्वदेशे वा चतुर्विधबलान्वितम् ॥ २९

विजिगीषोः सन्निवेशं शिविरं तत् प्रचक्षते ।

Śilparatna, Ch 5, *ll*. 58-9.

be a suburban town a little away from the main city guarding the latter at its main approach and thus commands a strategic situation.[1]

(iii) Skandhāvāra:—This and its suburb cherikā fall under the above category. Rivers, mountains and woods form its defences. Many people reside there as was always the custom with people of ancient India who invariably followed the royal camp in order to enjoy security under the king's protecting auspices. The Skandhāvāra contains the imperial quarters. It appears that a Skandhāvāra is nothing but a camp of the soldiers, not very remote from the actual battle-field, when two kings are fighting together.[2] Its plan is detailed in the appendix.

(8) Sthānīya:—Kauṭilya says: "There shall be set up a sthānīya (fortress of that name) in the centre of eight hundred villages." It is stationed by the king on the bank of a river or at the foot of mountains. There is a garrison

[1] सर्व्वजनैः सङ्कीर्णम् नृपभवनयुतं तदेव तथा ॥ ३०
बहुरचोपेतं यत् सेनामुखमुच्यते तज्ज्ञैः।
Mayamatam, Ch 10, *ll.* 60-1.

[2] Śilparatna, Ch. 5, *ll.* 60—1.
नातिदूरे तदेव स्यान्न पयोर्युध्यतोर्मिथः ॥ ३०
सेनानिवेशं तु पृथक् स्कन्धावार उदीरितः।
Also compare
नद्यद्रिवन समेतं बहुजनयुक्तं सनृपवासम् ॥ ३५
एतत् स्कन्धावारं तत्पार्श्वे चेरिका प्रोक्ता।
Mayamatam, Ch 10

of police there. It is a muffassil town and headquarters of the district or divisional officer. According to Śilparatna it is the headquarters of the dignitary who defends the frontiers of the kingdom.[1]

The radical import of the word sthānīya is local. Hence literally it is, a local fortified town. This refers us to a period of Indian history when her political state was in chaos and her condition was far from being settled and tranquil. Hence the king could not have a permanent sway over a fixed kingdom. His sway extended as far as his mighty arms could reach. The kingdom always followed him from place to place. Hence he had to quarter fortified capitals, wherever he could rest and settle for a while. In my opinion this clears up the following opinion of Kauṭilya. "With ready preparation for fight, the king may have his fortified capital sthānīya as the seat of his sovereignty (samudaya-sthānam) in the centre of his kingdom: in a locality naturally best fitted for the purpose such as the bank of the confluence of

[1] नद्यद्रिपार्श्वयुक्तं नृपभवनयुतं सवइरचम् ॥ २१
यत्र प्रतिस्थापितकं तत् स्थानीयं समुद्दिष्टम् ।

Mayamatam, Ch 10.

पर्व्वतस्याथवा नद्याः पार्श्वे राजबलान्वितम् ॥ २१
राष्ट्रस्यान्तकपालाय वा तत् स्थानीयं विदुर्बुधाः ।

Śilparatna, Ch 5.

the rivers, a deep pool of perennial water or of a lake or a tank, a fort circular, rectangular or square in form surrounded with an artificial canal or water, and connected with both land and waterpaths (may be constructed)."

(9) Droṇamukha :—It is a market town frequented by traders, lying on a river bank or sea shore, generally at their confluence, known also as Droṇīmukha. It is a harbour where many ships sail in and lie at anchor and also traders from distant islands fare to the place for traffic.[1] In other accounts, it is a small centre of traffic in the midst of four hundred villages. Local productions are offered to the market here. It may be that a police outpost is stationed here for the sake of administrative efficiency. There are five measures of its breadth varying from 400 to 496 daṇḍas with a common difference of 24 daṇḍas, the ratios of the lengths to the breadths being the same as before. If the Droṇamukha be a populous place in the midst of villages, it is also termed

[1] तद्दिवाब्धेश्च नद्याश्च सङ्गमागतपोतकम् ।। २८
द्वीपान्तरवणिग्जुष्टं विदुर्द्रोणीमुखं बुधाः ।

Śilparatna, Ch. 5, *ll*. 56—7.

नद्याब्धिदन्विपादन्विणभाग् वणिगादिसंयुक्तम् । ३२
सर्व्वजनावासं यद्द्रोणमुखं प्रोक्तमाचार्य्यैः । •
ग्रामसमीपे जनतालयमिदमुदितं विड्म्बमिति ।। ३३

Mayamatam, Ch. 10, *ll*. 64-6.

द्रोणमुखं जलनिर्गमप्रवेशं पट्टनमित्यर्थः ।

Viḍamba. It is mainly inhabited by peasantry. Its measurements vary from 200 to 500 daṇḍas, the common difference being 50 daṇḍas. From the measurements it appears that these cannot be properly designated as towns; they are only prominent village markets.

(10) Kotmakolaka :—It is a populous settlement in a hilly or wild tract.[1] There are five varieties of it varying in breadth from 100 to 500 daṇḍas, one greater than the preceding by 100 daṇḍas.

(11) Nigama :—It is a market mainly of artisans; but all the four castes of people also live here. It seems owing to insufficiency of space, the rule of allocating different sites to different castes and professions was not rigidly observed in this town. Nigama literally means a trade route. Hence it is a trysting place for traders and caravans. Again Nigama may be a market with a police outpost situated on the approaches to the capital or the kingdom.[2]

[1] *cf.* "वनमध्ये जनवासं"

[2] चातुर्वर्ण्यैः कर्मकारैर्नानाकर्मोपजीविभिः ।
पण्याश्वधनधान्याद्यैर्युक्तं तु निगमं स्मृतम् ॥ २२

Śilparatna, Ch. 5, *ll.* 65-6.

चातुर्वर्ण्यसमेतं सर्वजनावाससङ्कीर्णम् ॥ २४
बहुकर्मकारयुक्तं यन्निगमं तत् समुद्दिष्टम् ।

Mayamatam, Ch. 10, *ll.* 68-9.

(12) Maṭha or Vihāra :—Last but not the least in importance is the university town called Vidyāsthāna, Maṭha or Vihāra. Literally it means students' quarters or colleges. Hence it is a residential university where not only the learners board and lodge but religious itinerants (parivrājakas) or monks also reside. Savants from foreign lands also repair to the place, where there is provision for (free ?) supply of food and water. It is defended against hostile attack.[1] The student celibates who prefered religious pursuits and philosophical lore to a worldly life used to put up at this university town, it may be, in the capacity of professors. "And as the Brāhmaṇs became the custodians of Aryan traditions and culture, the Āśrama or Brāhmaṇ village developed into the university town to which Aryan youth of the twice-born classes went for instruction."[2]

Here closes the catalogue of all the noted types of towns, great and small, which ancient India knew and their number is by no means small. Diversity and architectural ingenuities or peculiarities in their planning are nowhere alluded to. Only we have their definitions—that too not

[1] आगन्तुकाणां च सर्व्वेषां नैष्ठिकानां निवासभूः ।
अन्नपानीयसंयुक्तः कैवलो वा मठो मतः ॥
विद्यास्थानं तु तद्वत् स्यात् बहुसेनासमन्वितम् ।

Śilparatna, Ch. 5.

[2] E. V. Havell.

distinctly differentiating, but on the contrary very vague—based on genetic causes and the purposes they served. Nevertheless these sufficed to endow them with characteristic features; for the sea ports, the halting places for caravans, the capitals and headquarters of the Government, the military stations during expeditions, all could not be shaped and planned in the same style, their temporary or permanent character and the houses therein built so as to suit different purposes constituting the distinguishing factors. Even in modern towns, it is not so much the peculiarity of street-planning which cannot strike the eyes of a pedestrain, as the civic centres and public places as well as natural beauties which emphasise their personality. And all of these peculiarities are natural and spontaneous rather than factitious, developing from local circumstances. It has been already mentioned that the shape, style, height, and the storeys of buildings were different for different people according to their ranks and avocations.

A reference to the relevant chapters will show that even in the planning of streets and distribution of public buildings and places there was a great diversity of arrangement. I have only to draw notice to the different types of towns known as Daṇḍaka, Nandyāvarta and so on. I may recount here that all the sites were not planned in the same style (*vide* Ch. VIII). As regards the planning of plots and distribution of public buildings, it is to be noted that the royal mansions, the council house, the quarters of the premier and other imperial officials, the tenements of the different castes, artisans and traffickers were variously distributed in various towns. The style of architecture after which the buildings were constructed also contributed to the development of the individuality. It should be borne in mind that diversity was not attained at the sacrifice of harmony and concord. Every building in a certain quarter or along same street was not constructed after a style different from the rest. Such an architectural chaos will be repugnant to the view. Indeed, on the contrary, a sort of structural unity and architectural uniformity, (but not of the Procrustean type), as in Jaipur, marked the buildings ranging along a particular street.

One proud glory of India is her temple-cities. Representing as they do India's national culture, they deserve special treatment. Temple-cities are generally those which had their origin in and evolved out of holy shrines with the spread of their fame and influence. Their peculiarities consist in the several successive rings of circumambulatory paths that writhe round and round their central plots whereupon the temples, their nuclei, are generally situated. These attest the successive stages of their growth and development. Another peculiar characteristic of these temple-cities lies in a good number of minor shrines set up in them. For many saints attached to the old temples set up their own shrines. Again their disciples raise others to their revered memory. It should also be noted that followers and preachers of creeds other than that represented by the original temple repair to the place either to measure their religious strength or from iconoclastic motives. A city like Benares offers the best forum for proselytization. Whatever may be the outcome of this trial of strength, the city, in consequence, soon outgrows its temple and develops a distinct corporate life. The new immigrants also settle here and raise their own monasteries.[1]

The corporate life of modern society being centralised in the city, people, a considerable percentage of them, now a days abandon their villages and settle in the city, some by their own choice, some by force of circumstances. The congestion of modern cities is the result. A narrow conception of town and town-planning

[1] *Vide* Ch. II, Conjeeveram.

has usurped every square inch of land and denuded the city of all trees or tanks, to make room for human habitations. The serried phalanx of cloud-high chimneys—the lofty pinnacles of modern civilisation—volleying forth incessant curls of smoke has imparted to the suburbs a most dreary and desolate appearance. Indeed the deforestation of the whole city, in and out, is complete. The aridity of this city life, devoid of the humanising and inspiring touch of gentle Nature, has reacted upon the life of citizens and they are therefore to-day looking for relief from this suffocating and artificial atmosphere. They have now realised their error in driving out Nature and are laying out garden-cities. These constitute rather a compromise between a city and a village, represent a harmonious combination of human art and soul-vivifying Nature. In these garden-cities there is symmetric distribution and allocation of parks, squares, gardens and tanks; trees are reared in rows along both sides of the streets, sometimes in the middle, sometimes in two or three rows on the streets thus segregating the different currents of traffic. Again every house has its own garden in the front. Some longitudinal portion of the street is sometimes kept evergreen with grass and installation of factories in large numbers is prohibited or discouraged.

In ancient India when congestion such as we notice in modern towns was out of question, tanks, parks or squares and even gardens were laid out in large numbers in every city. It must be remembered that modern water-taps were not then in vogue. Hence the large tanks or wells were necessary accompaniments to towns and were evenly distributed throughout the city. And their number could not consequently be small. We come across in the Śilpa Śāstras emphatic directions for excavation of tanks. Every tank with its high embankment overgrown with mighty trees affording shady rest to passers-by corresponded to the modern square or what is technically called 'place' in town-planning. Again Indian communalism required that there must be rendezvouses where citizens could assemble and discourse together. For this purpose there were the council trees with their spreading branches shading a large area. These grew into groves. There were gardens as well; and even orchards were not wanting. In Northern India reminiscences of these tanks and gardens can still be marked in Gaya, while they are still abundantly found in Southern India. It was the practice with the Aryan town-planners to dress the faubourgs of the city into fine gardens and orchards. This bespeaks sound economy and sanitation, let alone æsthetic propriety. Again the holy bæl (*ægle marmelos*), the shady baṭ (*ficus bengalensis*), the sublime kadamaba (*anthocephalus cadumba*), the febrifuge neem (*azadirachta indica*), the sacred aswatha (*ficus relegosa*), the flowering champaka or bakul (*plumerica acuminata* or *mimuspos' elengi*), and other plants whose flowers were offered in daily worship of deities, were copiously planted in the city so that Indo-Aryan cities partook much of rural aspect and wore a sylvan air. The Portuguese and Italian travellers who visited the kingdom of Vijayanagara in the early twenties of the 15th and 16th centuries have left detailed accounts of its capital. They called it a garden-city and their descriptions leave no room for doubt. From the stand-point of town-planning and town-expansion, the graphic description of the town of Vijayanagara, as left by them in their books of travels, presents a very interesting study. I think I need not apologise for quoting at length their description of the city at this place.

The city was founded by Harihar Deva in 1336 A.D. Its foundation in the middle of the 14th century notwithstanding, there is nothing to suspect that it was not laid out according to the canons of the Silpa Sāstras, especially when we remember that many cities, particularly the capitals of many principalities in Rajputana founded much later were planned according to the best Indo-Aryan town-planning traditions and this demonstrates beyond doubt that Indians never relegated this science to oblivion until the advent of European civilisation into this country. From the description of the city by Nicolo, an Italian traveller who visited it in 1420-21, we learn: "The circumference of the city is sixty miles; its walls are carried up to the mountains and enclose the valleys at their foot, so that its extent is increased." Here and there were wonderfully carved temples and fanes to Hindu deities with Brāhmaṇical colleges and schools attached to the more important among them. The narrative of Domingo Pæz, the Portuguese traveller (1520-22) is more extensive and minute: "The whole country (of Vijaynagara) is thickly populated with cities, towns and villages. The king allows them to be surrounded only with earthen walls for fear of their becoming too strong. But if a city is situated at the extremity of his territory he gives his consent to its having stone walls; but never the towns; so that they may make fortresses of the cities but not of the towns.

"Returning then to the city of Vijayanagara, you must know that from it to the new city (the reference here is to Nagalpur, a league off from the main capital) goes a street as wide as a place of tourney, with both sides lined throughout with rows of houses and shops where they sell every thing and all along this road are many trees that the king commanded to be planted, so as to afford shade to those that pass along. On this road he commanded to be erected a very beautiful temple of stone and there are other pagodas that the captains and the great lords caused to be erected.

"So that, returning to the city of Vijaya-nagara you must know that before you arrive at the city gates, there is a gate with a wall that encloses all the other enclosures of the city. This wall has a moat of water in some places and in parts where it was constructed on low ground.....From this first circuit until you enter the city there is a great distance, in which are fields in which they sow rice and many gardens and much water, which water comes from two lakes. The water passes through this first line of wall and there is much water in the lakes because of springs and here and there are orchards and little groves of palms and many houses.

"Returning then to the first gate of the city, before you arrive at it you pass a little piece of water and then you arrive at the wall, which is very strong, all of stone work, and it makes a bend before you arrive at the gate; and at the entrance of this gate are two towers, one on each side, which make it very strong. It is large and beautiful. As soon as you pass inside there are two little temples; one of them has an enclosing wall with many trees, while the whole of the other consists of buildings; and this wall of the first gate encircles the whole of the city. Then going forward you have another gate with another line of wall and it also encircles the city inside the first, and from here to the king's palace are all streets and rows of houses very beautiful, and houses of captains and other rich and honourable men; you will see rows of houses with many figures and decorations pleasing to look at. Going along the principal street, you have one of the chief gateways which issues from a great open space in front of the king's palace; opposite there is another which passes along to the other side of the city, and across this open space pass all the carts and conveyances carrying store and every thing else; and because it is in the middle of the city, it cannot but be useful.

"This palace of the king is surrounded by a very strong wall like some of the others, and encloses a greater space than all the castles of Lisbon.

"Still going forward, passing to the other gate you see two temples connected with it, one on each side.

"Close to these pagodas is a triumphal car covered with carved work and images, and on one day in each year during a festival they drag this through the city in such streets as it can traverse. Going forward you have a broad and beautiful street, full of rows of fine houses and streets of the sort I have described, and it is to be understood that the houses belong to the men rich enough to afford such. In this street live many merchants, and there you find all sorts of rubies and diamonds and emeralds, and pearls, and seed pearls, and cloths and every other sort of thing there is on earth and that you may wish to buy.....At the end of this street you have another gate with its wall, which wall goes to meet the wall of the second gate of which I have spoken, in such sort that this city has three fortresses, with another which is the king's palace. Then when this gate is passed you have another street where there are many craftsmen, and they sell many things; and in this street there are two small temples. There are temples in every street, for these appertain to institutions like the confraternities, you know of in our parts, of all the craftsmen and merchants; but the principal and greatest pagodas are outside the city.....A fair is held every day in different parts of the city. At the end of this street is the Moorish quarter which is at the very end of the city.

"...There are many groves within the city, in the gardens of the houses, and many conduits of water which flow into the midst of it, and in places there are lakes, and the king has close to his palace a palm grove and other rich bearing fruit trees. Below the Moorish quarters is a little river and on this side are many orchards and gardens with many fruit trees, for most part, mangoes and areca-palms and jack-trees and also many lime and orange trees, growing so closely one to another that it appears like a thick forest; and there are also white grapes. All the water which is in the city comes from the two lakes outside the first enclosing walls.

"This is the best provided city in the world, and is stocked with provisions such as rice, wheat, grains, Indian corn, and a certain amount of barley and beans, moog, pulses, horse-gram and many other seeds which grow in this country which are the food of the people and there is a large store of these and they are very cheap....The streets and markets are full of laden oxen without count, so that you cannot get along for them."

I supplement this exhaustive picture with extracts from the chronicles of Fernazo Nuniz, another itinerant :—

"The city was enlarged by Ajarao, the grandson of Bukkaraya who succeeded to the throne after Harihar Deva, the founder. This king made in the city of Vijayanagara many walls and enclosed it anew. The king desiring to increase that city and make it the best in the kingdom, determined to bring it to a very large river which was at a distance of five leagues away. So he did damming the river itself with great boulders. By means of this water they made round about the city a number of gardens and orchards and groves of trees and vineyards; and many plantations of lemons, oranges and roses, and other trees which in this country bear good fruits."

I venture to think that the Aryan traditions of town-planning preserved in the Śilpa Śāstras and handed down from generation to generation were recognised and followed in the planning of the city of Vijayanagara. This can be ascertained by comparison with the description of ancient cities found in such ancient epics as the Rāmāyaṇa, the Mahābhārata and other treatises chronologically following them. The city of Ayodhyā abounded in gardens and mangoe-orchards.[1] Bharata, the son of Kyakeyī, founded two towns in the country of Gāndhāra (this included the West Punjab and East Afghanistan), one Taxus at Taxila and another Puskal at Puskalwat. Treasures in large quantities and gardens of various kinds embellished both the cities. Intensive commerce and a great concourse of people lent fame to both. In both of them shops were symmetrically arranged in rows on both sides of the main thoroughfares. Many splendid shrines, useful trees like tāl (palmyra), tamāl, tilak, bakul and the like rendered these cities pleasing to the eye. Five years were spent in their foundation.[2] Mathurā is also described to have been rich in gardens and groves (udyānavana-sampanna). We learn from the Harivaṃśa that Dvārakā was adorned with tanks of pure water, troughs and sheds for drinking water, splendid squares and parks, orchards and gardens.[3] In this connection a glance at the description of Indraprastha given in the Mahābhārata which will be found in the appendix will shew

[1] The Rāmāyaṇa, Ādi Kāṇḍa, Ch. 5, sl. 12.
[2] The Rāmāyaṇa, Uttara Kāṇḍa, Ch. 114.
[3] Vishṇu Parvam, Ch. 58, *l.* 93.

that the renowned capital of the Pāṇḍavas was conceived and planned as a garden-city. Indeed almost all ancient Indian cities of note were more or less garden-cities. We will hardly be justified in attributing the descriptions of cities reproduced above and also in the appendix to the winged imagination of Indian poets noted for their fondness of imaginative hyperboles. Even such books on technical subjects as the Yuktikalpataru and the Mayamata lay great stress on this aspect of Indian cities. According to the former, a town should be, "trimmed with sheds for drinking water, shrines and halls, tanks, gardens and the like" (prapā-maṇḍapa-kāsāra-kānanādyopaśobhita)[1]; while the latter lays down: "There should be a fair distribution of reservoirs, tanks and wells." Only the necessity of defence and fortification lending a fortress-character to the cities of olden times hindered their full development into garden-cities as grand and magnificent as those of the modern age.

[1] Kāsāra really signifies artificial lotus lakes : कृत्रिम पद्माकरः ।

CHAPTER XII

CITY AS THE EXPRESSION OF CIVIC LIFE INTERPRETATION OF CIVIC ARCHITECTURE : CULTURAL AND SOCIO-POLITICAL

Art is expression. A true and great art is not a mere body; it shows a heart, a soul scintillating through the form. A national art not only expresses the matter, *i.e.*, the needs and interests of the nation, but also its spirit—its culture and ideals. Civic art therefore must express the needs, life and aspirations of the community in the outward form of their towns, portraying the community, as it were, on a gigantic canvas. "The city as a whole is but a visible symbol of this life behind it." I shall make here an attempt at an interpretation of Indian civic art, especially in its socio-political and cultural aspects; how Aryan master-builders not only attended to the needs of the community, but imparted to the city a permanent value and interest by embodying in its design the spiritual and cultural life of the race; how Indian cities are the most convincing records of the evolution and progress of India, more so than the edicts and the copper-plates. It is very difficult, if not altogether impossible, to do full justice to this vast and comprehensive subject; I have merely essayed to draw its bare outlines in this chapter.

The most conspicuous characteristic of ancient Indian towns—in fact, of all ancient towns, Greek, Roman or Indian—that cannot fail to arrest the indifferent eyes of the most desultory tourist, is their fortification,—the girdle of walls and moats. It is not for nothing that these constitute an integral part of the discourses on town-planning in the Silpa Śāstras where their construction is treated in elaborate details. It is because they were indispensable bulwarks of defence, that their structure was consummated to a skilful science. In India, as in Europe, there was no vast empire under one suzerain extending all over the country, in which case Nature would have furnished the most formidable breastworks in the shape of encompassing seas and mountains. But like the old Greek city-states, India was a congeries of many small principalities which were often engaged in guerilla warfare with one another to gain overlordship. The life of citizens was necessarily insecure due to these internecine conflicts and this insecurity was further accentuated by the barbarian aborigines, called the Rākshasas who were driven by Aryan might into the jungles and who with their anthropophagous propensities were ever ready to fly at the throat of the intruders upon their native home and hitherto undisputed realm. Besides, the whole country was interspersed with thick jungles alive with wild animals who, every now and then, carried havoc into human habitations. These causes combined to impress upon the ancient civic architect the indispensibility of effective defence against the inroads of deadly foes, rational or irrational.

To a student of history and sociology peering through the hazy past and groping for unmistakable milestones marking the various gradations of Aryan progress and civilisation, the mound—the most ancient and aboriginal abode of the uncivilized autochthones—, the subterranean rooms with superstructural houses walled round, with no windows or doors opening on the street, the quadrangular groups of houses all facing an open space in the middle and their back-walls forming a continued enclosure, with only small openings on the sides, the villages or the wards in the city with their girths of walls and moats, then the wards with a row of houses lined along the streets and opening on them; the city fenced round by similar ramparts, embattled parapets and wide ditches possessing but few gates; then the walled and ditched cities containing many arteries of communication with the country outside; finally the open city of the present day with no walls and ditches, all these are indelible landmarks and their comparative study opens up wonderful vistas of ancient Indian history. Let the student consider as well the following three types of cities—the fort capital; the capital with a citadel or fort in the centre containing within the fold all the important public buildings, to wit, the royal palace, the cantonment, the commander-in-chief's lodge, the court, the council house, the treasury, the minister's house, the city shrine; finally the capital with the fort at the side, some or all of the public buildings having been stationed without the fort.

In very ancient times the king was nothing but a redoubtable warrior-chief at the head of a large following, a band of soldiers, leading them by dint of his transcendent military prowess. In those times of disturbance and insecurity, when everybody had to depend for safety and self-protection upon the artful manipulation of his sword, it was the fighting capacity which measured the worth of men. Hence anybody who excelled in the art of fighting and surpassed all in bravery and fortitude, was willingly obeyed and followed by all. The leader of the combatants was the king and his martial ability struck awe and reverence into his followers. In the absence of any administrative machinery in those unsettled times, the military, the executive, the judicial, nay all the important functions of the State combined and centred in him. Later on when peace and tranquillity prevailed in some measure in the territory and a sort of constitution was elaborated, still the old notion of the supremacy of the chief in all matters of importance and responsibility, did not undergo any material change. Facts sometimes change faster than ideas. The king still remained the State in miniature, the fountain-head of all justice, the-head of the executive, *parens parenti*, Lord Paramount, the commander-in-chief of his valiant warriors. Hence it is that we find that the court, the treasury, the soldiers' barracks, the council-house and the minister's house were grouped round the royal castle, and formed part and parcel of it. Again in case of emergency the citadel was utilised as a fort, the ultimate resort.[1]

The very reasons which led to the elaborate fortifications of the city and its citadel and gave

[1] The above by no means seek to establish that no form of Government except military absolutism or paternal monarchy was known to ancient India. The labour of modern Indologists have, indeed, proved beyond doubt that republican or democratic forms of Government, technically known as Saṅgha or Gaṇa were also not unknown in this land. The most typical examples of this political Saṅgha were the Lichchavis or Vajjis of Videha and Kośala who had their capital at Vaiśālī and also the Mallas of Kuśinārā. In fact the observations I have made above are without any reference to the forms of government that obtained in ancient India.

rise to the foregoing political theory, were responsible for the origin of communalism in ancient India. I have already observed that blocks of houses under different ownerships were erected round an open space in the middle so that their back-walls formed a continued enclosure. In the common ownership of the central open space lies the seed of communalism. The communalist sentiments engendered by combination of mutual vigil and protection were crystallized by the patriarchal rule. We find therefore in the village communities of ancient India common pasture and common fields or tenure. Communalism remarkably expressed itself in the planning of the ancient city or village in the shape of a public square or common tank in the middle of the village, or in the village rest-house, in the council tree planted at the crossing of two main roads of the village with a pedestal raised round it or in the temple of its tutelary deity with its spacious maṇḍapa.[1] At all these trysting places the village elders congregated after sunset to discuss village politics; and at all hours of the day rural folks repaired to these places and enjoyed friendly chats. "The essential condition for the development of strong civic

[1] Note the temples in every street of Vijayanagara appertaining to the confraternities of all the craftsmen and merchants. ((*Vide* the preceding chapter.)

spirit lies in the maintenance of the communal life and consciousness, and this condition is fulfilled nowhere else in the world than in the oriental countries. This is to a certain extent the result of climate. Life, in the clear air and under the cloudless skies of India, is necessarily passed much in the open air. That the street is a kind of club, the very architecture, with its verandahs and stone-couches, bears mute witness to. The family-homes stand ranged behind the great open air *salon*, like a row of convent cells, for the stricter members of the choir. Sometimes there are added evidences of a larger social grouping, visible to the eye. Bhuvaneśwar has its great tree in the midst of the parting of three roads, and at any hour one may see there knots of talkers of one sort or another, seated at ease beneath it. Conjeeveram is like a city out of the old Greek or Assyrian world, so wide is the road-way that leads to the temple entrance, and so splendid is the arch that spans it just before, eloquent both of communal worship and rejoicing. Nor are women in India altogether without their civic centres and gathering places, though these are necessarily concerned chiefly with the bathing ghat, the temple and the well."[1]

Patriarchism also accounts to some extent

[1] Sister Nivedita.

for trade-guilds, as the castes or their sub-divisions really were, inasmuchas any profession used to be handed down from generation to generation, *i.e.* sons in almost all cases followed the trade and crafts of their parents. This guild system no less than the division of social functions and theory of decentralisation of government made the village community an autonomous unit and gave rise to that peculiar social organism of the Hindus known as the Varṇāśram-adharma. This Hindu sociology, dividing the whole Hindu community into four principal castes which ultimately disintegrated into many more sub-castes, stamped the Aryan town or village-planning with indelible marks of its own. For, we find, in the town or village, different building-plots or wards were assigned to different castes or subcastes and the Śilpa Śāstras are very much particular in their distribution. In this stratification of the society also, com-munalism asserted itself, for every building-block or ward of a town was planned exactly in accordance with the same principles as were followed in village-planning and consequently such communal centres as the council tree and the square were necessarily provided for in the wards or the building-plots. The evil consequence upon city-corporate life of segregating people into detached wards where they could be liable to develop different habits and customs was provided against by the large composite wards, villages in themselves, of the big cities ; or in small towns of simple residential blocks, by establishment of temples in the centre with magnificent maṇḍapas, debating halls, and rest-houses within the temple compound, where all sorts of people could freely congregate together irrespective of their caste. As in strictly religious matters there was no distinction of caste, so the holy ground of the temple was open to all. Varṇāśrama-dharma was a strictly a social institution and it could not stretch beyond the pale of social concerns. Every person belonging to any caste has his inherent right to make offerings and devotions to the tutelary deity of the city or village whose holy precincts can by no means be polluted by his sons. The influence of human organisation cannot enter and interfere with the equality and fraternity of devotees reigning in the consecrated compound. It is in this sense that it is said that Holy Benares is without the world. Inasmuchas every institution or performance drew its inspiration from a religious creed which was supreme in all matters, the true national spirit of the Hindus as embodied in their common religious susceptibility, permeated all strata of the society, strengthening the bonds of corporate life. It was in periods of degeneration that caste distinctions were carried also within the holy precincts of the temple. It was for this reason and also because non-Aryan gods, such as the Dravidian deities, were not recognised by the proselytising Aryans who, though they took the non-Aryans within the pale of their society, did not in some cases find niches for their deities in the Hindu Pantheon, that we meet with arrangement for temples to exclusive caste-deities in the villages or towns. The dirty habits of the low classes might have accentuated this untenable and ugly phase of Hindu society. It may not be at all improbable that actual conversion of many aboriginal tribes never took place. Their living and constant contact with a higher civilisation might have done its work of slowly and silently influencing them, until they, largely innocent of any pronounced consciousness of the integrity and individuality of their own race that marks the modern civilised races, became Hinduised in their ideas and habits to a certain extent. They formed of their own accord the lowest strata of the Hindu society. The victors have in all ages and climes claimed such voluntary converts to their own creed. Perhaps the victorious Aryans could not shed their superior airs and treated the vanquished non-Aryans much in the same way as alien rulers treat the natives of a subject nation professing a different creed and civilisation and belonging to a different race. In India too at present there are many persons saturated with western civilisation who have imitated European manners and customs. They are more European than Indian and they glory in that and are highly gratified if they constantly come in contact with the European community. If at any time Indian civilisation decays down in its land of birth, then they will first form the Panchama class of the Christian community. This is what has happened in the Deccan with respect to the "untouchable" Hindus.

Howbeit it cannot be gainsaid that caste-distinction prevented one thing; it did not make poverty a crime, a depressing disqualification. In the towns or villages building-blocks were not distributed exclusively on the basis of wealth, thus dividing the city into two parts like the East End and the West End of London. Though from the standpoint of city sanitation the difference mattered little, yet so far as corporate life and the building up of individual character and civic consciousness were concerned, it meant a good deal of difference. Freedom of religious belief, freedom of worshipping the tutelary deities, and communal instincts were the equilibrating and unifying forces that arrested the social disintegration that was likely to accrue out of social differences and consequent caste-acerbities.

It was the great Vivekananda who said in one of his speeches at Ramnad : " The secret of a true Hindu's character lies in the subordination of his knowldege of European science and learning, of his wealth, position and name to that one principal theme which is inborn in every Hindu child—the spirituality and purity of the race." At every stage of town-planning the master-builder's duties as laid down in the Śilpa Śāstras bring home to us the validity of this dictum. The religious predilections of the Hindus led the authors of the Śilpa Śāstras to enjoin some ritualistic and sacrificial observances in the selection, exorcisement and purification of site, We have seen how the whole site was divided into a number of plots ; how each plot was held sacred to and named after a god. Then a presiding deity of the vāstu was conceived, his various limbs occupying certain fixed chambers and then offerings were made to him. Some religious rites were also performed when laying the foundation of a city or of a building: "The gods such as Vishṇu, Hara, the Sun-god, etc., should be worshipped before founding a city and offerings should be made at the instances of the founder."[1] The assignment of causeways on the city-walls to sentinel-deities, the denomination of the various plans and gates of the villages, the annular strips demarcating the city-ground and their appellations were the notable characteristics which the pre-eminently religious character of the Hindus impressed upon the civic art.

The predominantly religious nature of the Hindu life and culture also inspired and manifested itself in the Hindu civic architecture in the shape of a large number of Aryan and non-Aryan gods and their magnificent edifices which were distributed throughout the city. Every street of note, every building zone or every district of the town was sanctified by these religio-communal centres where the patron deities were installed radiating bliss and brightening their jurisdictions with a halo of holiness. Thus we read in the description of Vijayanagara by the Portuguese traveller, Domingo Pæs :—" There are temples in every street, for these appertain to institutions like the confraternities, you know of in our parts, of all craftsmen and merchants ; but the principal and greatest pagodas are outside the city." All the expenses of worshipping the deities and the upkeep of their edifices were met by local subscriptions and these communal traditions of

[1] *Vide* Agni Purāṇam, Ch. 106, *l.* 11.

public worship of gods are kept up to this day in every Indian city and village.

In the village or the town the various gods were enshrined according to some scheme. The scheme of the Agni Purāṇa runs as follows:— "The phallic emblems belonging to the *chala* or removable class should be installed in temples situated at the eastern quarter of a city. The images of Lakshmī and Vaiśravaṇa should be established at each side of the eastern gate; and the temples of gods established on the western side of a city, should face the east, looking on the two above-said images. In the east or the south, the divine edifices should face the west and the north respectively. The images of Brahmā, Vishṇu, Īśa and other gods should be installed in a city, for the protection of and as the guardian deities of the latter." The Agni Purāṇa then proceeds to cite the evil consequences accruing from absence of divine installations in the city: "A city, village, fortress, or a house not having tutelary deity of its own, is devoured by the Pichāśas, and becomes infested with fell diseases or pestilences." The blessings that are due to the divine images raised in the city are as follows: "A city or a village etc. protected by a deity, becomes thriving and prosperous; and ensures victory, enjoyments of earthly good, and finally salvation to its inhabitants."[1]

[1] *Vide* Agni Purāṇam, Ch. 106, *ll.* 28-34.

Mayamuni's order is different, and more detailed and comprehensive. "Allocation of the gods is to begin from the east. The Aryan gods should all be set up within the compound of the village or city. The temple of Śiva may be established outside it. The Vināyaka is to occupy Bhṛṅgarāja or Pāvaka's chamber. Śiva is to be enshrined in the chambers consecrated to Īśa or Soma, or in those adjoining Soma. Surrounding Śiva are to be measured the sites for the temples of his attendant deities. The Sun-god is to be quartered at the chamber held sacred to Āditya ; the goddess Kālikā is to have her shrine installed at Agni's plot. Vishṇu's edifice is to be erected at the plot presided over by Bhṛśa, and the image of Shaṇmukha (the six-faced god) is to be constructed at the Yāmya square. To the north (Mṛga quarter) or the south-east of Mṛsha's chamber lies the temple of Keśava. The Lord of the gaṇas is set up at the chamber held sacred to Sugrīva or at the Pushpadanta's portion. Aryaka has his edifice at the south-east corner of the village and Vishṇu is assigned his shrine at the Varuṇa. The great Sugata (Buddha) should have his monastery at the Sugrīva, and at the Bhṛṅgarāja the deity of the Jainas should be located. The liquor-shop should be relegated to the north-west corner, and the goddess Kātyāyanī should occupy the Mukhya site. Kuvera (Dhanada) is to be stationed at Soma's chamber and the Mātṛs may also be assigned sites there too. Saṅkara may possess temples either at the Īśa, the Parjaṇya, or the Jayanta. Kuvera must occupy either of the two sites, the Soma or the Sosha, and if he occupies the one, the other should be allocated to Gajānana. The Mātṛs may occupy shrines at the Aditi. The edifice of Vishṇu should be erected at the centre of the village. To the south-east or the north-east of the Brahmā's site, the council-house is to be raised. To its north-west Hari should have his shrine. The dimensions and number of storeys of all the divine edifices should be commensurate with the size of the village or the city. If a divine edifice be too low for the village or the town, the men become also low-minded and the women acquire foul habits. Chaṇḍeśwara, Kumāra, Dhanada, Kālī, Putanā, Kālī-suta and Khaḍgī are the divine porters of the city. Īśa should face either the east or the west and Vishṇu can face towards all cardinal quarters. All should have their faces turned towards the village, or the city. All the gods barring Īśa and Vishṇu should face the east and the Mātṛs are to have their faces turned towards the north. The Sun-god's shrine is to have its door in the west."[1] Generally Brahmā is

[1] *Vide* Mayamatam, Ch. 10, pp. 31-33.

placed at the crossing of the two principal highways meeting at the centre of the city, with His four faces turned towards the four cardinal directions as if looking down the street and watching the city in all quarters. All the gods are posed as facing the village or city which symbolises their tutelage over it. The non-Aryan gods or goddesses are stationed beyond the village or city.

The above in a way is indicative of idealisation or deification of the abode. " The ground on which a city stands is in truth a great hearth-place of human love, a veritable altar of spiritual fire." As for instances of idealising the abode, " What of Benares, built about the Vedic hearth, that to-day is the golden grating of Biśweśwar ? What of Allahabad with her thousands of pilgrims bathing in the sacred waters of the Gaṅgā-Jamunā ? Kālikā—Kāṅgrā Rānī, Queen of the Battlements ? What of Calcutta, where appears Nakuleśwar, as guardian of the ghat of Kālī ? From end to end of the peopled earth, we shall find wherever we look, that man makes his home of a surpassing sanctity to himself and others, and the divine mingles with the domestic fire on every hearth."[1]

I have already remarked that religion is the be-all and end-all of a Hindu's life. Spirituality

[1] *Vide* Sister Nivedita, Civic and National Ideals.

is the fountain-head from which flowed his national currents. Hence the temples—embodiments of spirituality—were the centres where culture and education were fostered and promulgated. Again the same sages who were the custodians of sacred lore and expounders of Hindu theology, holding holy communion in meditation with God, were also the professors and propounders of Hindu sociology. Generally the wise and sagacious hermits, belonging to the sacerdotal class were also the persons who directed the legislation of society. A sequestered cloister away from the hustle and bustle of the city was the one most suited to their contemplative life and to the training of the young hopefuls of the race. And their hermitages took the place of modern colleges where students congregated from all parts of the country. The temples, hermitages or monasteries of ancient India formed the nucleuses of the university towns of later ages, such as Taxila or Nālandā, Naimishāraṇya or Benares.

Communal instincts of the Aryans were reflected not only in the great concourse of votaries in the temples irrespective of caste or rank, power or pelf, but were evident also in the common rejoicings on the occasion of any public worship. The conscious thought of the spiritual unity and kinship of all the citizens manifested itself in communal festivities. Every triumphal arch that surmounts the village gates or 'crowns a bathing ghat, on the banks of the Ganges' testifies to that feeling. It was this feeling which led to the institution of the grand ceremonial processions along the principal roads of the towns or villages. "Over and over again, in the Ṛg-Veda, the earth is referred to as the 'sacrifice' round which the path of light makes a friendly circle in the course of the year. It is one of the most beautiful and vigorous of similes. But it reminds us of the beautiful procession of the images which are so characteristic a feature of life in Indian towns. As the light encircles the earth, so verily do these ceremonial pilgrimages girdle our boroughs and villages; nay, it is not only the worshipper of Saraswatī or the commemorator of the Mohurrum who makes the circumambulation of communal home. The whole Indian idea of enjoyment is communal and even at a marriage, processions form the typical delight."[1] These processions exercised a salutary effect upon town-planning. It was the grandeur of these processions which necessitated the great width of the highways of Indo-Aryan towns; so that the stupendous cars, as for example, the Jagannāth's car at Purī, which were dragged by

[1] *Vide* Sister Nivedita, Civic and National Ideals.

huge crowds gathered from far and near, could easily pass through them. This is why we come across description of fine broad streets in ancient Indian cities. These processions prevented the narrowing of streets by buildings encroaching upon them. Quite akin to this, there was another ceremony which prevented the germination of bacteria of diseases in the stagnant waters of the tanks of Indian towns. I mean the water festival. It consisted of a floating car as a counter-part of the land car. It was also pulled and propelled to and fro, hither and thither. This had the effect of killing water insects, mosquito larvæ, all germs of diseases that stagnant waters generally begot, destroyed the aquatic plants that over-grew the water and polluted it and purified as well as sanctified it. What a far happier way of maintaining the purity of water than the modern method of filling up and doing away with the tanks of the town. The ceremony thus combined in itself religion, civic spirit, social unity, and sanitation.

The massive architecture of the public buildings and their fascinating details of ornamental decorations bear eloquent testimony to the high level of artistic skill reached by the Indian schools of architecture as also it speaks of the affluent economic condition of the citizens, their happy life and jubilant nature. The Indian town-planners were alive to the importance of the public buildings. They were not constructed in a perfunctory fashion. Their civic utility is too great for such indifferent treatment. Art is nothing if not an expression of culture and a method of inculcating and propagating culture. These public buildings offered therefore one of the most effective means of educating the citizens, training their eyes, inspiring them with religious and national ideals. The bas-reliefs sculptured on the walls, aisles, cornices, corridors, ceilings, capitals, and domes of the public buildings and shrines, also on the colonnaded pillars give pictorial illustrations of the soul-stirring achievements of the religio-national heroes like Rāma, Buddha, Hanumāna, Kṛshṇa, Vishṇu, and of other divine or deified heroes. The fresco paintings on the walls exhibited brilliant portraits, group-pictures illustrating scenes depicted in the Epics, the Purāṇas, folk-lore and the like national literature. They blazonned forth and inculcated humanising and ennobling sentiments, in a pleasing manner, all bearing upon religious and national culture. A more pleasing and effective method than the one through art and æsthetics, of disseminating national culture, preserving and encouraging art, emphasising glory and fulness of civic life, cannot be concieved. Cities are thereby turned into great schools of nationalism, in its most liberal and comprehensive sense. India's cities, maṭhas, and caves possess such admirable specimens of sculpture and fresco paintings without number as no other nation does and they will ever continue to excite wonder and admiration of the world.

APPENDIX A

Some noted ancient Indian towns

Descriptions of some typical cities of ancient India given in the Epics, the Purāṇas, the vernacular literature, and the accounts of foreign travellers, have helped me a good deal in studying the science of Indian town-planning and forming a proper conception of its practical working. Some of them are reproduced here because they are as much of supreme interest as descriptions of ancient towns, as of high importance to the reader who will find in them first-hand materials to judge and compare for himself.

Ayodhyā

This was a city twelve yojanas long, three yojanas broad. There were in it many fine wide streets, all symmetrically arranged; their level varied to suit the ground and to facilitate the circulation of traffic. They were regularly watered and occassionally strewn with full bloomed flowers. The king Daśaratha made large extensions of the city in order to relieve congestion. The city had stout arched gates with large door-panels, a fine lay-out of lanes and other minor roads, was fitted with mechanisms, equipped with a variety of weapons and wore a resplendent appearance. There lived in it many skilled artisans, craftsmen, and charioteers. Multitudes of lofty castles, countless flags flaunting on high, hundreds of guns (śataghnī), numerous gardens and mango-groves enhanced its beauty and magnificence. Surrounding the city was a belt of Śāla trees.[1] In all quarters of the city were special theatres for females. A deep-water ditch girding the city made it difficult of access. There were innumerable horses, elephants, cows, camels, asses, towering palaces of the best stone or marble, and sport-houses for the ladies. It was laid out on a plain and there were many seven-storeyed buildings. The houses were arranged one beside another so that there was no plot of land without human dwellings. The water of the city was limpid and sweet to the taste. The facades of all the houses, owing to a harmony in their design and symmetry in their arrangement, were magnificent to behold. There were town-halls and squares in the city. Ladies' parks too were not wanting.[2]

[1] The original text is 'śāla-mekhalā,' It may also mean 'wall-girdled.' But evidences are not wanting to show that there were cities in ancient India that possessed girdles of trees.

[2] The Rāmāyaṇa, Ādi Kāṇḍa, Ch. 5.

Indraprastha

It was adorned with sea-like ditches, defended by sky-high parapets and furnished with gates, towers and palatial buildings. There was a fine lay-out of large thoroughfares. There were magnificent houses, pleasant retreats, fine museums, artificial hills, numerous tanks brimming with water, beautiful lakes fragrant with lilies and lotuses and lovely with variety of birds, many charming parks and gardens with tanks at the centres and also numberless fine ponds.[1]

Pāṭalīputra

Pāṭalīputra, the capital of the Mauryya Empire, was planned on a magnificent scale. Megasthenes informs us: " The greatest city in India is that which is called Palimbothra, in the dominions of the Prasians, where the streams of the Erannoboas (this is Greek corruption for Hirannavati, modern Sone) and the Ganges unite....This city stretched in the inhabited quarters to an extreme length on each side of 80 stadia (nearly ten miles), and its breadth was fifteen stadia (nearly two miles), and a ditch encompassed it all round, 600 feet in breadth and 30 cubits in depth, and the wall was crowned with 570 towers and four-and-

[1] The Mahābhārata, Ādiparva, Ch. 217.

sixty gates."[1] There were smaller doors between the main gates and there were really three brick-lined moats in quick succession. The walls of the capital were made of timber. "The royal palace which occupied a central position and placed in a fine wooden park laid out with fountains and fish ponds, was described by Megasthenes as being more splendid than those of Susa and Ecbatana. Its pillars were plated with gold, and it was magnificently furnished with thrones and chairs of state, and great vessels of gold, silver, and copper set with precious stones." Mr. Havell supplements this picture with details given in Kauṭilya's summary of Indo-Aryan polity. This can be done only on the presumption that Kauṭilya's discourse on fort-planning was not based on what he considered to be sound principles of efficient fortification, but that he faithfully recorded what he found in his own favourite metropolis. Howbeit I do not append here extracts from his Arthaśāstra inasmuchas I have utilised his discourse on town-planning in more appropriate chapters.

Madurā

"Madurā, the capital of the Pāṇḍyas was a fortified city. There were four gates to the fort,

[1] Arrian, Ind., Ch. X.

surmounted by high towers, and outside the massive walls which were built of rough-hewn stone, was a deep moat, and surrounding the moat was a thick jungle of thorny trees. The roads leading to the gates were wide enough to permit several elephants pass abreast and on the walls on both sides of the entrance, there were all kinds of weapons and missiles concealed, ready to be discharged on an enemy. Yavana soldiers with drawn swords guarded the gates. Over the gates and walls waved many a standard which had been taken in battle. The principal streets in the city were royal street, the market street, the courtezans' street, and the streets where dwelt the goldsmiths, corn-dealers, cloth merchants, jewellers, etc. Outside the fort of Madurā resided those men who led a life of religious devotion and poorer classes such as the Panar and other lower castes."[1] This account I supplement from the materials furnished by Venkatarama Ayyar. The original site of Madurā was a forest of lordly kadamba trees whence another name of Madurā is Kadamba-vana. In this forest were a beautiful tank and a temple of God Śiva on its embankment. The then ruling king of the Pāṇḍya dynasty attracted by the site, caused a careful survey of it and finally evolved a city-plan starting with the temple

[1] V. Kanak avai, pp. 12-3.

as centre. Round this temple the king constructed in order, a Padma-maṇḍapam where the Vedas would be chanted, an Artha-maṇḍapam where festivals might be held, and a Nṛtya-maṇḍapam or kitchen for the temple, and other small temples around. Thereafter were laid out the main streets including the chief processional streets, and other small streets were constructed intersecting the former. And in the open squares thus formed public meeting places and other open places were also planned and constructed. He also erected several public platforms and planted fruit trees thereon. He did not disturb the existing streams and ponds, but added to their number. Such were the tanks, orchards, gardens, and flower gardens; and the walls and moats encircled the town.

Many years passed and the town was washed away by a huge flood. When it subsided, the town was constructed anew. The plan was drawn up afresh after a resurvey of the limits of the old city from a study of the extant traces and that on such a comprehensive scale as to satisfy the growing need of the swelling population. In this new plan, which was circular also, the old temple retained its central position.[1] The great

[1] *Cf.* Mānasāra: "In the reconstruction of old ruined villages, old shrine should not be disturbed; but on the other hand, the plan should start from it and centre round it." Ch. 9.

पौराख्यंदेवताहर्म्यं सर्वथापि न चालयेत् ।
तस्मात्तदनुसारेण कुर्याद्वास्तुविनिर्णयं ॥

entrance gate of the city was to the south, while the smaller gate on the northern side was its exit. Thus the city grew towards the south and had the river Vaikaki as a natural boundary on the north. This arrangement of a big entrance gate and a small exit gate is after the model of ordinary houses. The walls of the fort were constructed as the natural topography of the land would permit and hence admitted of several deflections and zig-zag shapes. It was henceforth called Tirumudangal or the beautiful city surrounded by meandering walls.

"The starting point and circumscribing walls having been decided upon, it then became necessary to allot the several classes of population to definitely marked areas and provide ample open spaces, public baths, public halls, schools, markets, gymnasiums, or public play grounds, and other appurtenances of the city. The portion for the palace having been duly apportioned, the remaining space was utilised for schools, streets, play grounds and separate quarters for the different classes. And all these were done according to the Śāstras, due importance being attached to the provision of groves and parks which were reared afresh in several parts of the newly planned city.

"There were not only big broad streets but

also crooked streets and small lanes in the new plan.....The four streets round the King's palace was occupied by the ministers, rich merchants,.. Brāhmaṇs, and others, mostly servants of the Royal household. The streets were provided with dustbins."

" Into the ditch was received all the drainage water of the city. The rural belt round the city gave it a desirable completeness and finish. A little from the eastern gate of the city and outside the walls of the fort, there was a spacious garden which was left for the exclusive use of saints and others who were engaged in meditation and prayer.

" On either side of the ditch next to the walls of the city, there was a small forest-growth (thorny thickets) which was one of the defences of the city. It was in the nature of a garden which, while serving the purpose of defence, had the other advantage of providing a use for the impure water of the city. This device of forming gardens and groves outside the city utilised the drain water of the city considerably....Triangular plots, and quadrangular plots or squares separated these streets from the royal palace proper."

Vaṁji or Karur

"The city, once a capital of the Chera Kingdom, now a deserted village known as Tiru Karur, was strongly fortified, and on the battlements were mounted various engines to throw missiles on those who attacked the fort. Over the gates in the walls, were towers plastered with mortar and adorned with flags. Surrounding the walls was a big moat in which man-eating alligators of large size abounded. The king's palace, a temple of Vishṇu called Adakamadan or the "the golden shrine," a Buddhist Chaitya, and a Nigrantha monastery which was outside the gate of the fort, appear to have been the most conspicuous buildings. If Madurā was noted for its many mansions and towers, Vaṁji with its flowers and tanks full of crystal water, limpid streams, and little islands, shady bowers and parks with artificial hills and waterfalls, was charming to every visitor. Outside the fort, in a part called Puranakar (Puranaceri) lived a mixed population of different social status including the soldiers of the Chera king. Ascetics and philosophers also dwelt in the silent and shady groves, far away from the din and bustle of the capital."[1]

"The water of the palace, public halls, and private residences fell into this ditch by means of a conduit sluice known as Tumbu.

"The royal palace occupied the centre of the city. Round the palace were placed four streets

[1] V. Kanaksavai, p. 15.

intended for the Brāhmaṇs, the ministers, the chief military officers and servants of the King's household. Besides the above, there were parallel rows of streets inhabited by peoples following different trades and occupations....There were platforms under single fruit trees. At various places between the several quarters alloted for the trades and occupations, there were public platforms with fruit trees planted over them, while the people may sit awhile and chat. Public halls find free accommodation there. And triangular plots and quadrangular squares were kept as open spaces that they may serve as lungs to the separate quarters of the several classes of the people.

" Starting from the outer portion of the city, there were first the residences of the soldiers who guarded the city gates. Then the Puranakar (Puranaceri) or the part of the city next to the ditch and the walls was set apart for the several classes of the people, mostly a mixed population of different social status including the soldiers in the army.

" Besides the ditch and the walls, then there was the defence created by the trees and shrubs specially planted so as to form an artificial forest. Such forests are known as *milai*. People were forbidden to interfere with them. Generally soldiers resided there and guarded the trees."[1]

[1] Venkatarama Ayyar.

APPENDIX B

CAMPS

In a previous chapter I have traced the origin of the most famous Indian cities to the camp-life of the Aryans. It was round the royal seats that the important cities of India were planned and laid out. Now these royal capitals, in ages of hoary antiquity, nay even down to the Pathan period, were nothing but, and could not be but, imperial encampments, inasmuchas the then state of the country was one of constant belligerency and consequently the boundaries of the dominions were bound to be singularly precarious and indefinite. Not unfrequently the warrior chief,—(for the king in ancient times was nothing more than a commander at the head of an army swaying his suzereinty over an area controlled by the over-awing might of his arms,)—had to move from place to place at the advance of a more puissant foe. Naturally therefore with the change of his kingdom his capital also changed and followed him to his temporary residence. The Saṃskrit synonym for the word camp is 'śivira'. The Śavdakalpadruma notes the following various imports of it:—(1) nibeśa *i.e.*, settlement or encampment; (2) āgantuka-sainyābāsa, *i.e.*, the temporary residence of an advancing or newly arrived army; (3) kaṭaka, *i.e.*, a capital or a town, a fort, an army, a belt; (4) nṛpasya mulasthānam, *i.e.*, the principal seat of the king. According to the Uṇādikosha, śivira means an encampment or military quarters in times of war. The foregoing synonyms imply a native affinity between a royal seat, a capital, and a camp. They refer to a period of history when all of them were more or less identified. The origin of the name of Cuttuck (written as Kaṭaka in Indian vernaculars) of the town of the same title also corroborates this. The Turkish word 'urdu' means a camp and the language Urdu originated in the camp-life of the first Muhammedan invaders of India when they had to make intercourse with the Indian kings who also lived in camp-like capitals. It is significant that Urdu was the court language of the time. Every Indologist who has ever cared to bestow any thought upon the the origin of the Indian towns supports the above theory. For example, Sir Henry S. Maine says in his " Village Communities" that " the most famous of all towns grew out of camps." Mr. Havell also subscribes to this view.

In support of the above theory, I give below a description of śivira or camp and also of skandhāvāra, *i.e.*, an encampment in the neighbourhood of the town about to be beseiged. The 103rd chapter of Śrī Kṛshṇajanmakhaṇḍa in the Brahmavaivarta Purāṇa deals with the following characteristics of a śivira or camp: "Camps have ditches with a girth of high walls furnished with twelve gates surmounted by lion-arches the doors of which exhibit variegated and fascinating painting and workmanship. No forbidden trees should be allowed to grow within them, while they should be rich with those trees which civic traditions have made them famous."[1] The chapter then proceeds with the enumeration of the suitable or unsuitable trees and creepers in the encampment, deals with water supply and other food-resources, treats of domestic architecture, the height of walls both of the camp as well as of a citizen's home, and the depth of the surrounding ditches.

The description of a skandhāvāra given in the Kāmandakīya Nītisāra is more minute :- "Having approached the vicinity of the enemy's fort, after fully reconnoitring the locality and the ground by experienced scouts, military quarters should be pitched by persons who are adepts in the art. The encampment should be quadrangular

[1] शिविरं परिखायुक्तमुच्चैः प्राकारवेष्टितम् ।
युक्तं द्वादशद्वारैश्च सिंहद्वारपुरस्कृतम् ॥
युक्तं चित्रविचित्रैश्च कृत्रिमैश्च कपाटकैः ।
निषिद्धवृक्षरहितं प्रसिद्धैश्च पुरस्कृतम् ॥

in shape, equipped with four gates, should have not very wide lanes but must possess large streets and massive walls with a girdle of a broad trench. The residence (āgāra; encampment ?) may be shaped like a square (cross-way), a semi-circle, a circle, or a rectangle (dīrgha) according as the nature of the locality permits. Spacious lodges should be symmetrically set up there separate from each other. The rooms should be well protected. All should be surrounded by a cloistered (? paṭākārai) boulevard. In the centre should be erected the royal palace charming to look at, the quarters of the premier standing hard by, and the treasury being located within the compound of the royal mansions. In the vicinity and in all directions should be quartered, in order of rank and position, the principal officials of the crown, the various trade-guilds, the loyal citizens, the twelve divisions of forces experienced in forest-fight. At the extremities should lie in a circle the butchers, the fowlers and other classes of low, abject occupations whose fidelity has been bought off with ample remunerations."[1] It is to be noted here that this description of the camp comprises all the salient features of a town.

Kauṭilya's planning of an encampment is different and more exact in particulars, as the

1 *Vide* Ch. 16.

astute deplomat always is. "On a site declared to be best according to the science of buildings, the leader (nāyaka),[1] carpenter (vardhaki), and the astrologer (mauhūrtika) should measure a circular, rectangular, or a square spot for the camp which should, in accordance with the available space, consist of four gates, six roads and nine divisions. Provided with ditches, parapets, walls, doors, and watch-towers for defence against fear, the quarters of the king hundred bows long and half as broad, should be situated in one of the nine divisions to the north from the centre, while to the west of it his harem, and at its extremity the army of the harem are to be situated. In his front, the place for worshipping gods; to his right the departments of finance and accounts[2]; and to his left the quarters of elephants and horses mounted by the king himself. Outside this and at a distance of hundred bows from each other there should be fixed four pillared walls as broad as a cart-pole.[3]

[1] It seems so refer to the head mason who directs and supervises the work,

[2] "The treasury and the court of justice" appears to give the more correct construction.

[3] "Śakaṭamedhī", *i.e.*, axle of the cart. Though the above is an extract from Dr. Shamasástry's translation of Arthaśāstra, I have altered his translation in the above line because his rendering is based on an obviously erroneous construction. The original text being "चत्वारः शकटमेधीप्रतोलीस्तम्भसालपरिक्षेपाः"; his endoring is "four cart-poles, pillars, and walls."

In the first (of these four divisions), the prime minister and the priest (should have their quarters); to its right the store house and the kitchen; to its left the store of raw products and weapons; in the second division the quarters of the hereditary army and of horses and chariots;[1] outside this, hunters and keepers of dogs with their trumpets and with fire; also spies and sentinel; also to prevent the attack of enemies, wells, mounds, and thorns should be arranged."[2] A comparison between this plan and the lay-out of sites within a fort detailed in Ch. VI will shew their striking similarity in the broad features.

The fact that Indian towns grew out of camps explains a peculiar phenomenon about them. Any antiquarian about ancient India, or any traveller who has traversed the vast expanse of this sub-continent cannot fail to notice and feel curious about the peculiar juxtaposition of

[1] An alternative reading adds the following lines after this: "सेनापतेश्च। तृतीये हस्तिनः श्रेण्यः प्रशास्ता च। चतुर्थे विष्टिर्नायको मित्रामित्राटवीबलं स्वपुरुषाधिष्ठितम्। वणिजो रूपाजीवाश्चानुमहापथम्।" *i. e.*, "and also the commander-in-chief. In the third division, the elephants and their controllers (trainers ?); in the fourth. mercenaries and their leaders, and forest-fighters of the mitrāmitra nature with their heads. The traders and the public women should be settled along the great road (boulevard ?)". This reading seems to be more faithful and appropriate.

[2] Arthaśāstra, p. 437.

many cities, some or all of which are to-day deserted and lie waste in ruins. Thus there are seven cities of the name of Delhi, some of which lie at present in debris, all in close proximity to one another. Again "within the valley in which the remains of Taxila lie and within three and a half miles of each other are the remains of three distinct cities: (1) Bhir mound; (2) Sirkap; (3) Sirsukh."[1] This phenomenon is at first sight quite inexplicable. One explanation I have sought to give elsewhere.[2] The genesis of Indian cities as partially formulated in the foregoing lines furnishes the clue to two other reasons. The mode of warfare and laying seige as disclosed by the above description of a skandhāvāra or military necessity accounts for one; for these military encampments projected and laid out in the light of the highest science of civic architecture were nothing short of miniature cities. These, more often than not in the event of victory, were turned into royal capitals to the rejection of the conquered city, or in case of reverses, were deserted to be utilised by the victorious adversaries as a suburban colony or extension of their own metropolis. Again the state of perpetual warfare which necessitated camp-life as the inevitable order

[1] A Guide to Taxila by Sir John Marshall.
[2] Chapter II, pp. 39-40.

of the time was responsible for many of these deserted cities. The fourth reason I have given in connection with the expansion and improvement of towns. There were some other minor reasons peculiar to the individual towns. Indian cities were not however always destroyed at the caprice of the monarch who had to abandon it, either chased from it by the enemy or led by a vain-glorious policy as well as suspecting diplomacy to found another. "Some peculiar manufactures had sometimes so firmly established as to survive desertion, and these manufacturing towns sometimes threw out colonies."[1]

This genetic peculiarity of Indian towns probably influenced domestic architecture, at least, in the towns or cities. Almost every house in some Indian cities had an underground chamber. Though internecine conflicts subsided with the progress of time and these underground chambers fell into desuetude, yet their characteristics did not entirely disappear from posterior domestic architecture. The first storeys of the houses had no windows often no doors opening either upon the streets or upon the quadrangular courtyard. "A remarkable feature of these houses is that, although in some cases there are no doors com-

[1] Maine's Village Communities.

municating between two or more rooms, there are no doors giving direct access from these rooms to the interior court or to the streets outside,—the practice having apparently been to enter these lower chambers by means of stairways or ladders descending from the room above."[1] This had the effect of giving every ward in a town the appearance of a walled stronghold. The practice was done away with in later periods. Another feature of Indian towns due to the selfsame cause lay in the copious provisions and food-stuff stored up in the towns. "Nearly all the movable capital of the empire or kingdom was at once swept away to its temporary centre, which became the exclusive seat of skilled manufacture and decorative art. Every man who claimed to belong to the higher class of artificers took his loom or his tools and followed in the train of the king. This diversion of the forms of industry which depend on movable wealth to the seat of the court, had its first result in the splendour of oriental capitals. But at the same time it made it easier to change their site regarded as they continued to be in the light of the encampment of the sovereign for the time being."[2]

[1] A Guide to Taxila by Sir John Marshall, p. 71.

[2] Maine's Village Communities, p. 119.

APPENDIX C

Distribution of City Gates

The construction and distribution of city gates have been briefly discussed in proper places in some previous chapters but the separate treatment of the subject in orthodox treatises of Śilpa invests it with an importance that necessitates its special discussion *in extenso*. Construction of city gates does not obviously come under town-planning. It is with their allocation that I am therefore concerned here.[1] The main directions about the latter operation will bear repetition here in view of its full, complete treatment contemplated in this chapter. The arrangement of the gates has been made with reference to the division of the city into a Paramaśāyika pada, *i.e.* into eighty-one rectangular blocks, the fundamental operation upon which the whole science of Indian town-planning has been based.

[1] The principal directions regarding this distribution have already been noted. The details, actually some prohibitory injunctions, will interest none but the academic antiquarian. I have considerable doubt if these restrictive regulations were actually followed by the Indian civic architect at all. Certainly the modern town-planner has nothing to do with them. The grounds adduced for these prohibitions are like so many dogmatic assertions savouring more of superstition than of reason, which is a stereotyped characteristic of Indian treatises in such cases. Nevertheless, their description is a necessity to make our investigation complete and exhaustive according to the Indian town-planning code.

All authorities on Silpa Sāstra agree that four principal gates (Mahādvāra) should be constructed on the four sides of the town. The Eastern gate should be located at the Mahendra (*i.e.*, at the chamber dedicated to Mahendra); the Southern gate at the Rākshasa; the Western gate at the Pushpadanta; and the Northern gate at the Bhallāṭa. The Mahendra gate is said to be conducive to prestige and glory (māhātmya); the Rākshasa gate is conducive to wealth and prosperity (sampad); the Pushpadanta gate to all good qualities (guṇa); and the Bhallāṭa gate to the singularity of the king and his citizen. It should be noticed that the site of a principal gate is one pada or chamber removed to the left from the central one. The gates are therefore not situated in the middle of the sides, so that the two principal roads of the town that run through its centre east to west and north to south are confronted by the walls of the city.[1] It is difficult to surmise the reasons which weighed with the civic architects to enjoin this deviation of the gates from the central position and to have the principal roads blockaded at their extremities by

[1] Strange as it may seem, it is exactly similar to the Chinese system. "In many Chinese cities, where the streets are straight and run at right angles to one another, the gates towards which they point are nevertheless not *vis-à-vis*, but the main thoroughfares between the gates make two right-angled turns at some point in their otherwise straight course."

walls. This also detracted from the beauty and splendour of the roads as well as of the gates which, under this peculiar arrangement could not have over-arched, like many magnificent crowns, the stately streets lying before them. The arrangement also spoiled the splendid vista that would have otherwise spread out before an on-coming visitor. The arrangement, in all probablity, was an institution of those unsettled times when the necessity of defence preponderated over æsthetic needs or the requirements of naturalness and convenience and impressed upon the city its fortificatory character. The conservative habit of the Indian may have preserved and handed down this quaint practice from generation to generation. This is the only plausible explanation about the recommendation of a system that one meets with in almost all the the Śilpa Śāstras. It may be observed here that this rule of establishing the gates a little removed from the middle of the sides extended to the doors of houses and also gates or entrances to the compound[1] of a homestead.

The natural, the æsthetic asserted itself in some measure in later periods when comparative

[1] MM. Dr. Ganganath Jha writes in the *B & O Research Society Journal*, Vol. II, Pt. II, *June*, 1906 :—Every house should have doors on all four sides ; but no two doors should be exactly opposite each other. Even the modern village mason is very particular about this. In spite of the strictest orders of the master, he will never allow two doors to be exactly opposite, but will shift them at least an inch or two. The preventing of direct draught appears to be the motive underlying this rule.

peace and tranquillity settled in the land. The rectification of the doors or gates was first made for the gods, Brāhmaṇs, and the kings.[1] This modification of the old rule in favour of these high classes may indicate that the alignment of the gates with the central streets or the opening up of the doors just in the middle of the wall of the house was looked upon as an improvement upon the previous practice. This was therefore first sanctioned to the rank as a special privilege or it may be that, being the intelligent class, they were the first to realise the advantage and utility of this simple arrangement and the Vaiśyas and the Śūdras who, belonging to the lower grades of the society, were by nature more conservative and unimaginative, continued the old practice even after the higher classes had abandoned it in favour of the natural and more convenient rule.

Gradually however all classes of men became conscious of the advantage of this system and they came to accept it. Perhaps the Mānasāra was compiled at a period of transition when the old usage of arranging doors or gates was giving place to the new and the natural. In

[1] मध्यद्वारच देवानां द्विजानामवनीभृताम् ॥

Mayamatam, Ch. 30, sl. 42,

this book we find that in some village-plans the old rule has been retained and also recommended, while in others the new has been advised. Thus in the Nandyāvarta town-plan Mānasāra directs a peculiar arrangement of the principal gates. The principal gates of the village, instead of being constructed along the sides, were located in the four corners. The eastern gate was situated at the Īśāna; the southern gate at the Agni (hence it was also called Agni-dvāra); the western gate at the Pitṛs (therefore known as Pitṛ-dvāra) and the northern gate at the Vāyu (hence also called Vāyu-dvāra). And in the same village-plan again he would seem to recommend another set of four principal gates on the four sides and located on the central lines running towards the cardinal directions.[1] This way of distributing the principal gates he has adopted in the other village-plans as well. On the other hand he has not totally discarded the old practice to which he makes a general reference.

The author of the Śilparatna makes the following commendatory observations about the old arrangement of main gates which bears semblance of their classification according to different castes:

[1] Probably these two schemes of arranging gates point to the two types of the Nandyāvarta town-plan, the circular and the rectangular. In the former may it be that the gates were opened in the corners, while the latter was provided with gates on the sides.

"The gates constructed in the Mahendra and the Gṛhakshata (Rākshasa) are respected by the Brāhmaṇs (Brāhmaṇapūjitam); the gates raised in the Gṛhakshata and the Pushpadānta by the royal class; the gates set up at the Pushpadanta and the Bhallāṭa by the Vaiśyas; and the gates located in the Bhallāta and the Mahendra by the Śūdras." It should be noted that the same gate obviously does credit to two castes. For example, the eastern gate situated at the Mahendra befits both the Brāhmaṇ and the Śūdra. This is an anomaly. A plausible explanation seems to be that the assignment of the gates to the various castes is a metaphorical way of classifying and arranging them according to their rank, determined by their magnitudes and grandeur, the rank of the caste attached to a gate only pointing to the rank of the gate.[1] Hence the cyclical order of the four principal gates according to their rank may either begin in the east at the Mahendra or in the south at the Gṛhakshata.

The natural plan of locating the gates was always emphasised upon in the northern school of Indian town-planning, if the author

[1] It may be these directions applied to the houses of the castes or to settlements exclusively of a single caste. The Śūdras should have therefore opened their doors or gates at the Bhallāṭa or the Mahendra, and so on.

of the Purāṇas may be said to form such a school. I have already had occasion to notice that according to the Matsya Purāṇa, the two central cross-roads should terminate at four stately structures. The Agni Purāṇa's instructions are more definite on this point. It lays down that the eastern gate should be raised at the chamber of Sūryya (Āditya); the southern gate at the Gandharva;[1] the western gate at the Varuṇa and the northern gate at the Soma.[2] That this was the oldest scheme in northern India will be evident from the directions about the distribution of gates given in the Kauṭilya's Arthaśāstra.[3] Kauṭilya would place the southern gate at the Yama and this was a necessity inasmuchas its location in the other chamber would clash with other gates.

The author of the Śilparatna would erect another set of four main gates situated, in order, at the Jayanta, the Gandharva,[4] the

[1] It should be noticed that this gate does not occupy exactly the middle position in the south. But the Matsya Purāṇa and the Kauṭilya have overcome this apparent aversion to the chamber of Yama (the Lord of Death).

[2] ईशादि त्रिंशत्पदके पूर्व्वद्वारं च सूर्य्यके ॥
गन्धर्व्वाभ्यां दक्षिणे स्याद्वारुणे पश्चिमे तथा ।
सौम्यद्वारं सौम्यपदे कार्य्या रुद्रास्तु विस्तरा: ॥ २ ।

अग्निपुराणम्, १०६ अध्याय ।

[3] *Vide* Chapter IV.

[4] The location of the gate at the Gandharva instead of at the Vitatha violates the symmetry of the distribution.

Sugrīva,[1] and the Mukhya and all these gates make for the weal of all the castes in contradistinction to the other set discussed above. The merits of the gates of this system are described as follows: The Jayanta gate brings in victory (jaya); the Gandharva gate is auspicious for all functions; the Sugrīva gate conduces to all sorts of gain; and the Mukhya gate gives immediate rise to Brāhmaṇya (good of the Brāhmaṇic culture).

The Mayamata would, on the other hand, set water-passages or water-gates (jala-mārga or jala-dvāra) in these chambers: to wit, Jayanta, Vitatha, Sugrīva, and Mukhya. It should be noticed that the Mayamata replaces the Gandharva in the order of the Śilparatna by the Vitatha, and this adjustment restores the symmetry of the arrangement. These water-gates or water-outlets are of doubtful significance. The lie of the ground, according to its levelling, was towards the east and the north. Consequently these jala-dvāras could not possibly be gates through which the drains of the town fell into the outside ditches inasmuch the two of the gates, namely, the Vitatha and the Sugrīva gates lie in the south and the north. The

[1] The text gives Dauvārika, but I have cancelled it in favour of Sugrīva, not only to maintain the symmetry but also in diference to the injunction contained in the same text against a gate at the Dauvārika.

Īśānaśivagurudevapaddhati would make provision for the water-gates, along the eastern and the northern sides in the space between the Mahendra and the Argala *via* Īśāna as the water would flow towards the east and the north.[1] The Mānasāra's directions are more specific on this point; it would open the water-gates at the Mukhya, the Bhallāṭa, the Mṛga, the Aditi, the Jayanta, the Mahendra, the Satya, and the Bhṛśa.[2] Thus the water-gates were confined to the north and the east. And this scheme stands to reason as well.

All authorities recommend the construction of some eight subsidiary gates. They are generally located at the Bhṛśa, the Pūshā, the Bhṛṅgarāja, the Dauvārika, the Śosha, the Nāga, the Diti, and the Parjjaṇya.[3] According to the Mayamata

1 जलमार्गास्तथैन्द्रतः ।
ईशार्गलान्तं प्रस्ताः स्युः प्रागुदीचीप्लवो यथा ॥
Pt I, Ch. 25, sl. 63.

2 मुख्यके वा भल्लाटे वा मृगे वा चोदितावथवा ।
जयन्ते वा महेन्द्रे वा सत्यके भृशेऽथ वा ।
एवमेव जलद्वारं कुर्य्यात्ततो विचक्षणः ॥

3 महेन्द्रे गृहरक्षे च भल्लाटे पुष्पदन्तके ॥
महाद्वाराणि चैव स्युरुपद्वाराणि सन्ति चेत् ।
भृशे पूषणि भृङ्गाख्ये दौवारे शोषनागयोः ॥
दितावपि च पर्जन्ये जलमार्गास्तथैन्द्रतः ॥—
ईशानशिवगुरुदेवपद्धति, Pt I, Ch. 25.

these are also known as tunnels (Suraṅga).[1] This designation of the subsidiary gates may indicate their original character. It strikes me as an anomalous paradox that the author of the Śilparatna who relates the demerits accruing from construction of gates on these sites, recommends them, in case of necessity, as fit places for the subsidiary gates. Such self-contradiction is inexplicable unless it argues a concession to necessity.

The Śilparatna recounts the disqualifications of the chambers that it discards in the choice of sites for gates. In its opinion erection of a gate at the Āditya causes son's death; a gate at the Satya makes for rupture with allies or friends. A gate at the Bhṛśa leads to the obstruction of path. If a gate is constructed at the Antarīksha, the owner goes to rack and ruin. The lord of the habitat meets with death in case he erects a gate at the Agni. Ruin from his domestic elephants overtakes him who raises a gate at the Pūshā. The Vitatha gate portends death of the owner. Death and utter annihilation will come in the wake of location of a gate at the Yama. A gate

[1] उपद्वारं प्रयोक्तव्यं तत्सुरङ्गमिति स्मृतम् ।

मयमते त्रिंशोऽध्याय—५२ श्लोकः ।

at the Bhṛṅgarāja portends danger; that at the Mṛsha destruction of crops; that at the Nirti mortality; and that at the Dauvārika causes apprehension. A gate at the Asura means perennial pestilence. A gate at the Śoshaṇa sucks up all merits. Leprosy is likely to follow if a gate is set up at the Roga. A gate at the Vāyu exposes the citizen to blasts of wind. There is every fear of snakes, if a gate is opened at the Nāga. Watery grave awaits him who would make a gate at the Argala. A gate at the Aditi portends abdomenal distempers. A gate at the Diti spells ruin of the wife or spoilation of reservoirs. A gate at the Rudra stands for conflagration. A gate at the Parjjaṇya augurs ill for the kitchen.

The above sum up the grotesque and fantastic reasons that the exponents of Indian civic engineering philosophy have adduced in support of their interdicting the aforesaid positions in the matter of location of doors. They are too dogmatic and mysterious to appeal to a modern architect. But then it should be noticed that the principal and subsidiary gates make up, between themselves, as equable and symmetric distribution of the gates as possible. I am disposed to think that these fastidious regulations marked the inchoate stage of Indian town-planning, especially the period when the towns were no bigger than a small ward of a corporation in a modern city. Small dimensions of a town can favour such likes and dislikes of the civic architect. With the growth and expansion of the towns, such meticulous distinctions fell into desuetude and gates were opened wherever necessary. Thus Megasthenes has left accounts testifying to the existence of sixty-four gates in the city of Pāṭalīputra. It seems the civic architects of ancient India do not favour a large number of entrances into the city.[1] By the side of every gate a temple should be raised to the lord of the quarter. It may be interesting to note here that the renowned residential Universities of ancient India, *e.g.* Vikramaśilā, fortified that they were with walls, possessed splendid gates and a renowned savant, so was the rule, was placed in charge of each gate. He therefore had his lodge beside the gate and any student wishing to enter the University by the gate had to pass through an examination by him. Vikramaśilā had six such gates and Prajñākaramati, a renowned Bengali Pandit (savant) of the time was the guardian of the southern entrance.

[1] बहुप्रवेशमार्गश्च मार्गविद्धश्च गर्हितम् ॥
मयमते तृतीये अध्याये १६श श्लोकः ।

BIBLIOGRAPHY

Among the multitudes of books scrutinised for materials, the references to the following will generally be found in the book :—

Agni Purāṇam.

Ancient and Mediæval Architecture, by E. B. Havell.

Ancient Town-Planning, by Haverfield.

Āpasthambha Dharma-sūtras.

Archæological Survey of India, Reports of.

Arthaśāstra of Kauṭilya, translated by R. Shama Sastry.

Bhavishya Purāṇam.

Bijapur Architecture, by Cousens.

Brahmāṇḍa Purāṇam.

Brahmavaivarta Purāṇam.

Buddhist India, by Rhys Davids.

Chips from a German Workshop, by Max Müller.

Civic and National Ideals, by Sister Nivedita.

Devī Purāṇam.

Early History of India, by V. Smith.

Essay on Architecture of the Hindus, by Rām-rāz.

Garuḍa Purāṇam.

Guide to Taxila, by Sir John Marshall.

Harivaṃśa.
History of the Aryan Rule in India, by E. B. Havell.
History of Indian and Eastern Architecture, by Ferguson.
History of Vijayanagar, A forgotten Empire, by Sewell.
Indian Architecture, by Ananthlwar and Rea. (My references to the Kāmikāgama are derived from this source)
Jātakas (Buddhist).
Journal of the Behar and Orissa Research Society, March (1916).
Kālikā Purāṇam.
Kāmandakīya Nītisāra.
Kāmasūtra of Vātsyāyana.
Mahābhārata, The.
Mānasāra.
Mayamatam.
Matsya Purāṇam.
Manushyālaya Chandrikā (Trivandrum Sanskrit Series).
Modern Review, The (1919 & 1920).
Nārada Saṃhitā.
Rāmāyaṇa, The.
Śavdakalpadruma.
Śukranītisāra (Jivananda Vidyāsāgar's edition, Calcutta).

Summary of the Mānasāra, A, by Dr. P. K. Acharyya.

Tamils Eighteen Hundred Years Ago, by V. Kanaksavai.

Town-Planning in Ancient Deccan, by Venkatarama Ayyar.

Town-Planning in Practice, by R. Unwin.

Varāha Purāṇam.

Vāstu Vidyā (Trivandrum Sanskrit Series)

Vāyu Purāṇam.

Vedic Index, by Macdonell and Keath.

Village Communities, by Sir H. S. Maine.

Viśvakarmaprakāśa.

Viśvakarmavidyāprakāśa.

Vitruvius, translated by M. H. Morgan.

Vṛhat Saṃhitā, by Varāhamihira.

Yuktikalpataru of Bhoja (edited by Pandit Iswar Sastry; Calcutta Oriental Series).

INDEX

(The numbers refer to pages)

A

F

H

I

M

N

U

W

Y

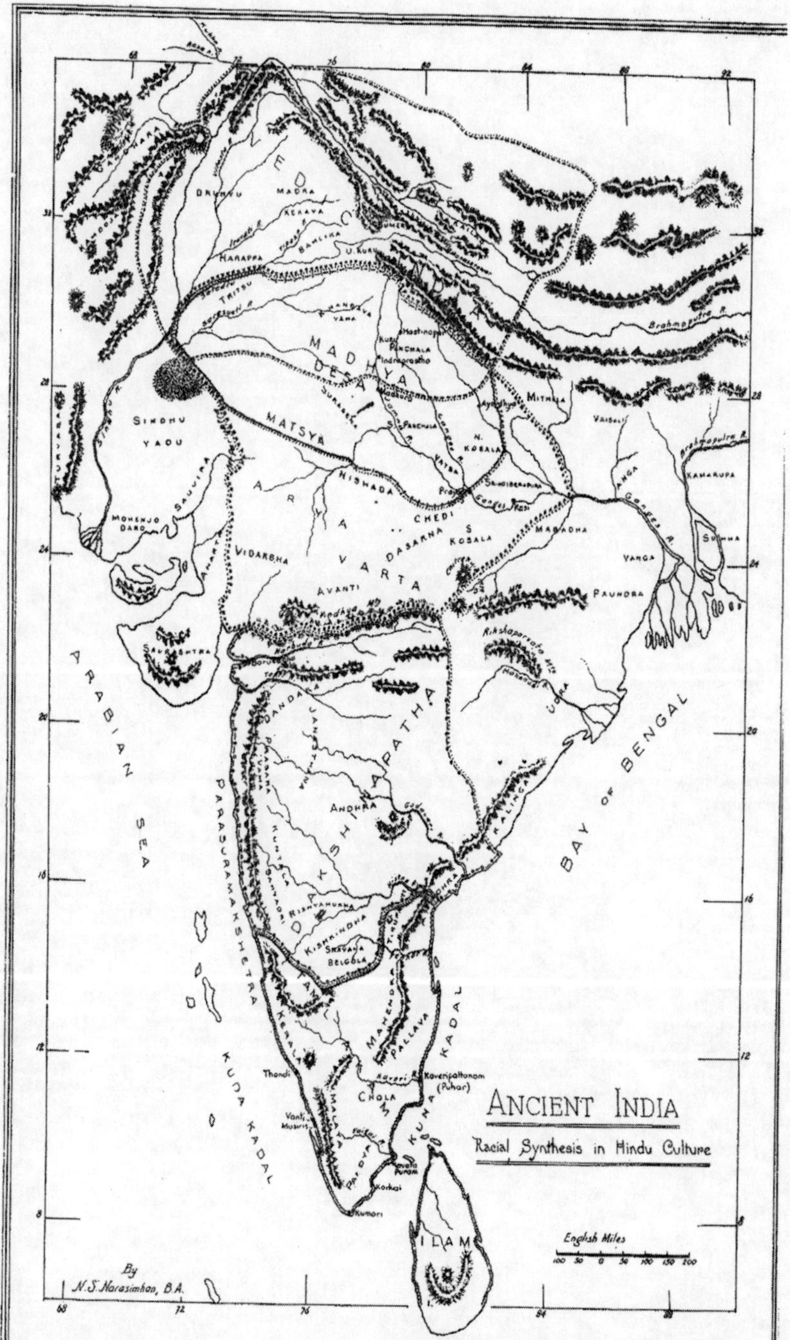

ANCIENT INDIA
Racial Synthesis in Hindu Culture
English Miles
100 50 0 50 100 150 200
By
N. S. Narasimhan, B.A.
SINDHU
YADU
MOHENJO DARO
HARAPPA
MADRA
KEKAYA
MADHYA DESA
MATSYA
PANCHALA
Hastinapura
Indraprastha
Ayodhya
N. KOSALA
VATSA
NISHADA
CHEDI
DASARNA
S. KOSALA
MAGADHA
MITHILA
ANGA
VANGA
PAUNDRA
KAMARUPA
Brahmaputra R.
Ganges R.
ARYA VARTA
VIDARBHA
AVANTI
SAURASHTRA
Rikshaparvata Mts.
DAKSHINA PATHA
ANDHRA
KALINGA
KISHKINDHA
PARASURAMAKSHETRA
KERALA
CHOLA
PALLAVA
Thondi
Kaveripattonam
(Puhar)
Korkai
Kumari
KUDA KADAL
KUNA KADAL
ILAM
ARABIAN SEA
BAY OF BENGAL